Copyright © 2019

All rights reserved. The Copyright Act of 1967, codified in Title 17 of the United States Constitution covers this book. Any form of reproduction of all or part of the contents in this book is prohibited and a punishable offense by the law.

Disclaimer

While every effort has been made to guarantee the accuracy and effectiveness of the information given in this book, it happens that the author is not responsible or liable for direct, indirect or any consequential damages as well as personal grievances resulting from the use of this information. This book shouldn't be a substitute for the advice of a professional. Nevertheless, we have been able to make sure that all information in this book is effective and correct. Note that the author would not be blamed for any misuse or misrepresentation of information.

1

Contents

INTRODUCTION

Okay, you've bought a Cricut machine, and you are excited. You have thought so much on what you are going to do with it. Now you have it. You really don't know the process. Well, that is why I am here. We would talk extensively about Cricut project ideas. Whatever you have in mind, maybe you want to become this craftsperson, or you just want to do it for fun in a school or office we have several ideas for you here.

I know you're probably hungry for projects, you desperately want to do something with this new machine, so let us get you started. The Cricut projects would be divided into steps each project has its unique number of steps. However, I have been able to separate these projects based on their difficulty. So we have the simple, medium, and hard. You don't need to be alarmed the projects under the *difficulty* session are

4

not difficult. They just require longer procedures. Most of the time, they are compound combinations of simple processes.

Feel free to play around, explore, and do something different. You should not consider this body of work as a complete instruction. Yes, it is but you are not limited to the contents of this book. If a procedure doesn't seem right or you just have this strong gut that it should be done in another way. Don't hold yourself back. Don't close your mind to new suggestions and procedures. Let your creativity flow.

Happy circuiting!

GETTING STARTED

Defining objects requires you to use other similar objects to drive home your point and to give the reader a clearer picture. The very available way we can describe a Cricut machine is to say that it is a machine that has so much resemblance with the printer, but it is used majorly for cutting designed pieces. That is a very simple and easy definition you don't need to bother yourself about that. Just picture a printer in your mind and think of a cutting device. Oh, no, you already have the Cricut machine with you, right? You would notice that it uses precise blades and several templates or rollers during cutting.

Against what people think. The machine isn't meant for scrapbook keepers or makers alone. I still don't know why this idea has become so much rooted in the minds of people that we've grown to allow this thought to dominate our reactions and attitude towards any new innovation. I was like that some few years back not until I saw the demo of this wonderful machine. Then the Cricut explore came and blew my mind away.

Several templates, designs, ideas were just rushing towards me. Before I knew what was going on, I found myself in the Cricut world playing with different projects and trying something new every single day. The Cricut process involves; designing your template on the design space software, attaching the cutting mat, confirming your settings and boom! Getting what you need.

The world has been transformed with that machine as its products have been able to add those special visual beauties to the simple paperwork that we know. The Cricut machine has several models and versions some of them include; Cricut Expression, Expression 2, Cricut Imagine, Cricut Gypsy, Cricut Cake Mini, Cricut Personal Cutter, Cricut Crafts Edition and Martha Stewart and the Cricut Explore air. The tool obviously fits into any type of craft you are working on. And there is also a die cut machine which gives you that extra-precise, sharp and smart cutting. The process of cutting materials by hand during crafts has been reduced drastically, thanks to this wonderful machine. More also, you can perform multiple projects all at the same time due to the effectiveness of this device. It contains several cartridges which are always available to help you explore different forms and shapes of several designs. More also that move from one project to another has been made possible with the use of this Cricut machine.

Any material can be shaped into that design you want it to be. Furthermore, you can also create patterns which are already pre-installed in the software that comes with it. The design software tool becomes very much available with pre-loaded designs for instant use. I am sure you must have been able to purchase this machine from your local craft store on the online store. You are aware that the price was based on the kind of model you are using and I am sure that you've been able to narrow down your needs for you to be able to get your machine because anything which makes your work easier and faster is a very important investment and the Cricut machine is definitely one. Due to the efficiency of this machine, we now have it in several places we never thought it would be in years. We have them in offices and specific workshops. If you think that the Cricut is a home-only tool, you are quite wrong. This time-saving device allows your work to be very professional, and the beautiful thing about it is that we have no limits to what it can do. I am sure that you're reading this to gain more ideas and you hastily want to jump into making things and doing some stuff. Yes, that is cool; however, we need to understand some basics else we would be making serious mistakes or the process would look very confusing.

The machine has lineages, and I am sure you are aware of that. It wasn't like this some years back but who really cares about the past more than the future. Remember we have the Cricut maker which is this cloud-based online software having this particular series and design which obviously cannot function alone because it has to be attached with the desktop or laptop computer having an available internet connection. But today, this Cricut maker has several offline features present in that design app which has so much compatibility with several devices like the iOS device and Windows also. What this suggests is that if you have this kind of machine you can work without the use of any internet connection, and you can also make use of an iPad/iPhone or Macbook. This general feature is also included in the Cricut Explore Air, but the difference is that you don't need a connection through a cable because you already have a Bluetooth connection in place.

This Robert Workman's invention in collaboration with other investors like Jonathan Johnson, Phil Beffrey, and Matt Strong has a bizarre pronunciation. People call it *cricket*. Same as the name of an insect. It was able to gather so many profits from sales all within a very short time due to its handiness and helpfulness. A.K.A Cricut expression machine, this device shapes out images from paper, cardboard, vinyl, wood, and several other materials that you can think of. Use this machine to replace the job of scissors or a blade, and you are definitely in for something that would blow your mind. The makers of this machine are not stopping as they keep bringing new inputs, which increase the value of the machine. Cuts made by this big boy machine ranges between 1" – 5.5" high and up to 11.5" long. And we have several cartridges which are always available to give you different measures, dials, and shapes for different materials apart from paper and cards. What if you need something bigger? Well, the latest addition from the Cricut cutting system is the Cricut Expression 24" Personal Electronic Cutter having several cutting mats in the measurement 12" × 24" and 12" × 12" It allows for different languages, measurement and other settings too, it is universal. Some designs have screens which would display your work during the designing process. They have an LCD screen for you to enjoy the display. You might be interested in the Cricut create which is a smaller version of the very large machine and permits 0.25" cuts to 11.5" while sitting on a 6" by 12" cutting mat. Your finished work can be completed in several modes all peculiar to the kind of Cricut machine design you have.

There exist several modes to get the finished product of your work. This isn't meant for the Cricut design or not, but you can also get that from the Cricut machines. If you can decide to do something different from the convention of others. He Cricut design space provides you with different modes. You may decide to fit page mode, portrait mode for taller pictures, the center point function, flip function plus the auto-fill mode also. We are aware that this machine comes in different sizes and hardware designs also. Some have buttons, and others don't have. Others also have display screens while some are touch enabled. We are also aware that there are different cutting mats, cutting blades, storage tote, and some other stuff which we already know. The machine you have on your table or workspace can work on several materials. In fact we have over 100 plus materials which include; adhesive cardstock, flocked cardstock, flock paper, Kraft board, Kraft paper, dry erase vinyl, Holographic Vinyl, Metallic Vinyl, Metallic iron, printable iron, Duct tape, Magnet Sheet, Soda Can Velvet, flocked cardstock, Velvet, etc. we would definitely give you project ideas on all these materials and more. I shouldn't forget the fabrics also. Any type of fabric can be cut into several shapes making use of the rotary blades. The Cricut cutter would allow you to cut several fabric materials like the heavy denim, sailcloth, burlap, sequined fabrics, leather fabric with glitter, faux fur, etc. it has a FabricGrip which would help you to hold the fabric firmly to the mat during the cutting process. For the Cricut design space, you need to be very intuitive. Make use of designs that jump at you through the screen. Allow your creativity flow. The software is easy to use and has several ready-to-use projects installed so that would be very easy for you. You should learn to twist or modify several designs to soothe your desire. I have been able to break all these procedures into detailed steps. You can do the following project with Cricut machine; a leather cuff bracelet, monogrammed water bottles, customized tote bags, coloring pages for children, paper flowers and bouquets, felt coasters, scrapbook, stencils for wood signs, paper gift boxes and tags, greeting cards, paper pennants for parties, iron-on Vinyl for T-shirts, etc.

If you are looking for an example of an open-ended question it would be; *what are the uses of a Cricut machine?* The definite answer you may get is that it can be used to cut anything. However, a cutting tool can have multiple uses. Cricut machines have peculiar markers which can definitely work smoothly with the machine. People use Cricut machine to create those homemade greeting cards. That sounds so weird, right? Okay. Let us make this quick analysis. You need a greeting card, and you walk up to a store, pay let's say some $5-10 for a card. First, you've spent a lot because with less than $5 you can make yours. Which would have your kind of design and unique words which you all need. You must have noticed that people obviously appreciate homemade cards even more than those cards that you purchased in the store. Another instance that comes to mind is when you are thinking of making seasonal decorations. This is when you need a Cricut machine more than before. Halloween, Christmas, Easter, Thanksgiving, etc. those dazzling Christmas trees, those special valentine hearts or Halloween ghost which would place your heart in your mouth. I am yet to see an individual who doesn't enjoy creativity. Everyone loves to do something, create something special; it is an innate ability from God. This machine would bring out your creativity within seconds of use.

We should not forget that the cool thing about Cricut is that projects are endless. You might decide to have your own wall lettering, or you might choose to make a nursery at home, and you would need to make that distinct wall painting with several letters. Instead of you to spend several hours cutting with blades and carving with knives or any other cutting device, you just need a Cricut machine. You don't even need to hire a muralist for your hand painting because you can do that yourself. In fact, people like these are happy that you are not exposed to this knowledge so that they can make some cash from you. The die cut machine produces those precise cuts which children and other professional needs. There are several die-cut stickers you can get from this machine. This machine also allows you to render wedding favors and party favors easily by helping in the creating process of tags, bags, boxes, and several other party creations. These pieces can come in several forms like gift bags, banners, hats, etc. these and many more can fit the theme of any party because you are making them. As much as I would love to shy away from the scrapbook stuff I just can't. Now, just picture your daughter or your son getting married and you present him/her with a scrapbook having pictures from the very first day they stepped into this planet to where they are now. Gifts like this sound odd, but they are invaluable because you are not giving out a utensil or a tool you are giving out those memories. Scrapbooks carry out a lot of memories and those feelings you cannot give through your regular gifts.

If you have a Cricut machine and you've not gotten these supplies I would advise that you get them as soon as possible. We are aware that these supplies are grouped into different categories. First is the paper category which includes; adhesive cardstock, cereal box, copy paper, flocked paper, cardboard paper, Notebook paper, flocked cardstock, foil embossed paper, Freezer Paper, Glitter Paper, Kraft paper, Kraft Board, metallic Paper, Metallic Poster board, Photographs, Photo Framing Mat, Poster Board, Rice Paper, Wax Paper, Solid core Cardstock, White Core Cardstock, Photo Framing mat, Watercolor Paper, Freezer Paper, Foil Poster Board, etc.

We shouldn't forget that the Vinyl is another material which you need to make your work on the Cricut machine smooth. The Cricut machine can work on those beautiful materials which can be used to make decals, stencils, graphics, and those beautiful signs too. You can cut through the following vinyl materials; chalkboard vinyl, dry erase vinyl, holographic vinyl, stencil vinyl, printable vinyl, Matte Vinyl, Adhesive Vinyl, Printable Vinyl, and Glossy Vinyl also. Furthermore, you may have so much experience in the fabric and Textile world, and you want to infuse the Cricut machine. Some of the materials or fabrics that you can work with are; canvas, denim, cotton fabric, linen, leather, flannel, burlap, duck cloth, felt, metallic leather, polyester, printable fabrics, silk, wool felt and many more others. If you have not got your Iron on Vinyl. Which is meant to be the heat transfer vinyl. You make use of this vinyl to decorate a T-shirt, tote bags and other kind of fabric items that you can think of like; Printable Iron On, Glitter Iron on, Glossy Iron On, Flocked Iron on, Holographic sparkle iron on, Metallic Iron on, Neon Iron on, Foil Iron on, etc.

We should not narrow our minds to the materials mentioned above because there are several other materials which the Cricut can cut through or even work on some of them include; adhesive wood, cork board, Balsa Wood, craft foam, aluminum sheets, corrugated paper, Embossable foil, Foil Acetate, Paint Chips, Plastic Packaging, Metallic Vellum, Printable Sticker Paper, Stencil material, Shrink Plastic, Wrapping Paper, Window Cling, Wood Veneer, Washi Tape, Birch Wood, Wrapping Paper, Wood Veneer, Plastic Packaging, Soda Can, Glitter Foam, Printable Magnet Sheets, etc. The Cricut maker can work on materials which are up to 2.4mm thick and other special materials and special fabrics like the; Jersey, Cashmere, Chiffon, Terry Cloth, Tweed, Velvet, Jute, Knits, Moleskin, Fleece, and several others.

This machine can be found anywhere and everywhere, so much paper artwork is done. What this suggests is that you can see these machines in schools, offices, craft shops, etc. you can make use of this Cricut machine for a school project, card stock projects as well as iron-on projects too. Making use of this machine to cut out window clings is not a bad idea at all. I did mention faux leather projects that would require the use of faux leather are perfect for the Cricut machine. It is not limited to this because you also engage in projects that have to do with adhesive stencil and stencil vinyl also. You would remove the stencil vinyl after it is dried. This would leave a distinct imprint. You can also make use of this machine to create lovely fashion accessories like several pieces of jewelry. The Cricut machine allows you to make use of the faux leather for exceptional designs. Recall that we talked about school projects. Preschoolers and their instructors can benefit from this machine. Furthermore, you can print out photos or images from your computer while making use of this machine, especially from the printable magnets to those sticker papers, customized gifts, bags, etc.

The aim of this chapter is to create that awareness for the supplies that you need for the use of the Cricut machine. And I have been doing that systematically while introducing you to the general capacity of the machine. For the supplies, I have been able to draft out that long list of supplies and you can recall that I did talk about several materials the Cricut machine can work on. These materials are supplies too. The Cricut provides you that service and provision based on your area of specialization. But we shouldn't miss the fact that there are some basic supplies that you need. Those supplies are so elementary that I think they should come with the Cricut machine. I would begin with those basic cutting materials. I may have failed to mention them when I was talking about materials that the Cricut can work on. But I wouldn't miss them this time.

- The Basic Vinyl supplies: this is the perfect option for those indoor items which you can't stop from getting wet. This is also meant for wall sayings and canvas also.
- The Glitter Vinyl: This is similar to the basic vinyl. However, it includes glitters in the material.
- The Dry Erase Vinyl: materials that are used majorly for labeling
- The Holographic Vinyl: This is just the basic vinyl having the holographic effect. That is several

colors staring at you when you look at it from different angles.

- The Chalkboard Vinyl which should be used for labeling and making calendars also.
- Printable vinyl which is an ideal sticker material.

We shouldn't forget the adhesive foil which has so many similarities with the vinyl but adds the nice shimmer to it so it becomes something that you'll need to get. Next on the list is the transfer tape which you would also need in your Cricut experience. The transfer tape provides that strong grip which can be used to transfer that vinyl with the glitters.

Iron on materials shouldn't be ignored here too. These supplies are always added to shirts, pillows, hats, and other clothing materials. Your Cricut experience should be complete with; iron on lite, Glitter Iron, Holographic Iron on, Printable Iron On, Foil Iron on, etc.

I would be listing some very pivotal materials which are required for the smooth Cricut experience;

- Cardstock: should be a combination of several cards, cardboards, gift tags, gift boxes, and other scrapbooking materials too.
- Faux leather
- Window Cling
- Felt; perfect materials for finger puppets and other dress ornaments. You might even want to use them for that distinct mask and those headbands too.
- Window cling: for your temporary window projects and designs.
- Faux leather perfect for making jewelry, baby moccasins as well as key holders and chains too.

We did talk about materials, but we should not forget those tools like pens, mats and other accessories. The fundamental tools include:

1. Mats: which may come in several sizes; 12 by 12 12 by 24 etc. it is advisable that you have several sizes for different uses and you should have more than one. Furthermore, the material you are working on should decide the kind of material that is in use.

Nevertheless, you should be able to get all or at least one of the following:

- The standard grip mats. The color green mat which is specially used for the vinyl and iron on materials.
- Fabric Grip is that color pic mat used for fabric materials only.
- Light Grip mat. The color blue mat which is used majorly for papers and cardstock projects too.

2. Pens: You can't be a craft person if you don't have a wide variety of pens available. You shouldn't get so much, but you should have those basic colors and even more.

3. Other tools like the Spatula, scissors, tweezers, scraper, weeder, etc.

4. Extras which are required for comfortable use of the Cricut machine. Like; bright pads, easy press, cuttlebug, etc. they are not fundamentally needed but having them as your Cricut supplies isn't a bad idea at all. The bright pad, for instance, is used for weeding and makes weeding very easy, especially if you are working on

those low light sections. This would be very useful if you are working on a material that has so much glitter. The cuttlebug is a non-necessary die-cut machine which produces sharp edges cut. The Cricut machine should also be supported with the easy press. This is a portable, easy heat transfer which is used with the vinyl. You can also decide to store your tools in a tote bag. They would keep the supplies safe and properly organized also. Machine tote, shoulder bag, rolling storage tote are all those types of bags which can be useful for you.

The Cricut Machine should contain some supplies in the box from the manufacturer. Let us take the explore air machine 2, for example. The Cricut Explore Air 2 comes in a box which would have the machine, the power cord, USB cord, Blade and Housing (which are pre-installed), Pen, Welcome Book, 12 by 12 StandardGrip Cutting Mat plus the Cardstock samples.

Where can I get all these supplies? All these supplies can be gotten online or from the local craft store around you. The other part of this book would focus on the project and projects alone.

Now that you have been exposed to the supplies you need. I am sure you're probably thinking. *Even if I get all these, how can I use them?* Well, that is why I am here to help with several project ideas and procedures. This is hands-on information for you. Consider it a detailed guide. You should not forget that your Cricut workspace is very important. The workspace I am referring to here isn't the workspace you have on the design application but the physical workspace, i.e., where you place the Cricut machine. It is an electronic machine, and like every other electronic machine, you should keep it far away from liquid.

CRICUT PROJECT AND PROCEDURES

This chapter is dedicated to only Cricut projects and procedures. I have been able to divide these projects into three segments; the easy, medium, and hard. These projects have a similar structure, which makes it look so much like a hand-on guideline that you can follow and execute within minutes. I would begin with something quite simple and easy before we move to those seemingly *complex* projects. Like I have mentioned, these projects are not as complex as you think they just require additional processes from the simple procedures.

We have been able to divide the project into three categories; Easy, Medium, and Hard.

EASY

PROJECT 1- HANDMADE FLOWER CORSAGE

Easy level

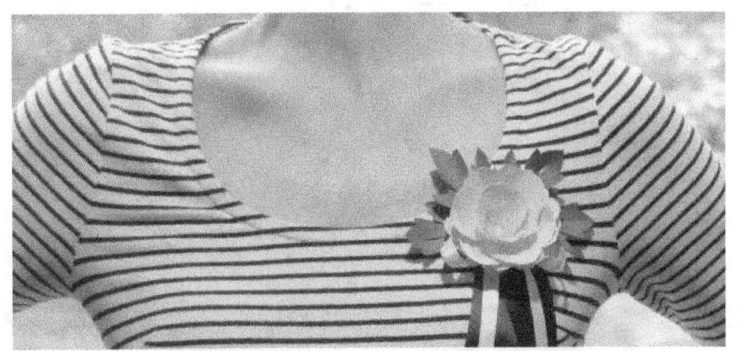

PROJECT THANKS TO MELANIE FROM SIMPLE MADE PRETTY

You are probably interested in making this year's Mother's Day extra special. I have been able to create this simply made flower corsage just in five easy steps. Furthermore, this paper corsage is also good for Prom, especially when you make it to match your Prom gown.

YOU'LL NEED THE FOLLOWING SUPPLIES

- Glue
- Scissors
- The Cardstock (which would obviously be the choice for the flowers and the leaves)
- Ribbon or pins
- Templates

STEP 1

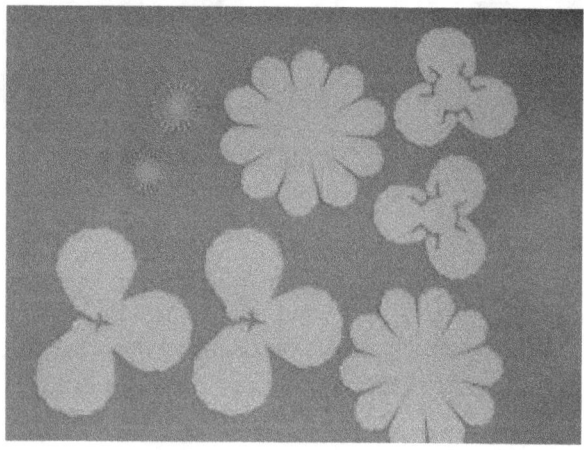

There are some pre-installed designs, so you just get them and pint them on the color of your chosen card. The Cricut explore would be used to cut it.

STEP 2

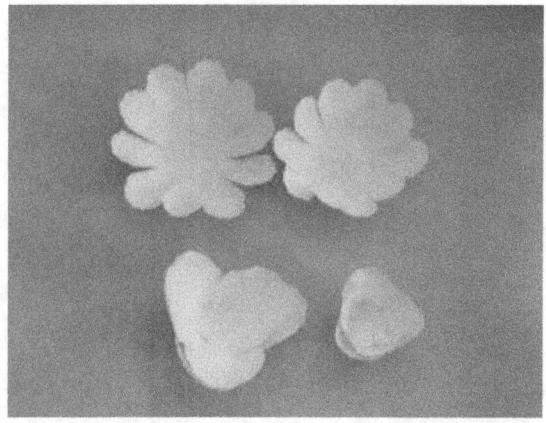

We would gently spray the paper with water. This would allow the paper to curl into that desired shapes and make the paper to form several shapes.

STEP 3

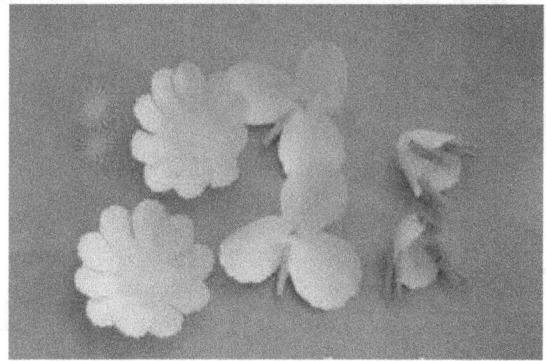

You make use of the glue to join those tabs together on each section and make sure it dries. I make use of clothing pin so that it would stick together while it dries.

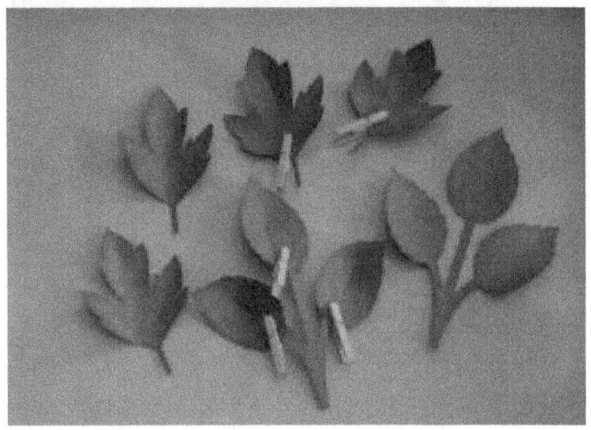

STEP 4

Make use of watercolors or makers to add colorful edges around before you glue all the petals and the leaves to form that flower and allow it to dry.

STEP 5

You may decide to make a wrist corsage. Doing this would require you to cut the desired ribbon length then you glue it with the finished flower. Simple. You may decide to make use of a pin on the back of the flower.

YOU CAN DO THIS NOW!

PROJECT 2- CRICUT PRINT AND CUT DIY HALLOWEEN TREATS

Level- Easy

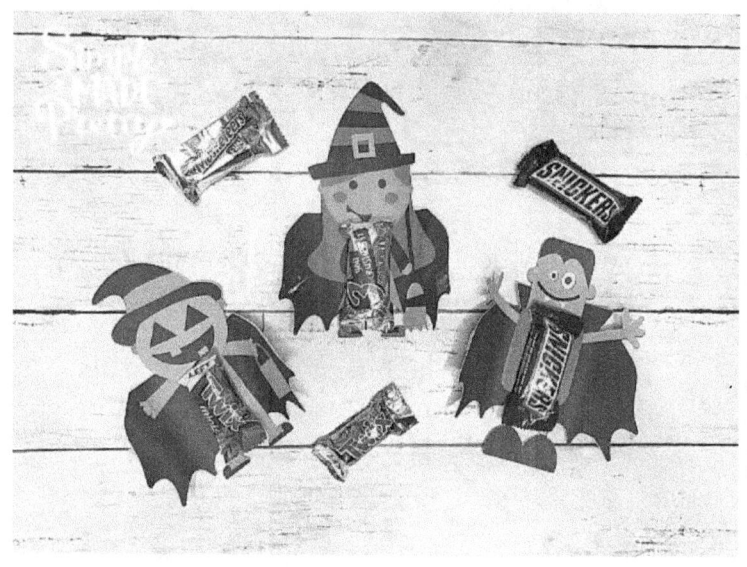

CREDIT- SIMPLE MADE PRETTY

You definitely want your Halloween trick or treat candy to be the talk of your neighborhood. This project would make you achieve that with just these few steps you would be able to make this year's Halloween special. These Candy

Treat Favors are very easy to make. You can fit one or more of these treats inside this favor.

SUPPLIES NEEDED

- Strong or Tacky Glue
- Halloween Candy
- Cricut Explore machine
- The SVG file or you can make use of your own personal design
- Heavy White Cardstock. In this project, I made use of 110 Ib weight

STEP 1

Get your supplies, download the SVG file, and upload it to your Cricut Design space or construct your own design and make sure you save it as print files. Don't forget to resize the image to contain the candy. I made use of 5.8 by 6.7 in this project. Then cut the images. Note that they are front and back for each character.

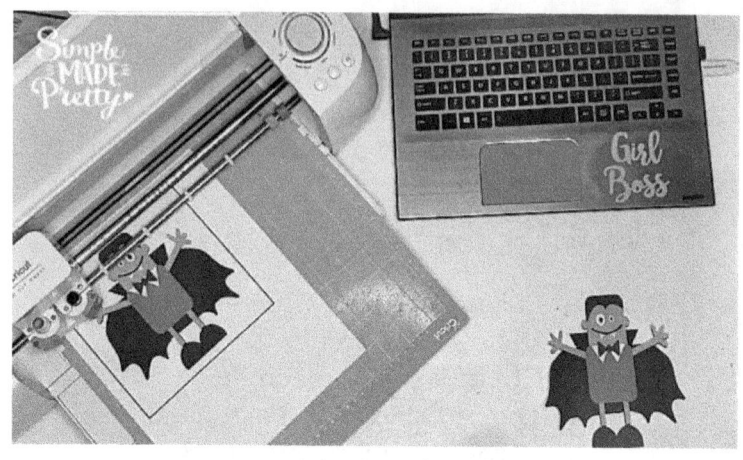

STEP 2

After you have been able to print it out, then you glue the front and back to make it a single piece.

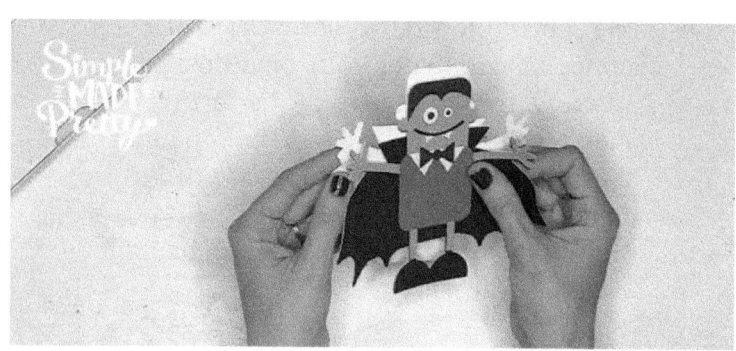

STEP 3

Place the candy bar on the character. Wrap the *arms* of the character around it so that it looks as if it is holding it. Then you make use of the double-sided tape to hold these together.

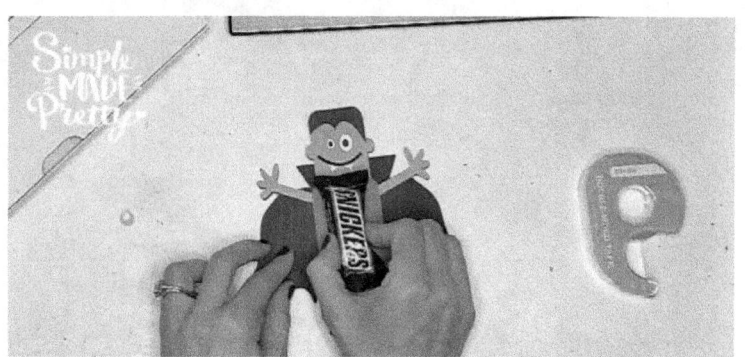

Repeat this process for each character; the pumpkin man and the witch.

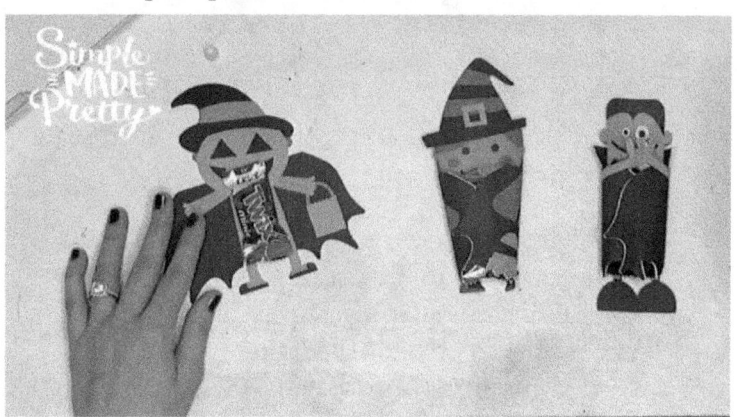

YOU CAN DO THIS NOW!

Level- Easy

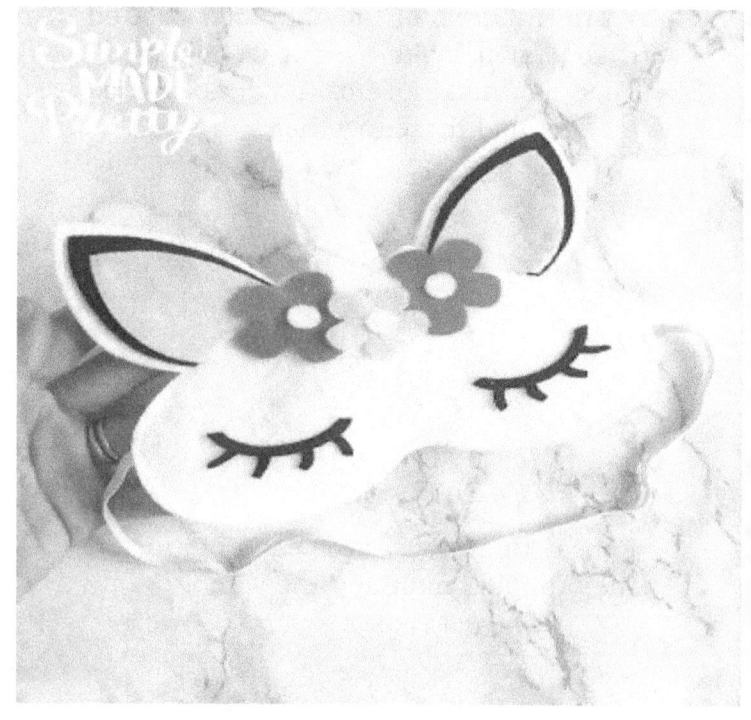

CREDIT- SIMPLE MADE PRETTY

This project is very easy and shouldn't take more than five minutes. It is very useful as a sleepover gift or a travel accessory. You would make use of the Cricut machine and SVG, DXS, ESP or

PNG file depending on what Cricut model you are using.

SUPPLIES NEEDED

- Felt materials. I used 2 different sheets of White plus 1 sheet of black, purple, light pink, hot pink, and yellow.
- The Cricut Explore machine.
- White Elastic
- Sewing Machine (this is optional because you may decide to glue it)
- Glue

STEP 1

Gather all of your supplies. Download the SVG, DXF, ESP or PNG file online then you upload it to the Cricut Design Space, or you work on yours. But remember that when you are uploading you should edit the image. I made use of 7.5 by 6.65 inches.

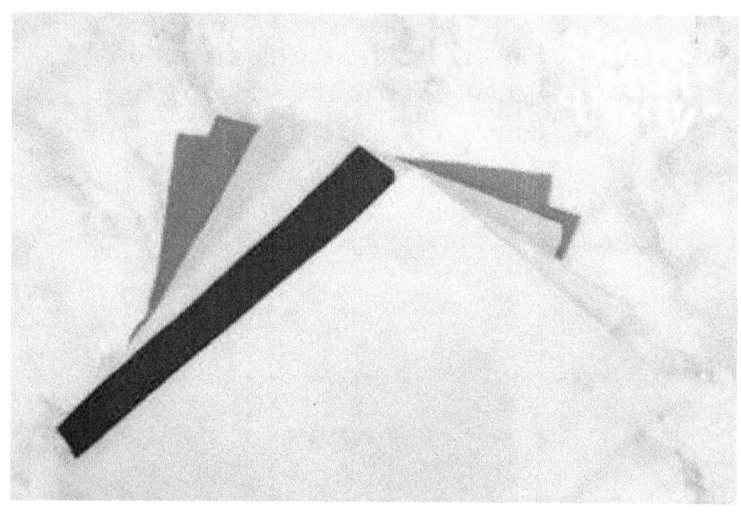

STEP 2

Cut the Images that you have been able to construct or re-size.

STEP 3

Blend those images perfectly to create that unicorn face then glue it carefully with every other material on the first layer.

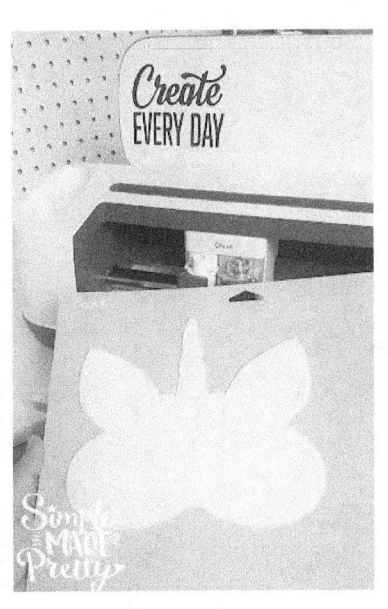
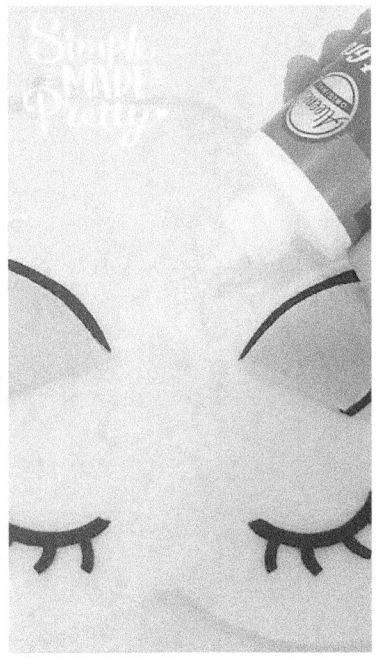

STEP 4

Put those elastic ends in between the two sides of the 2 white layers to make that strap around the mask. You can either glue both sides together then allow it to dry or you stitch around the edge to hold all of it in one piece as I did here.

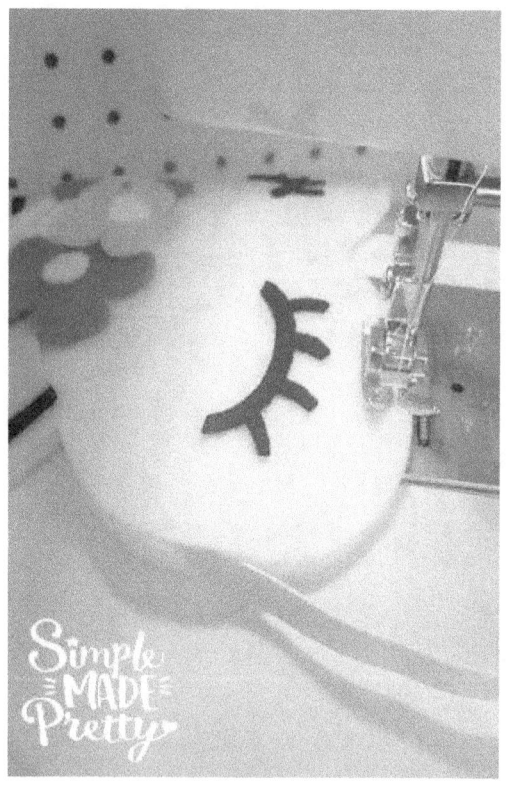

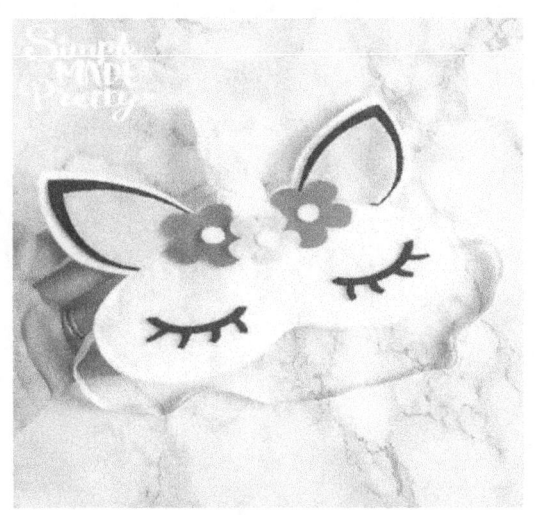

YOU CAN DO THIS NOW!

If you use glue you shouldn't wash, spot cleaning should be preferred, but if you were able to sew it together, then you are quite safe to do so. This unicorn sleep mask would come together in no time.

PROJECT 4- BUTTERFLY CANVAS WALL HEART ON CRICUT
Level- Easy

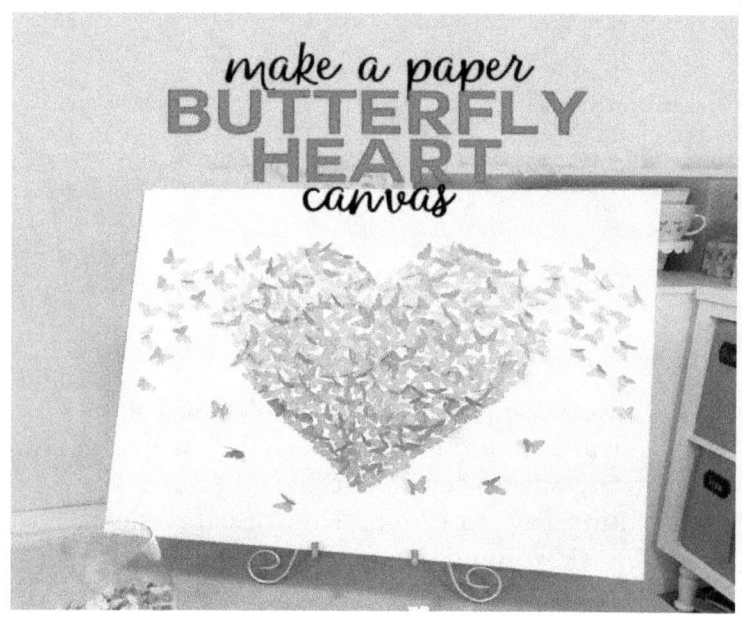

CREDIT- JENNIFER MAKER

The beauty of this project is that you don't need much to make it. It is very simple and easy. This project brings out the peculiarities of butterflies, especially the way they are arranged. So instead of arranging all the butterflies into that single love shape, I have been able to scatter them all around so it looks as if the heart's wings can soar. This means that there is a specific way to arrange these butterflies. You may decide to use these pieces to create a giant butterfly also. Just be creative about it.

SUPPLIES YOU NEED

- Four or more sheets of 8.5 by 11 paper. For the picture above I made use of Seafoam green paper
- 1 A sheet of 12 by 12 paper. This can be in any color that you want to create. You make use of it to make that heart template.
- A canvas, board, or sign. (In this project I was able to use 16 by 20 stretched canvas on a frame)
- The Cricut machine
- Free SVG/DXF/PDF cut files or patterns which are available online or you might just get the template from your pre-installed design bank and tweak it a little.

STEP 1

Get your butterfly designs from online downloads, or you can construct yours by arranging these designs on the Cricut design space and give them a uniform measurement. I also made a large heart design to house these butterflies. To add that touch of beauty to it, you should use several types of butterflies in this heart like; the blue morphos, emerald swallowtails, monarchs, and even the scarlet peacocks. I used all of these in my design.

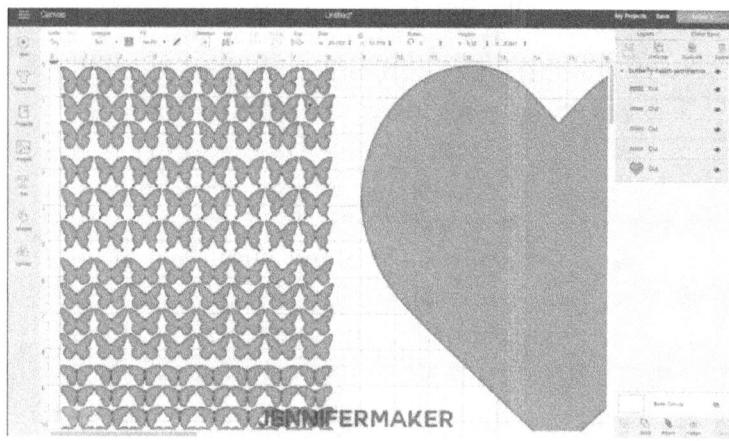

STEP 2

Load the images on your Cricut machine and cut them out.

STEP 3

Fold the butterfly wings

STEP 4

Trace the heart or other shapes on the canvas with a pencil. Make sure that the traces are very light.

STEP 5

Glue those paper butterflies on the canvas forming any pattern you choose.

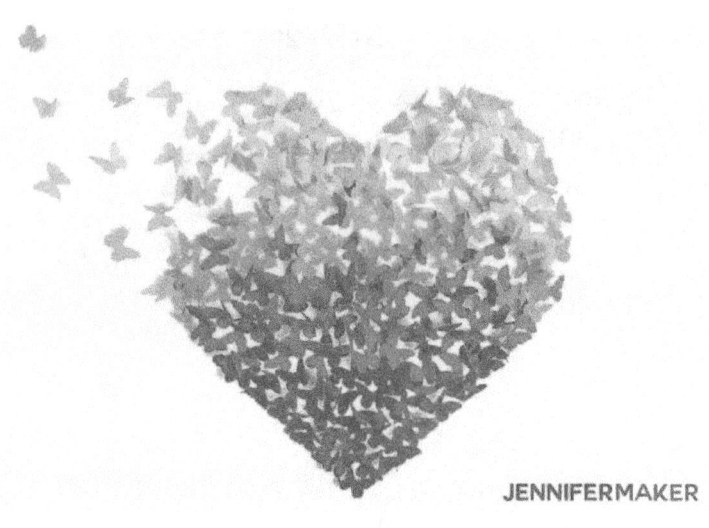

JENNIFER**MAKER**

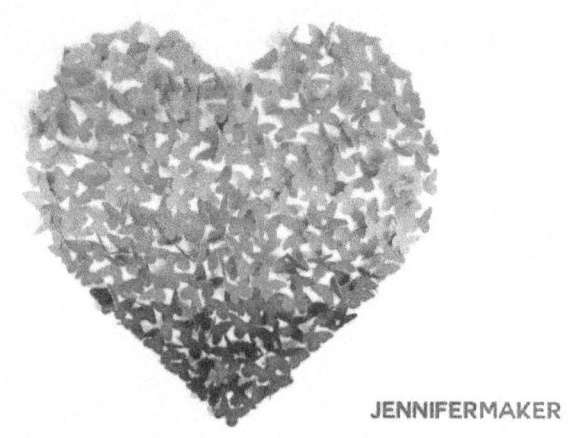

JENNIFER**MAKER**

46

PROJECT 5- DIY FLOAT KOOZIES
Level- Easy

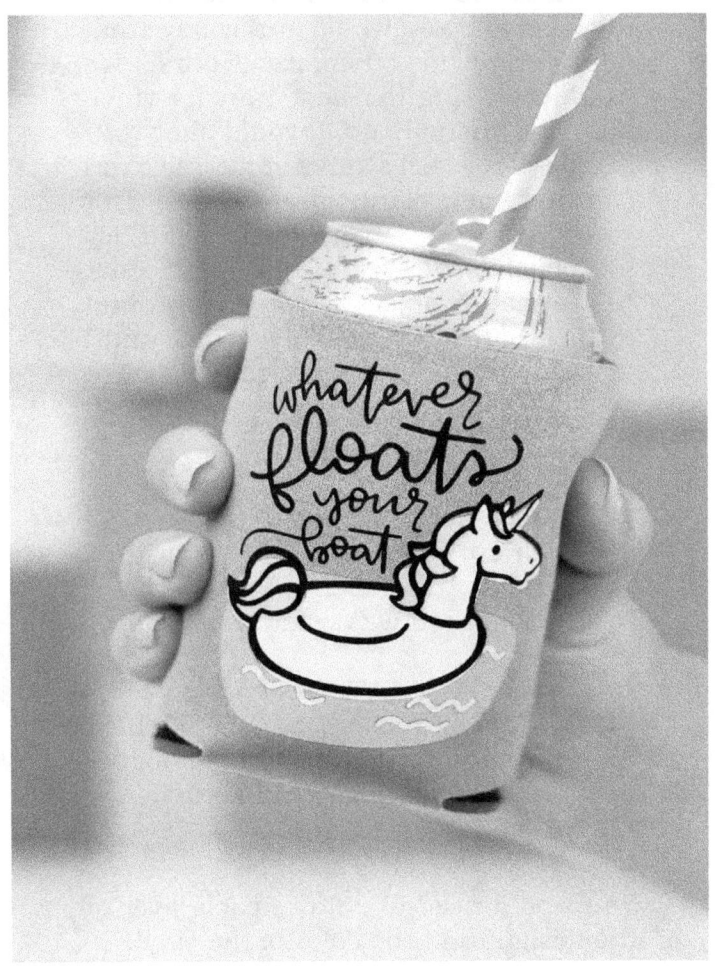

CREDIT- XOXO ALXSIS

You would learn how to make those beautiful pool float koozies. They are fun to make, and you would surely have that opportunity to customize yours. We would be using the heat transfer vinyl, and just I usually do, I would show you all the steps. Let's have some fun. You can just get blank can koozies. But yours would be colorful and definitely inexpensive. It would give you that perfect handy object as you float around in the pool. I love them so much, and I am sure you would love them too.

SUPPLIES NEEDED

- Blank Koozies
- Any Weeding Tool
- Cricut Maker
- Heat Transfer Vinyl. Siser Easyweed was what I used here.
- Iron
- Pool Float SVG Designs
- Multi-purpose paper. Which would contain parchment paper or that think cotton Fabric

STEP ONE

You would need to cut out each layer of the design from the color of the vinyl.

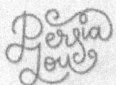

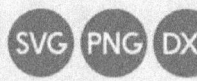

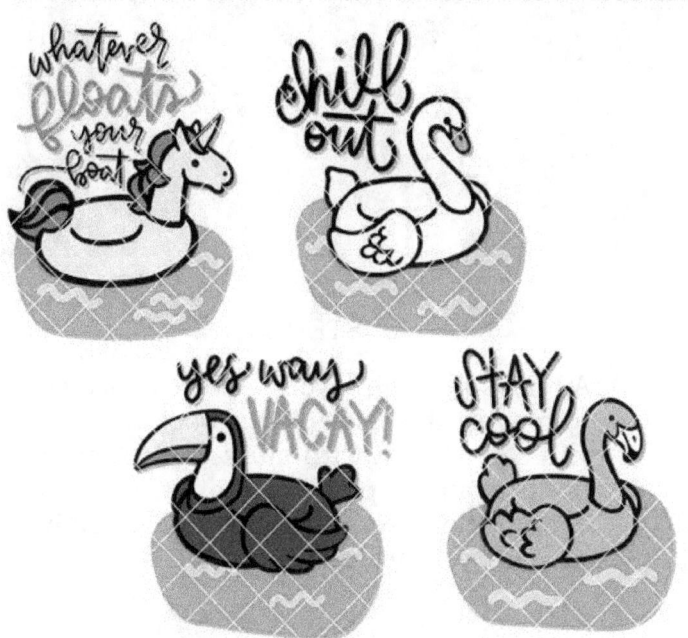

STEP TWO

Make sure you use the top layer to help with the lower layers. So, when you are laying the heat transfer vinyl, you would not only need the iron to lay for some few seconds which you would need to get it to stick since the layer would need more heat plus the application of an extra layer.

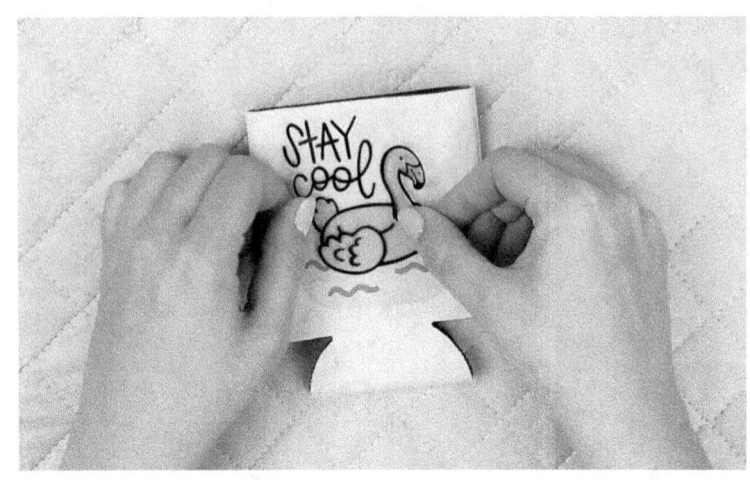

STEP 3

After using each layer, you are expected to remove the clear plastic backing then you can cover it with multi-use paper or the parchment paper or that thin cotton cloth which would protect the already spread over layers.

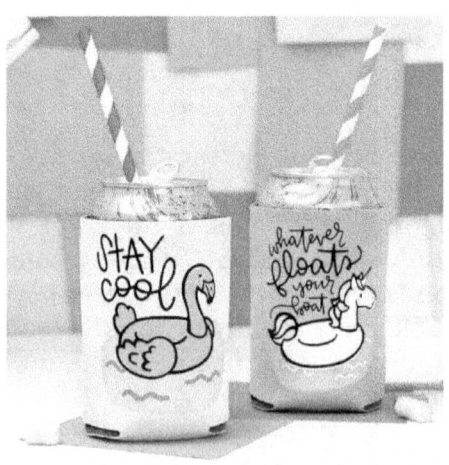

And there you have it! After the final layer has been applied, your koozie is ready to be used to keep your drinks cool!

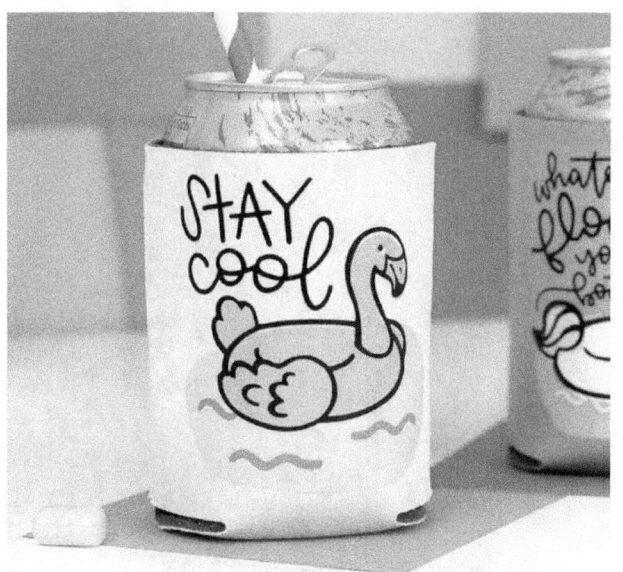

YOU CAN DO THIS NOW!

PROJECT 6- CRICUT MAKER FAUX LEATHER BASKET
Level- Easy

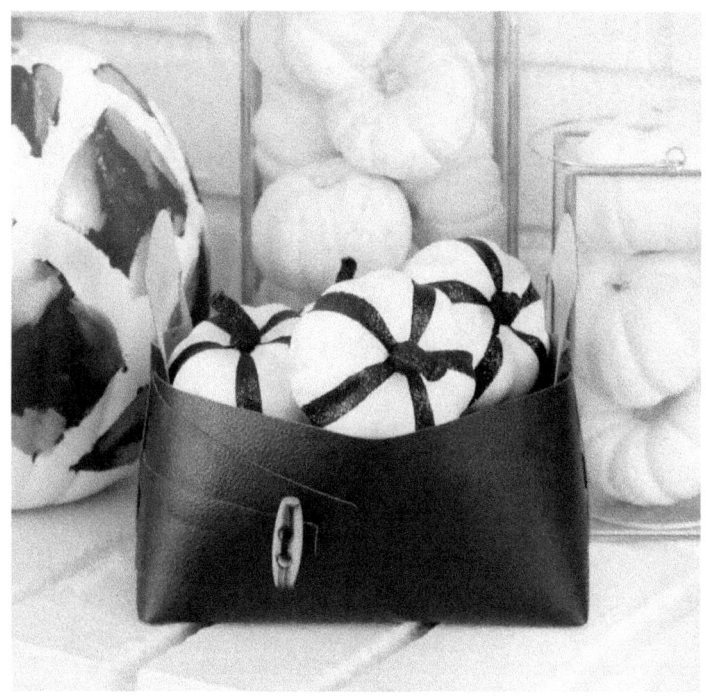

CREDIT-
THECRAFTEDSPARROW.COM

The Cricut machine can cut through any material; leather inclusive; so that is why I have to talk about this project. You can see how beautiful the leather basket is. You can do this by just following the simple steps below. Just gather your supplies, get your design or make yours, blend everything perfectly well, and you are good to go.

SUPPLIES NEEDED

- The Cricut Maker Cutting Machine
- The Cricut Faux Leather, 12 by 24 inches
- Cricut 12 by 24 inches cutting mat
- Your Cricut Scoring Stylus
- A small Buckle or a Button
- Glue Gun

STEP 1

For a project like this, you would begin with making use of real leather or faux leather. I chose faux leather because that was what I had in hand, and besides, it doesn't cost much.

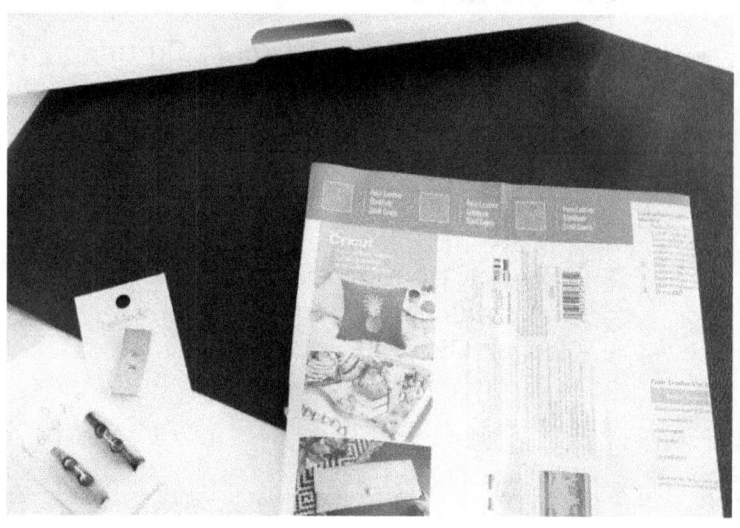

I also chose to make use of a small button. The wood toggle buttons were so appealing to me instead of the metal ones. But the gold one would have been perfect also if I had gone with that.

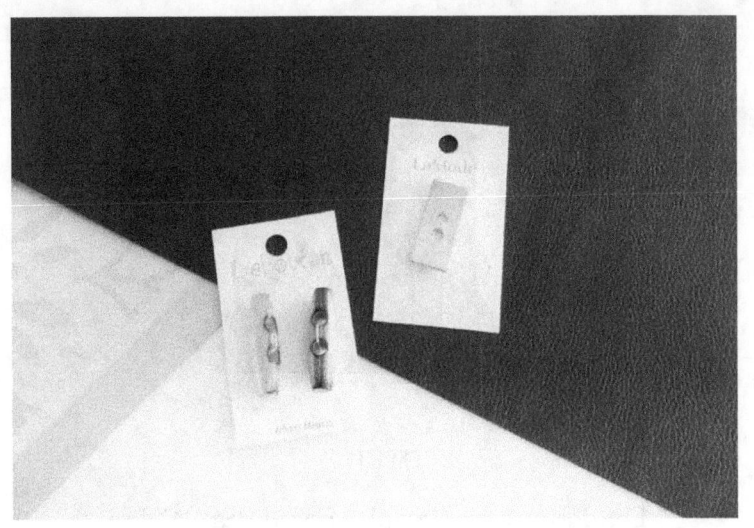

STEP 2

After you have gotten your design,
downloaded or you decide to just make
yours. You resize it into that perfect
shape that you need. Then choose the
material you are working with. You can
also decide to cut out that stiffened felt
too. In case you want to make the basket
smaller than the way it is, you click
customize not *make it*. Then you make
necessary adjustments.

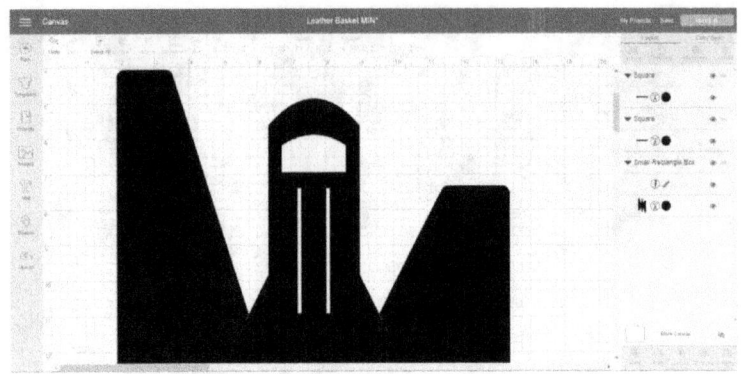

STEP 3

Load your materials onto that Cricut mat, and press GO! The material would cut great with its fine pointed blade. Easy and simple right?

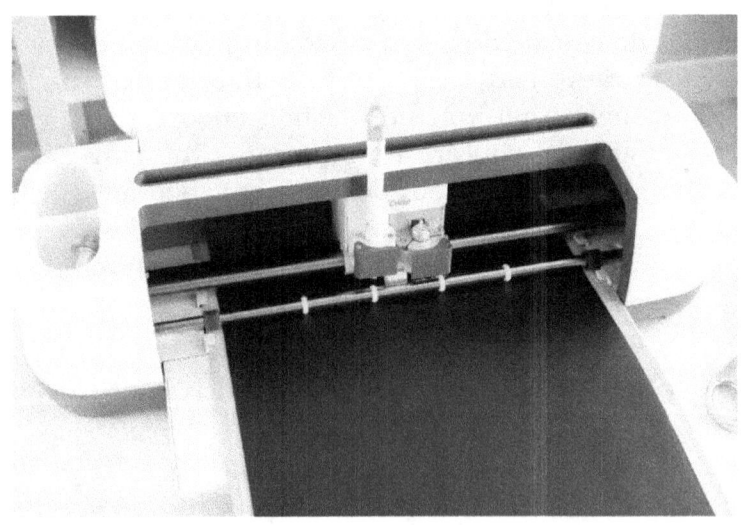

STEP 4

After the cutting process, you remove it gently from the Cricut mat, and you peel away those excess materials, and you have the pieces needed for the next step.

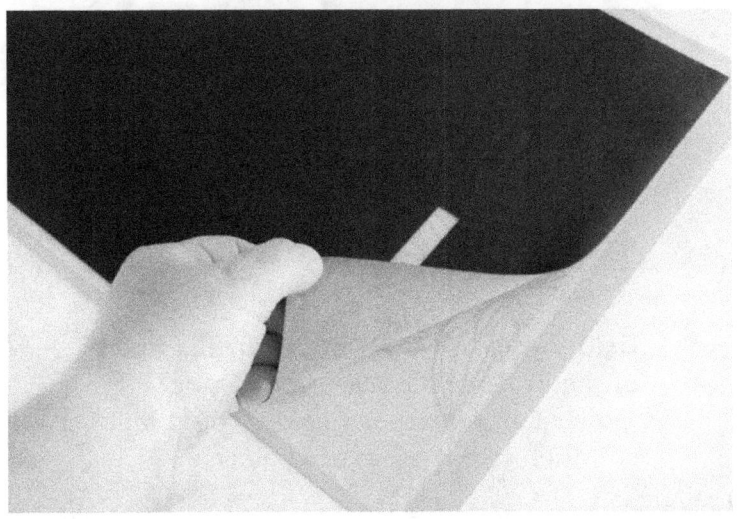

You should follow the detailed instructions on how you can make it. It is very simple. Just use a small amount of hot glue to hold down the basket pieces into position.

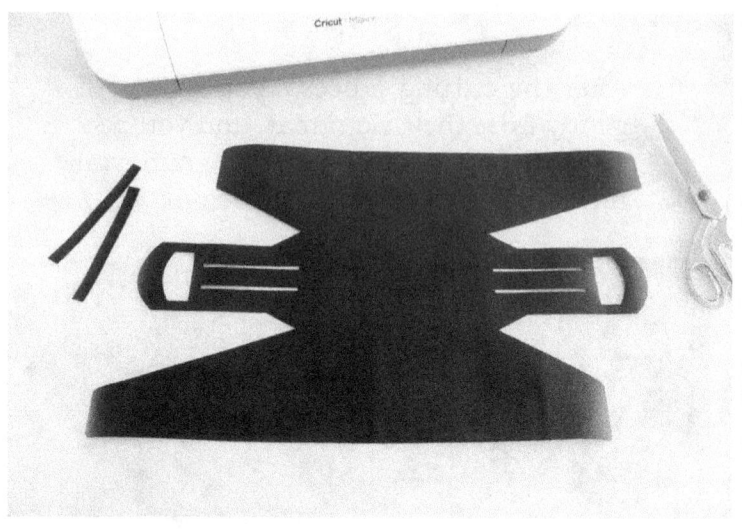

Before you add that final embellishment of the button or buckle your Cricut Maker Faux Leather Basket would look so much like the picture below.

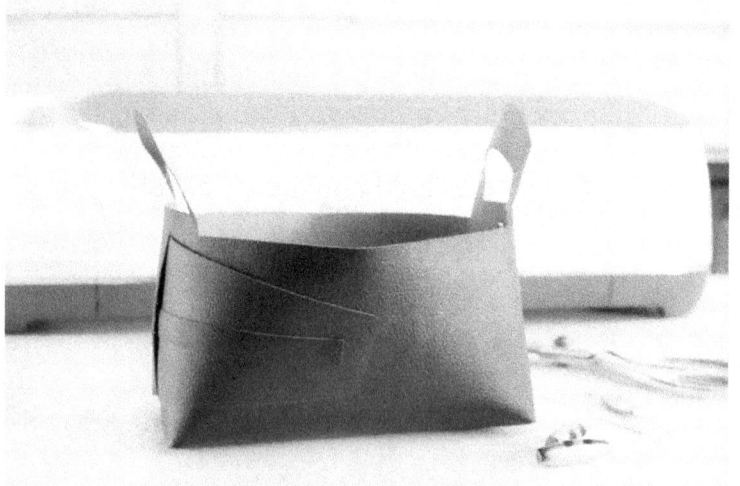

Remember, I made use of that toggle button and not a buckle. I also made use of black embroidery floss to build that *faux stitch* on the button, and then I made use of the hot glue to place the button on the basket.

It is so cute, right? This is something you can do within minutes. You can use this little basket to add some interesting home décor to your harem. And it is also cute for gifting purposes.

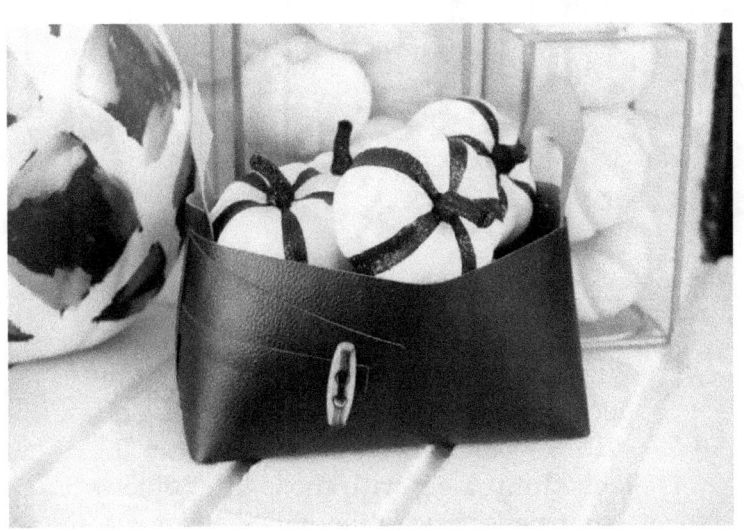

Level- Easy

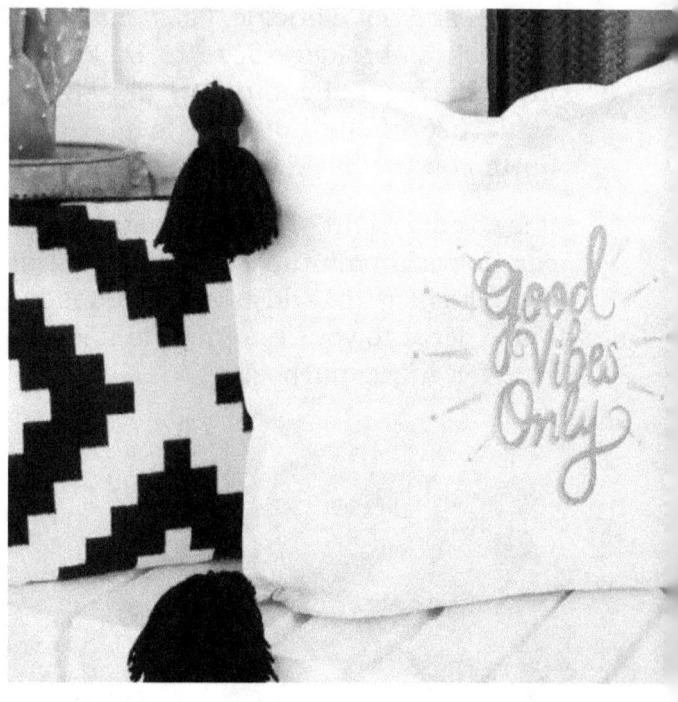

CREDIT-
THECRAFTEDSPARROW.COM

Whenever I am thinking of changing my décor; I always begin with switching out a throw pillow. I usually freshen up the look of my room with those little pillows that make huge differences. From all the projects that we have been doing, you must have noticed that starting something from scratch can be real time -consuming. I love a new quick DIY design, which is why I make use of the Cricut Iron-on designs. You are going to be taught how to do so.

SUPPLIES NEEDED

- Cricut Iron-On Designs (personal or downloaded to later upload on your design space)
- The Cricut Easy press
- The Cricut Easy press Mat
- Ikea Pillow Cover or any beautiful already made pillow cover
- Pillow inserts
- Some Yarn Tassels or Some Extra-Large Pom-Poms

STEP 1

You begin by making sure your pillow is covered with smooth pillow edges. You get your pillow cover ready by making it smooth. While making use of these, you should think of your personal design or wordings. I chose *Good Vibes Only* here. Before ironing the design, you must set the EasyPress to that correct temperature for your material. I had a

pillow cover cotton, so I placed it at 340⁰
With that time setting a record of 30
seconds. You might decide to reduce and
increase the level because they would be
divided into several heat settings which
are required for each surface.

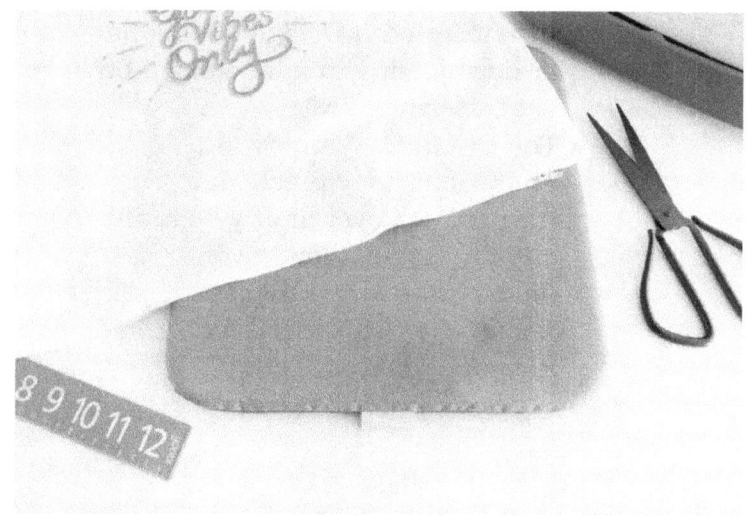

STEP 2

You should make sure that the design
on the pillow cover is placed strategically
at the center. You use your Cricut Easy
press to hover around and hold it firmly
in place for some 30 seconds. Don't
forget to use the timer. Once the timer

beeps, you know it is time to move to the next fragment of the design and don't forget to do the same.

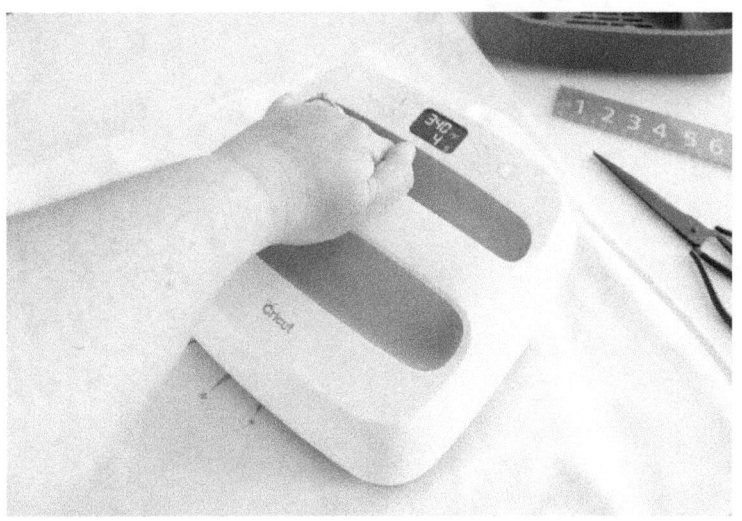

STEP 3

The Cricut EasyPress is very convenient and very easy to use. I should tell you that you can use the EasyPress for everyday ironing also. Are you aware? The EasyPress is very good stuff because it covers a very large surface area more than your regular iron. You are to reveal the iron-on design by doing a *cold peel.* What this means is that you should let cool off completely before removing that protective clear sheet that is over it.

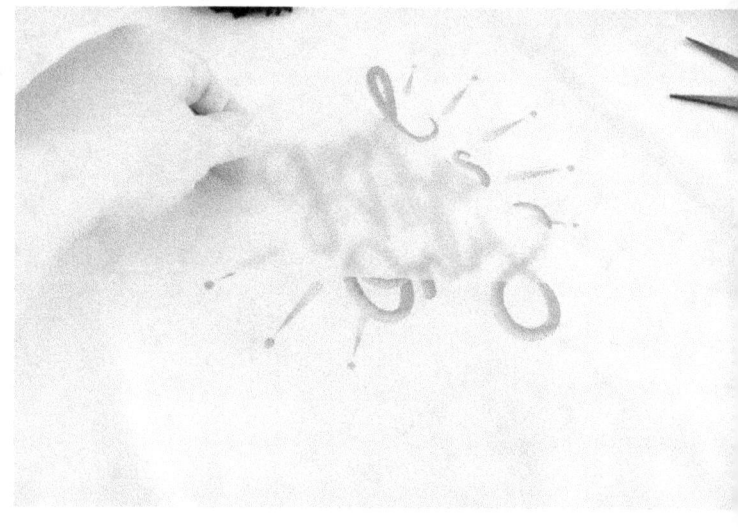

STEP 4

After this, you can decide to embellish your pillow. This is completely up to you. In this project, I was working with a premade pillow cover, so I decided to go with something simple and very easy. I went with the DIY yarn tassel for the project. You might decide to do pom-poms, pom-pom trim or you might just leave it the way it is. That is your decision, but I am sure you would want to make some designs.

For the tassel, you would wrap that your yarn around that piece of cardboard. For this project, I wrapped mine over and over again like a hundred times because I wanted them to be big and chunky. Next was that I trimmed them with those sewing shears.

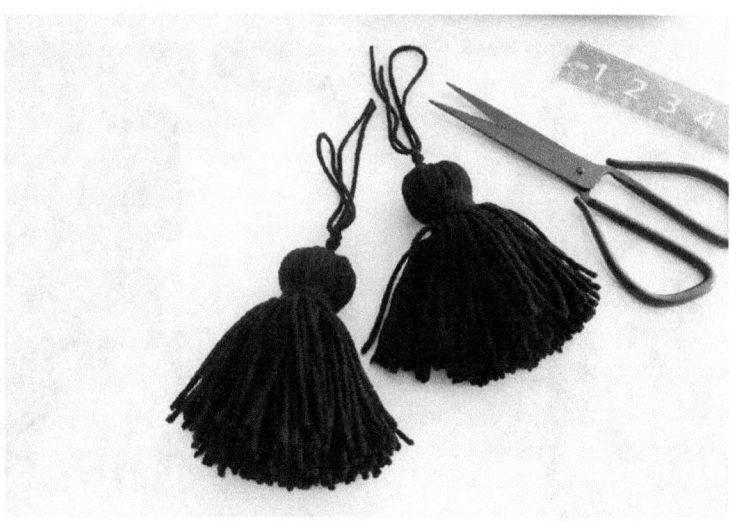

STEP 5

To add those tassels to the strategic corners, you would unstitch a very tiny spot on each side of the pillow cover with your seam ripper. Then you would insert the shot tassel string making use of some hot glue to seal it shut and secure it. Then you can also stitch them into that place that you want. I made use of a quick and easy way with the hot glue.

Lastly, you add your pillow to that corner of the room. Simple!

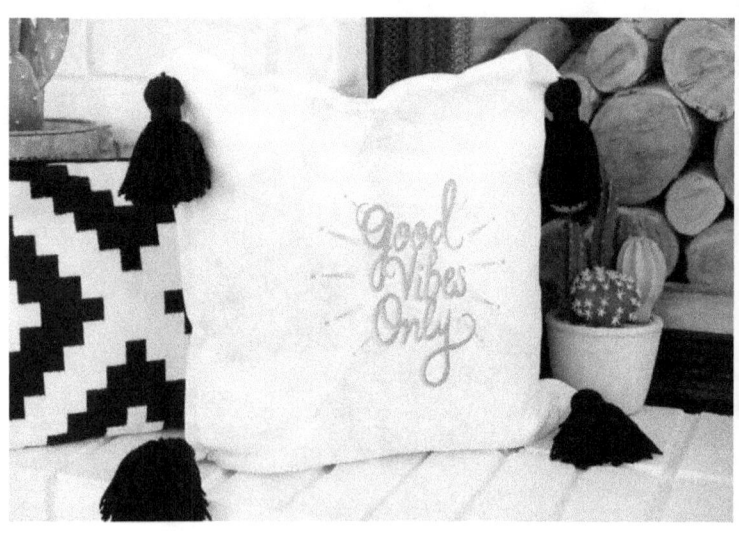

YOU CAN DO THIS NOW!

PROJECT 8- HYPER-REALISTIC CREPE PAPER PEONY FLOWERS

Level- Easy

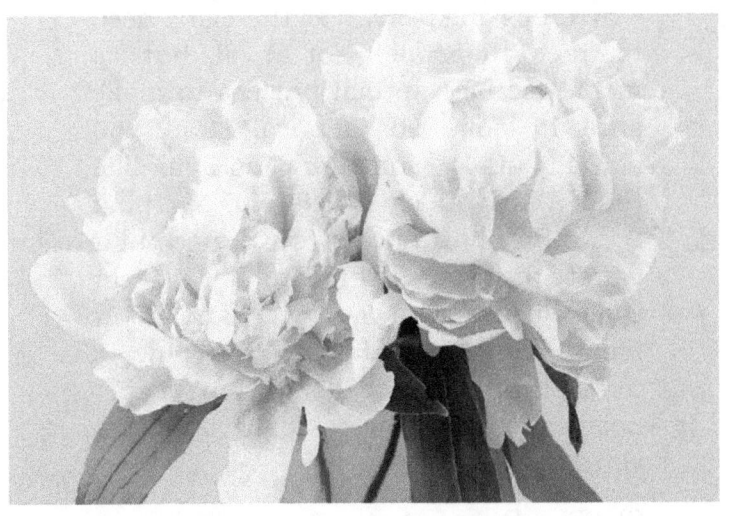

CREDIT- JENNIFER MAKER

I call it hyper-realistic because it looks so much like the original; in fact, we take objects from the real flower to make it. The flower looks so real that you'll forget that they are not real at all. This project is a product of Sarah Bernhardt double peonies. Like all Cricut projects in this book, this is fun.

For the Sarah Bernhardt peonies, I specially removed all the single petal on that peony. I was able to pull the petals away carefully, and this allowed me to prepare a wonderful pattern on the Cricut design space. Was there any need to trace all petals? Not at all, but we made use of a special process to make sure it looks so identical. Can you actually make something so real like this? Yes, you can. This delicate pink Sarah Bernhardt peony is a very popular variety that you can't ignore. It is a décor that you would always want and never ignore. So, I would show you how to make that hyper-realistic crepe paper peony for your flowers that would last you for so long.

SUPPLIES

- Fine Crepe Paper in Pink, green and yellow. I made use of the exact brand so you should do the same.
- Green floral wire
- Green floral tape
- Glue. It would be tacky glue and a hot glue gun
- A Cricut Maker

- Free files online or your own designs.

STEP 1

First, you cut your crepe paper making use of free SVG, DXF or the PDF files which can be found from several resource library or you make use of your own designs by cutting petals from the peony.

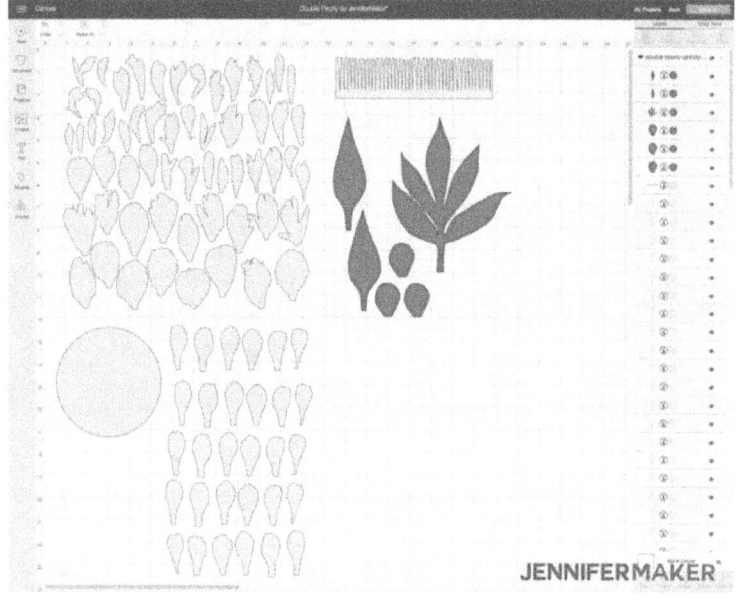

You should be sure that when you are gutting the crepe paper, the grain of the paper must be vertical and not horizontal.

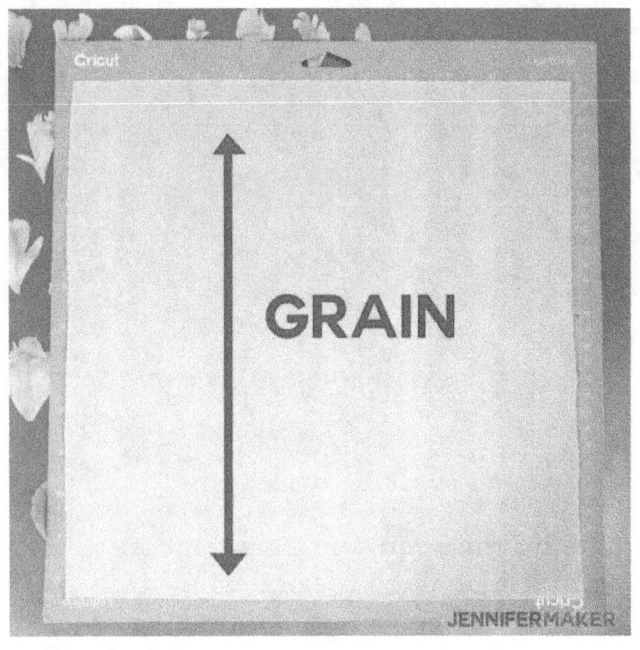

STEP 2

Then you take your cut crepe paper pieces away from the mat, and you can keep the petals in the order of the shown file. You might decide to cut your crepe paper with your hand making use of a PDF pattern, but that would just make the Cricut machine useless. What you would do next is to crumple a sheet of your scrap crepe paper. I set the petals into a ball in the picture below

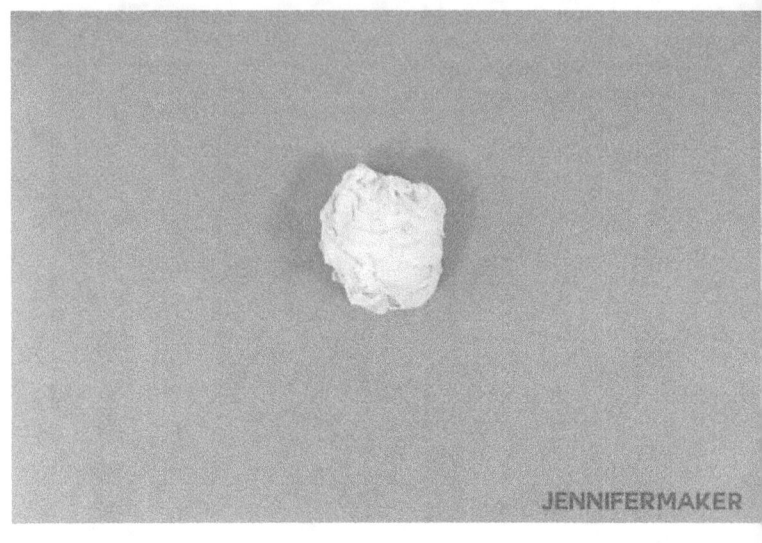

After that, you would now cut out a 12-inch long piece of floral wire which you can use to glue it into the center of that paper ball.

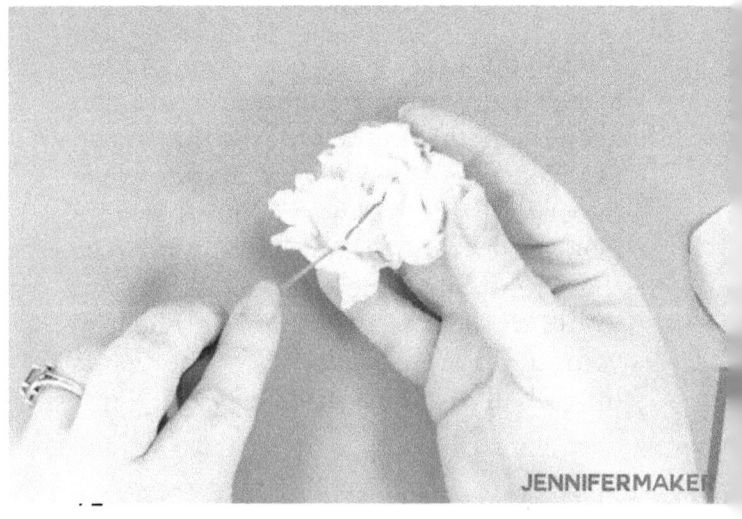

STEP 3

Then you would place the ball and the wire on the center of the crepe paper circle that you have been able to cut out. Then put the line of glue around the perimeter of that circle.

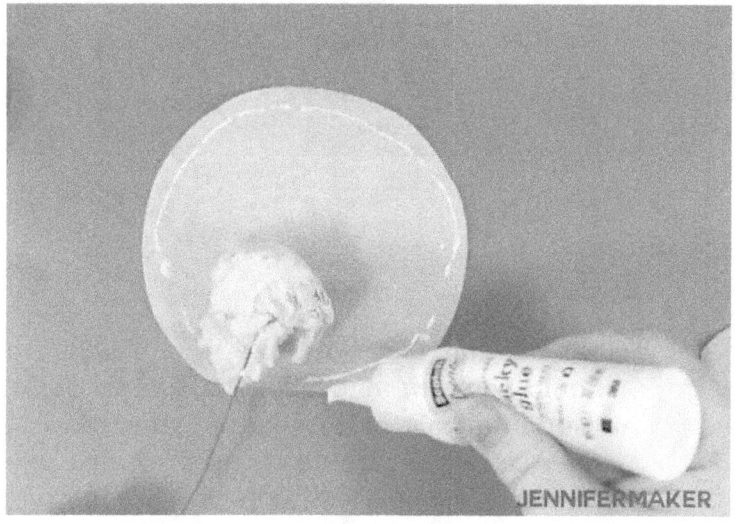

Then you would wrap the circle all around the crepe paper ball before pressing it down alongside the edges that you have been able to glue. This would make that crepe paper peony bud form properly like the flower around.

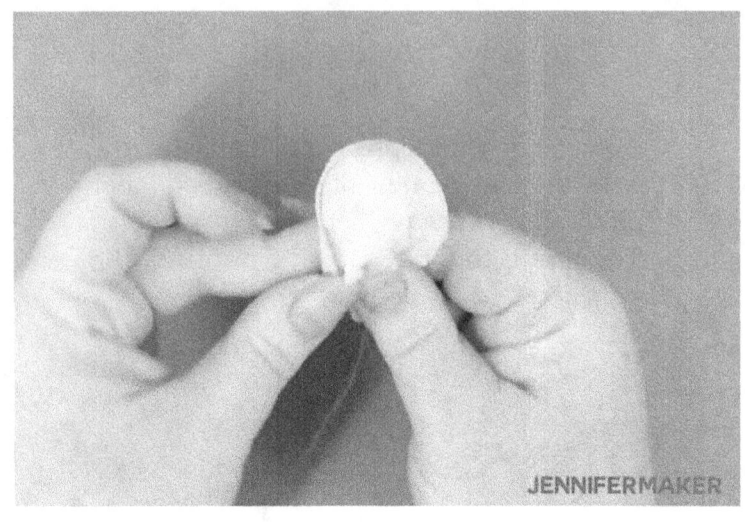

JENNIFERMAKER

STEP 4

Tear off that piece of floral tape which should be a few inches long and wrap it around the base of the edge of that crepe paper circle that would be used to tuck everything in perfectly. Below is the finished crepe paper peony flower bud.

Now let us focus our attention to the petals. There are several types of petals, one for each of the two "blooms" for the double peony. But the first set you

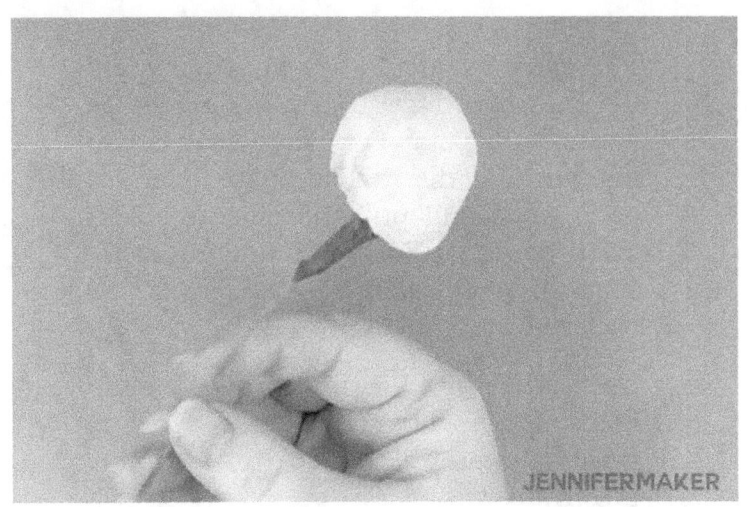

would need to attach that peony bud
with simple petals that should look like
the picture below

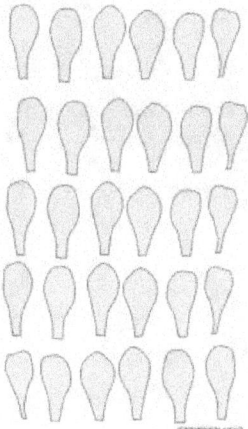

For every particular petal, you would need to *cup* it gently by pulling those edges of the petal. For you to do this, you should hold the middle of the edge for each petal and pull them gently. That crepe paper would stretch and form that kind of depression in the paper. It's super nice.

It would be nice for you to ruffle the top ideas of the petals to make it real peony petals. I was able to do this with my fingernails.

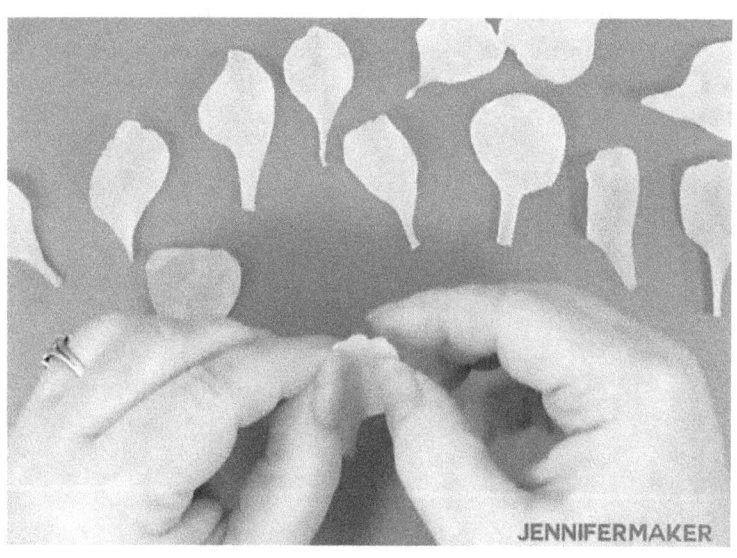

STEP 5

After you have been able to cuff all your petals cupped and ruffled you can start gluing them to that bud. Make sure that you use ALL of the first set which is above to show the bud. Make sure that you glue them so that the petal's cup would be in line with the curve of the bud.

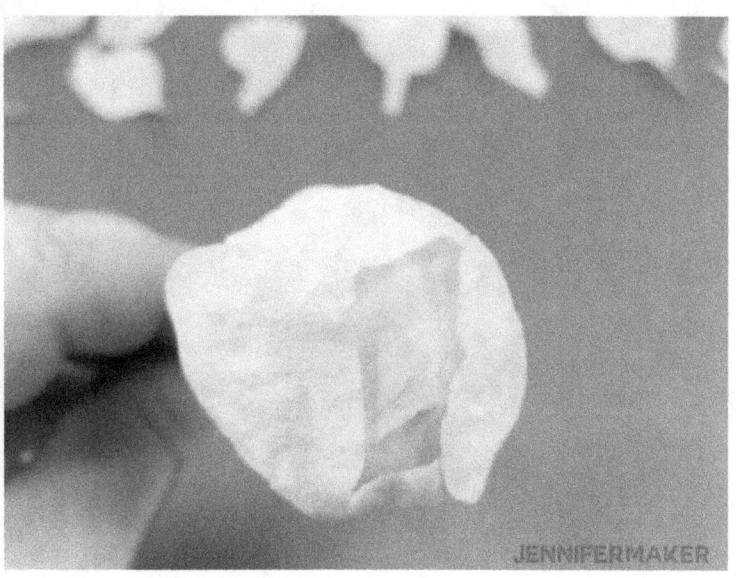

Don't stop. You continue to glue the bottom of the first set of petals to the bud in a clean circular fashion which would be around the base. Then you keep going around that flower. Keep doing it until you run out of the first set of buds. These crepe paper peony flowers would surely look like the picture below

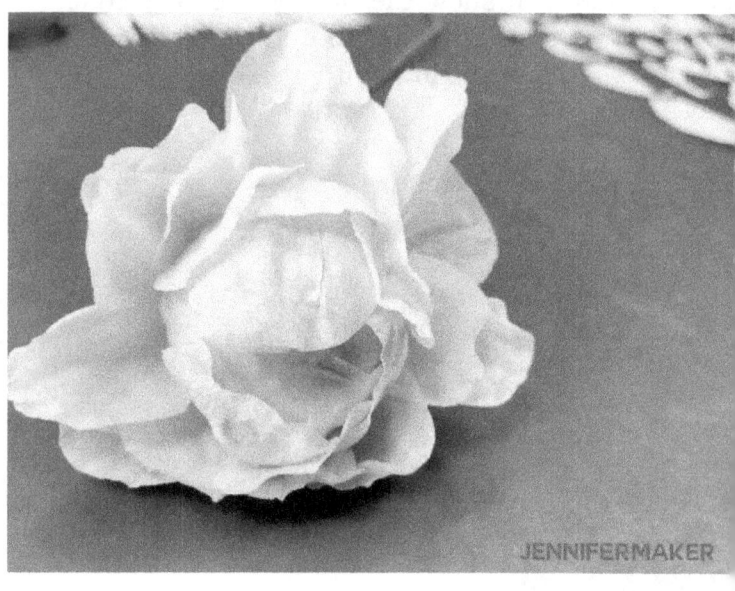

Start making the stamen by twisting those long strands that you have been able to cut between your fingers like this

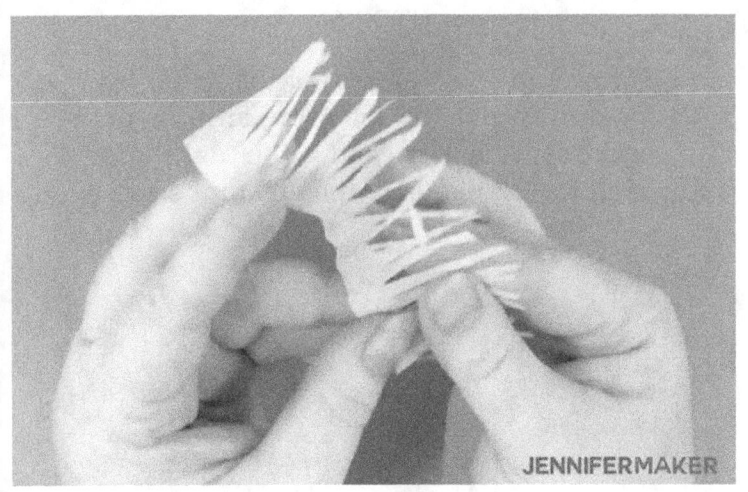

After doing that the stamen should be shaped so that it would look less like strips of paper, and this would look so much natural. Don't forget to glue the base also.

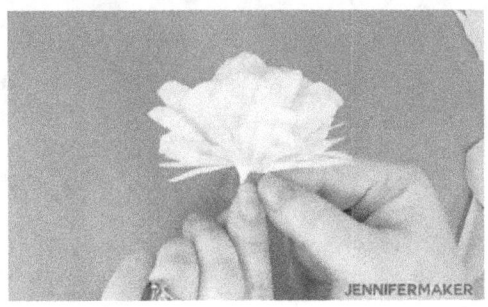

STEP 6

You would glue the rest of the metal by making use of the following formula or pathway. It is very good if you make use of all the 60 petals of the different sizes.

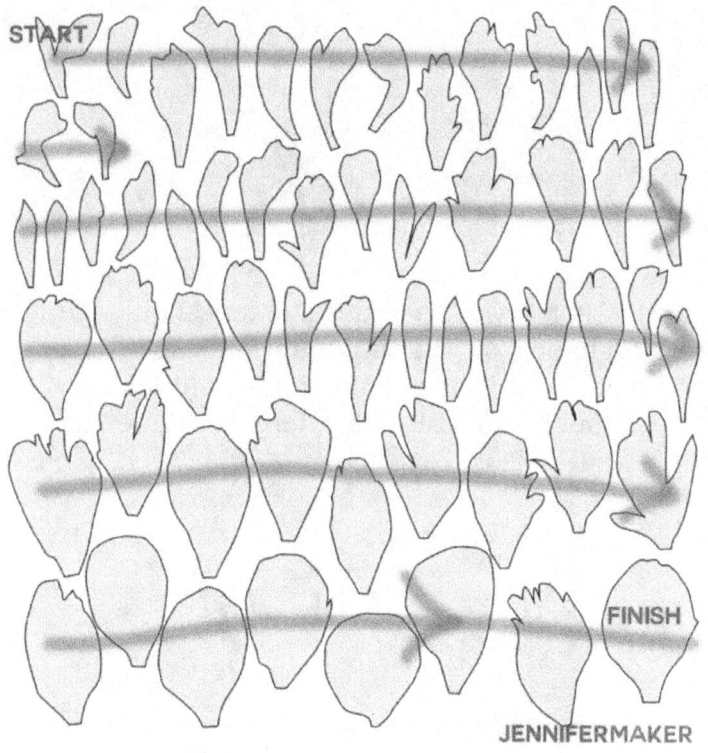

Then you would join the petal of the peony by touching it with glue with the base of the crepe paper peony flower. You should make use of the peony flower and stick it to the bottom.

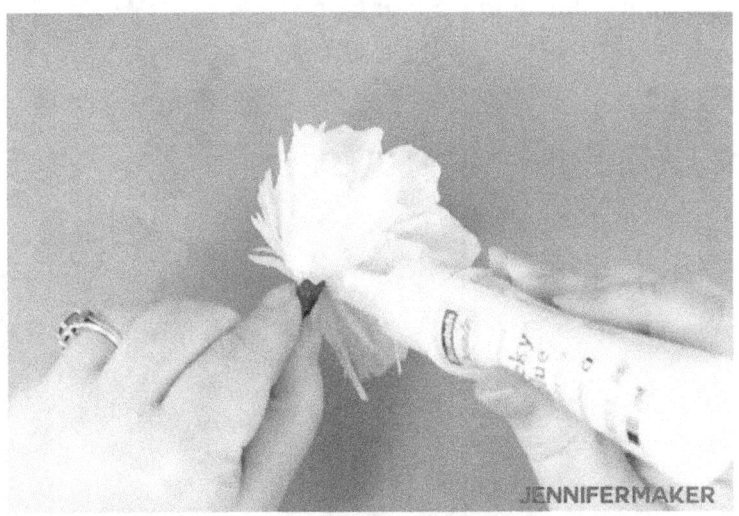

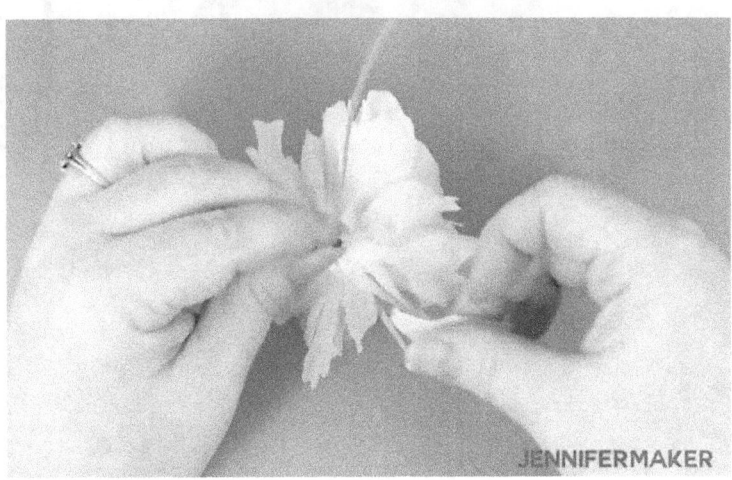

Then you would continue to glue the petals on the base of the peony in that circular fashion like below:

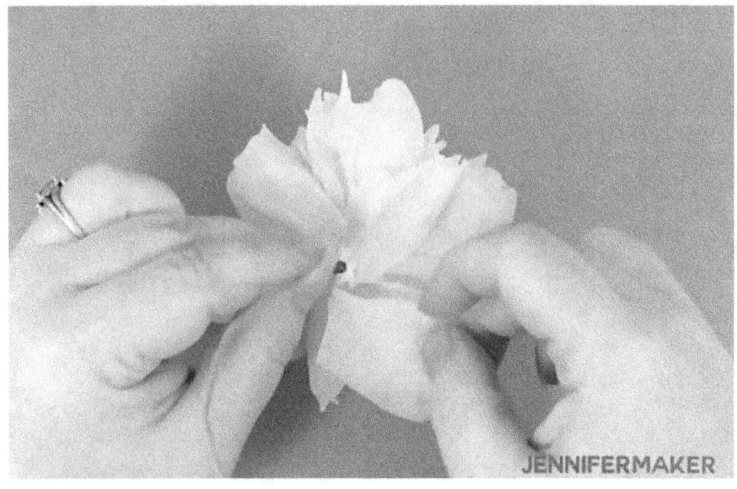

When you get to the end, you will glue the largest petals. It would look so much like this

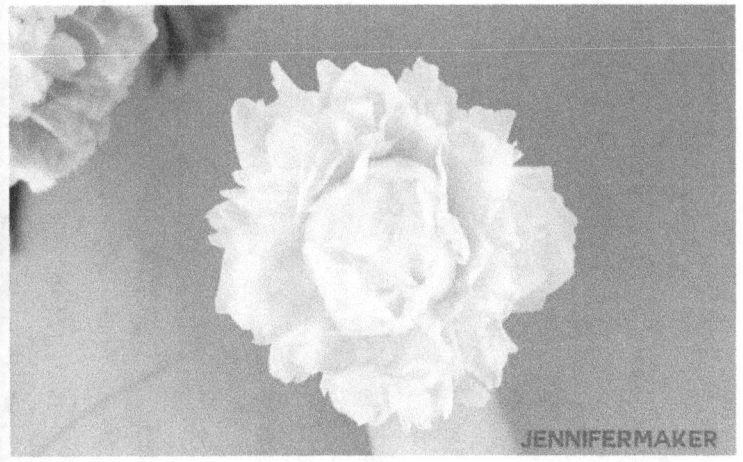

Turn the peony over and glue the three green sepal petals to the underside also.

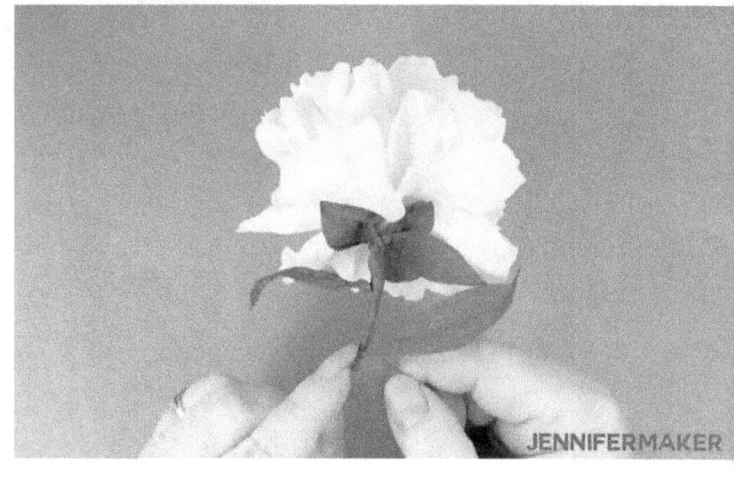

If you want the leave to be very realistic, you should glue that strip of floral wire to the underside to give it more structure.

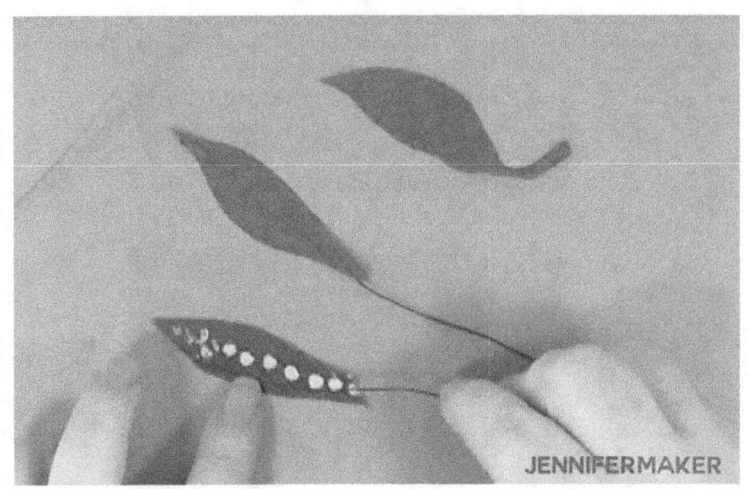

Then you finish it by wrapping the floral tape around the stem.

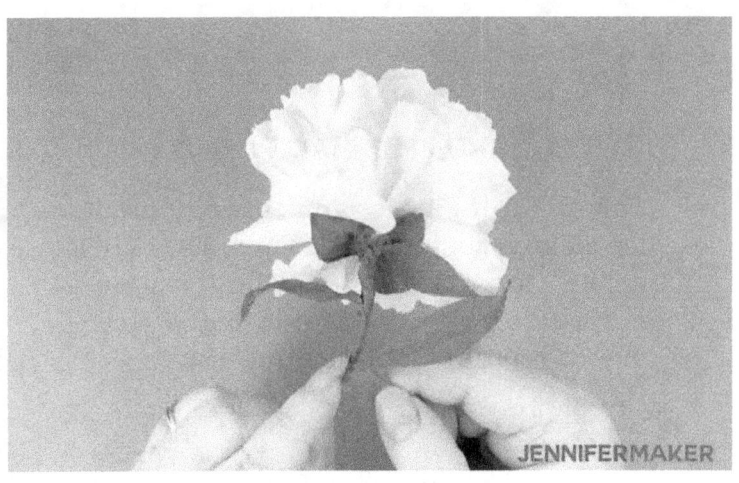

YOU CAN DO THIS NOW!

Level-Easy

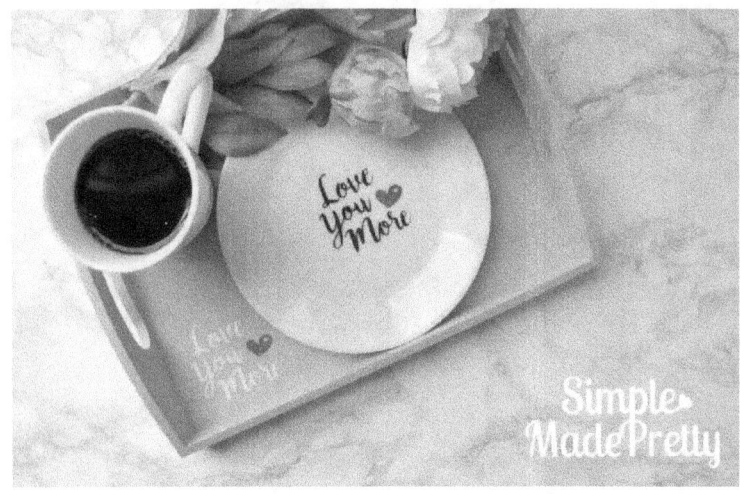

CREDIT-SIMPLE MADE PRETTY

This DIY Cut File design is majorly used for making customary designs. They are meant for romantic celebrations to surprise that special him or her, which makes it perfect for Valentine' Day.

SUPPLIES NEEDED

- The Cricut Explore
- Vinyl. I made use of a black, red, pink and white variety

- Serving Tray, Mug, Drinking Glass or Plate
- The Contact Paper

STEP 1

Get the SVG, DXF or PNG file and upload to the Cricut Design Space or you can work on your own personal design.

STEP 2

You should edit the image according to the size of the cup or plate that you are going to use. I used 3 by 3 inches for all the items in the picture above. Then you would weed the cut image.

STEP 3

Add the contact paper and paste it with the serving tray, mug, drinking glass, or plate. Note that you can only hand-wash these utensils do not use the microwave.

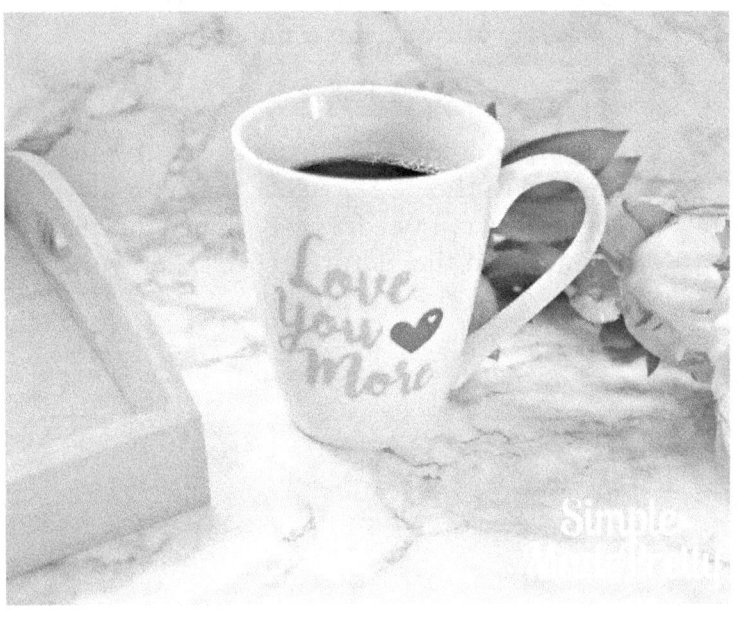

YOU CAN DO THIS NOW!

PROJECT 10 – DIY PERSONALIZED OUTDOOR LOUNGE CHAIRS

Medium level

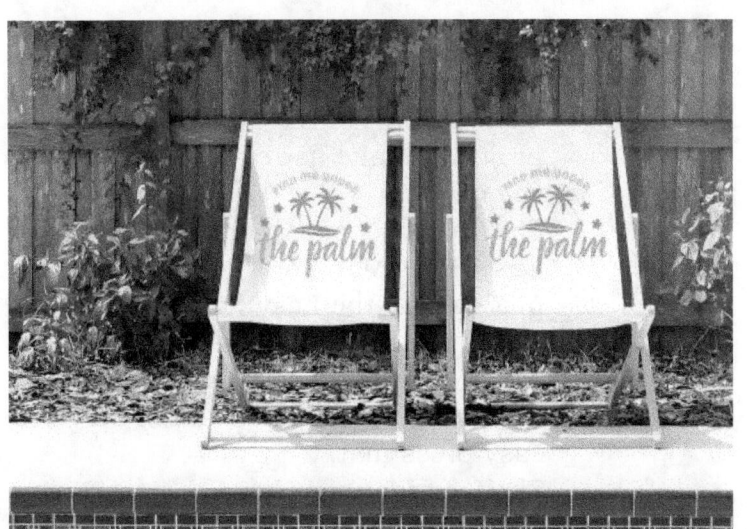

CREDIT- SIMPLE MADE PRETTY

These personalized outdoor lounge chairs give that exceptional look that would brighten up your pool or the beach. These fun, personalized outdoor lounge chairs are very easy to make, and like any other Cricut project, the possibilities to these projects are endless. You can possibly add names, fun quotes to the backside, and many more.

YOU'LL NEED THE FOLLOWING SUPPLIES

- The Cricut Explore cutting machine
- Iron-on Vinyl or the HTV. For this project, I make use of a variety of colors.
- The ironing board or Cricut the Easy Press Mat. For this project, I made using the Easy Press Mat.
- You'll be needing the ironing board or the Cricut easy press mat. I was able to make use of the easy press mat.
- The fabric lounge chairs.

STEP 1

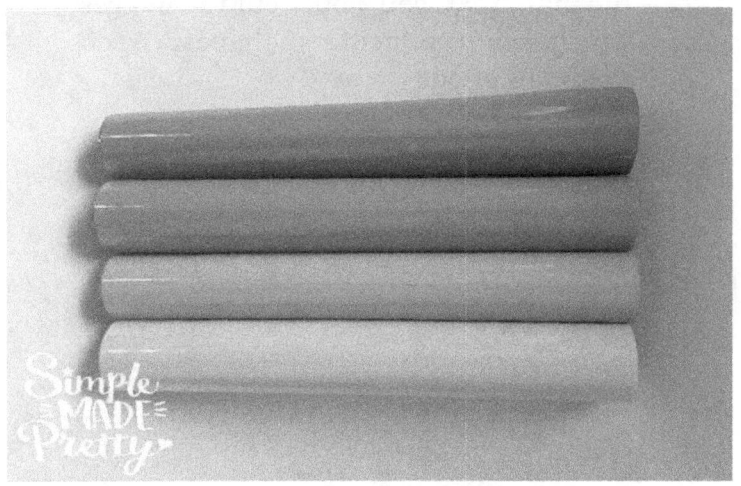

You make your design on the Cricut Design space, or you get the SVG or PNG file online and upload it. The size of the image must be in accordance with the size of the chairs.

You should mirror the image and place that shiny side on the material down on the mat. Next, you would cut the images which are rudimentary shapes. Weed the images too.

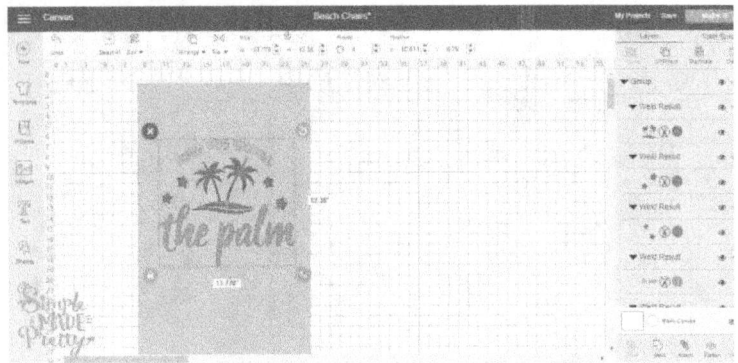

STEP 2

Remove the fabric from the chair. I made use of Ikea chair fabric, which is very easy to remove. You can slide the wooden dowels from the top.

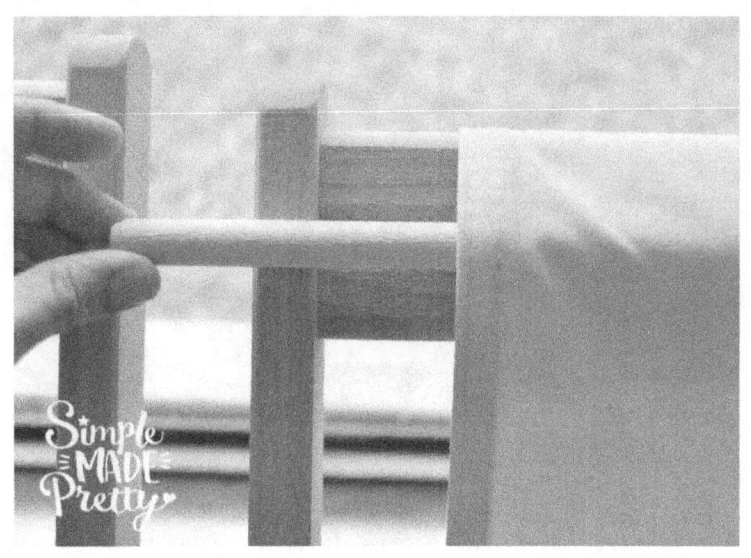

STEP 3

Carefully arrange the image on the fabric. You may decide to cut more than one color that makes it very interesting and cool.

STEP 4

Make use of an iron or the Cricut easy press to iron the image to the fabric.

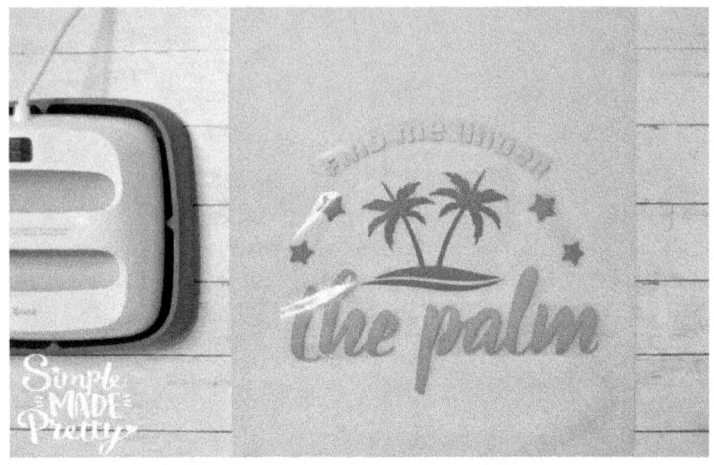

Most times, what you need to do is to hold the easy press down for just about 30 seconds at 300 degrees. This doesn't take so much time at all. Then peel the back to reveal that clear imprint.

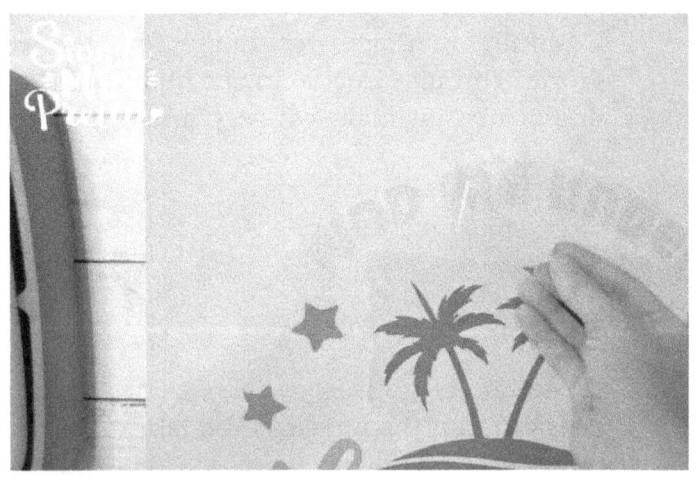

STEP 5

Place the fabric on the chair and enjoy your relaxing day at the pool, backyard, or beach with your personalized chairs.

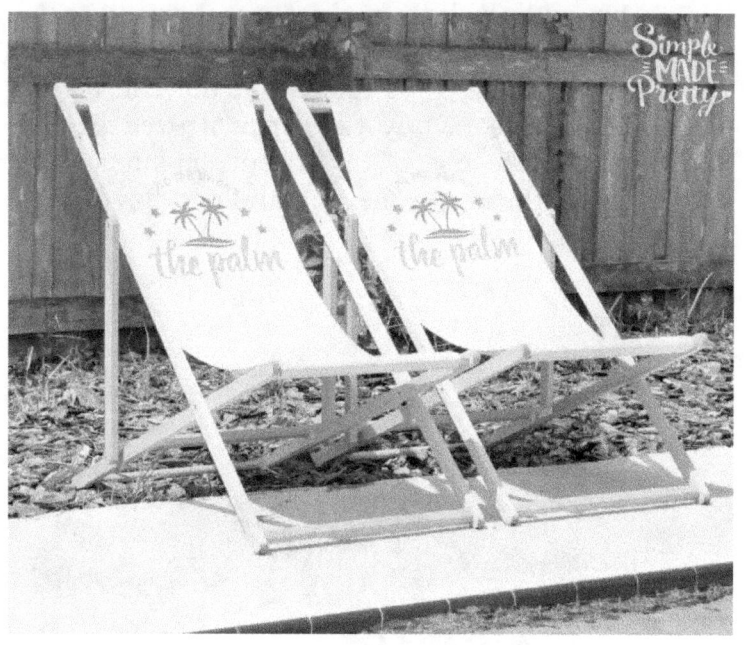

YOU CAN DO THIS NOW!

PROJECT 11- MAKING SUMMER APPAREL (T-SHIRTS, BAGS AND MORE)
Medium Level

Most of the time, I find very good ways to upcycle those old t-shirts, tank tops, and bags. A very good way to do this is by adding fun graphics to them. So, what happens is that I would get a plain t-shirt, tank tops and all at the end of each season, buy new ones if need be and make use of my Cricut explore to make those summer apparel designs on them.

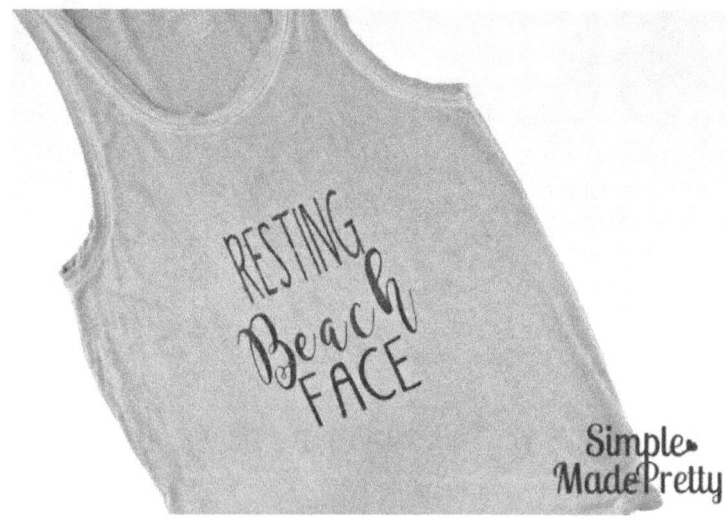

CREDIT- SIMPLE MADE PRETTY

SUPPLIES NEEDED FOR THIS PROJECT

- Old or new Plain shirts, pants or bags
- The Cricut explore machine
- Cricut Vinyl
- Cricut Transfer Tape
- Weeding Tool
- Sponge Brushes
- Fabric Paint
- Free SVG files or you can make use of your own designs.

STEP 1

First, you either upload your SVG files to the Cricut Design Space, or you create your own image in the design space. However, when you are uploading this image, you should clear the crop tool or remove those corner images and save them also.

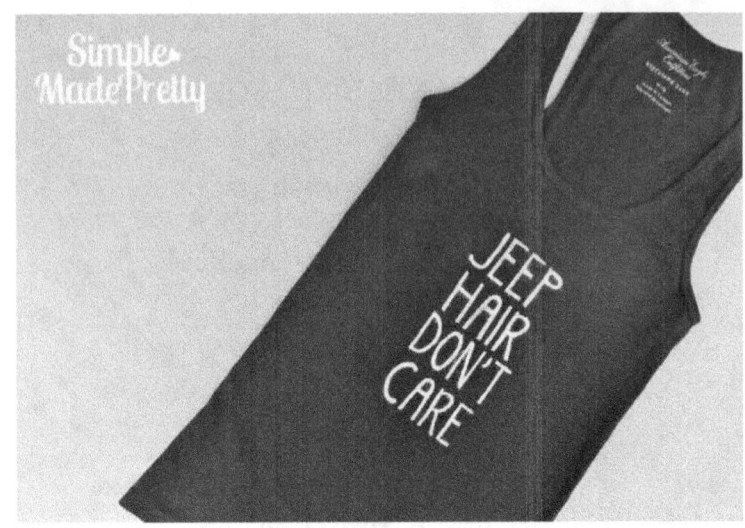

STEP 2

Load any color vinyl of your choice on the Cricut standard grip cutting mat on your Cricut cutting mat. Then you set the machine dial to vinyl. Then you cut the image making use of the Cricut Explore. The next process would require you to weed out the image, but you should make use of the image because you will be making use of this as the *stencil.*

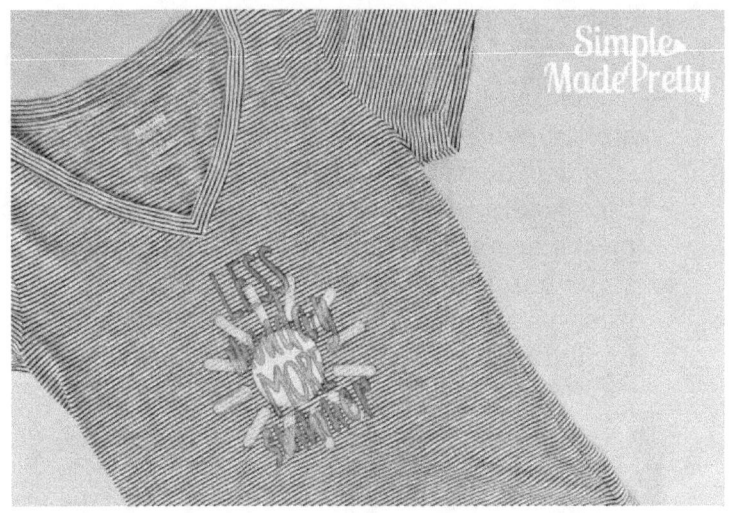

STEP 3

Make use of the transfer tape over the
vinyl and place it over the T-shirt, bag,
or any other apparel item. Then you
carefully remove the transfer tape. You
can use a sponge brush to gently dab the
fabric paint on your stencil.

STEP 4

Immediately after the covering of the stencil with paint, you should gently remove the small pieces. I made use of the weeding tool to remove those small pieces around. Definitely, you would get some paint on your fingers and the tool, but you should just wash them immediately.

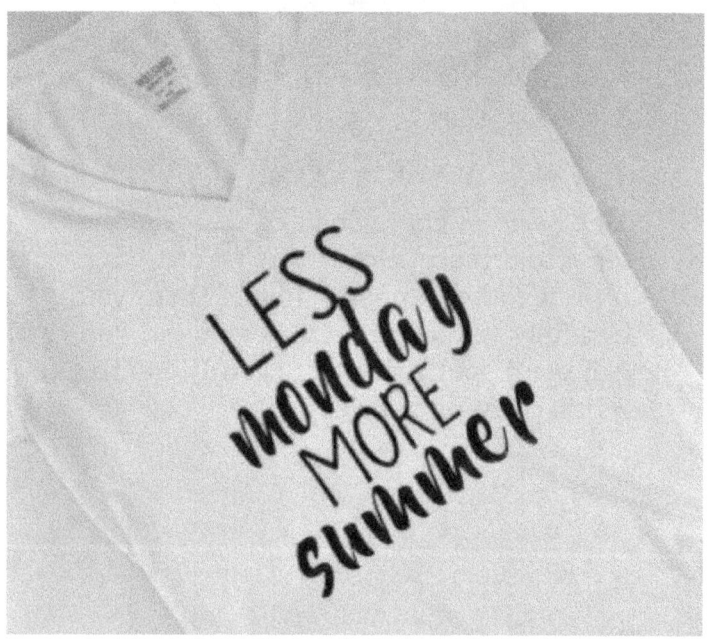

STEP 5

Allow it to dry for 24 hours straight, and you shouldn't wash the item for 72 hours!

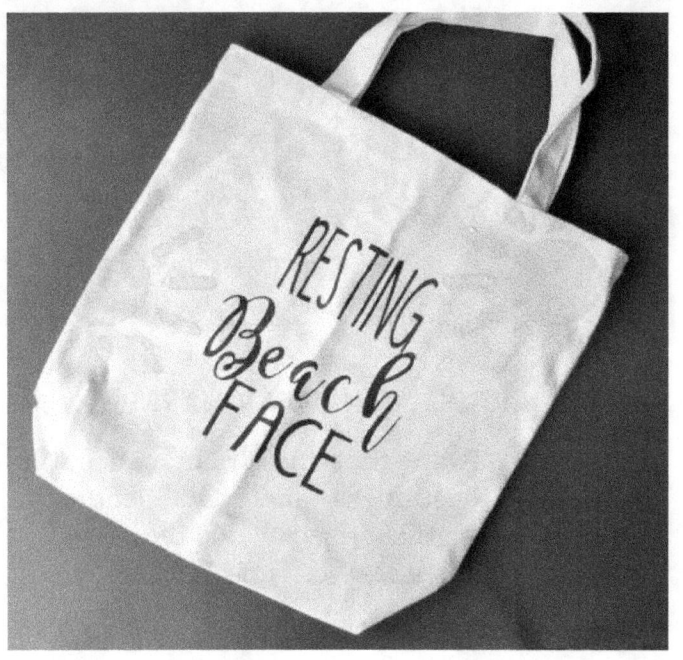

YOU CAN DO THIS NOW

PROJECT 12- DIY LEATHER CUFF BRACELET
Medium Level

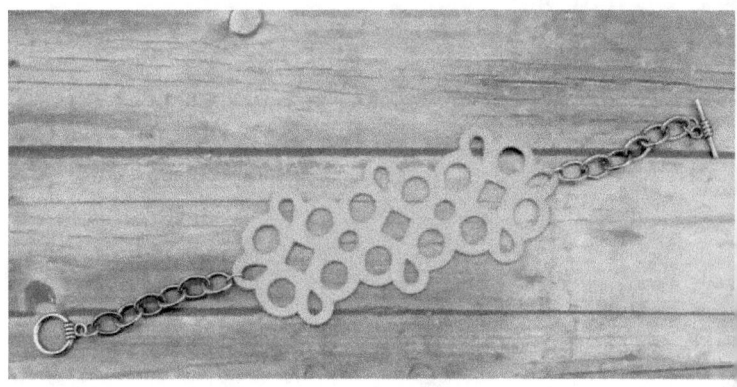

CREDIT- JENNIFFER MAKER

We are aware that the Cricut can cut through countless materials leather inclusive so this project would have to do with making a leather cuff bracelet

SUPPLIES NEEDED

- A small piece of leather. You can get that anywhere you wish to.
- A silver coated bracelet chain or cording. Any color you want is preferable.
- Some round nose jewelry pliers. You can also use some regular old

needle nose pliers. Also, they would work just fine.

- The Cricut explore which has a deep cut blade
- Little jump hoops. (optional though)

STEP 1

You create a design, or you just pick one from your design space. I made use of lace here, and I changed the size, then you cut it into a paper to have that exact measurement first before I cut the expensive leather. You can't just start with the leather or else you'll end up wasting it.

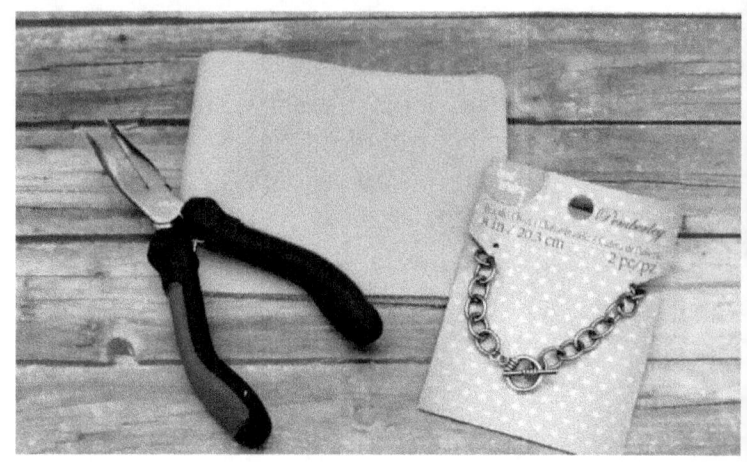

STEP 2

After cutting the leather into the shape I want, then I began to assemble the bracelet. Remember I made mention of a silver coated bracelet chain. Net is to check if the size of the chain is yours. So that you can make that nice bracelet.

STEP 3

If you want to do something of this nature, you can add the links into the leather. Never tear the leather to support the links. I don't think that is even possible.

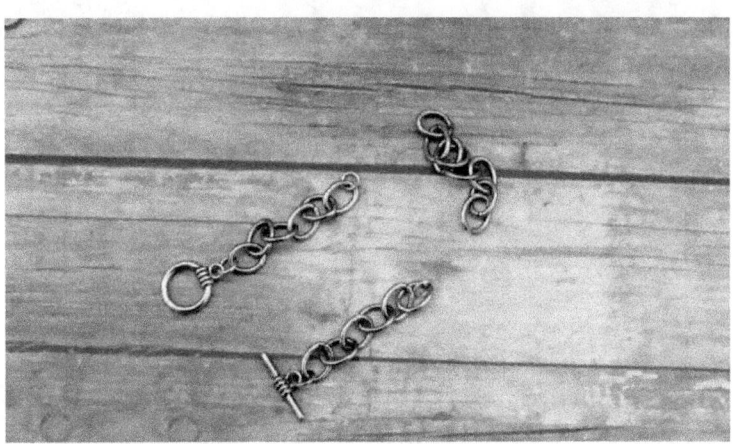

STEP 4

A design of this nature would look intricate for the first time, but when you practice it, and you frequently visualize the end product even before you start, you would be able to finish it without any stress.

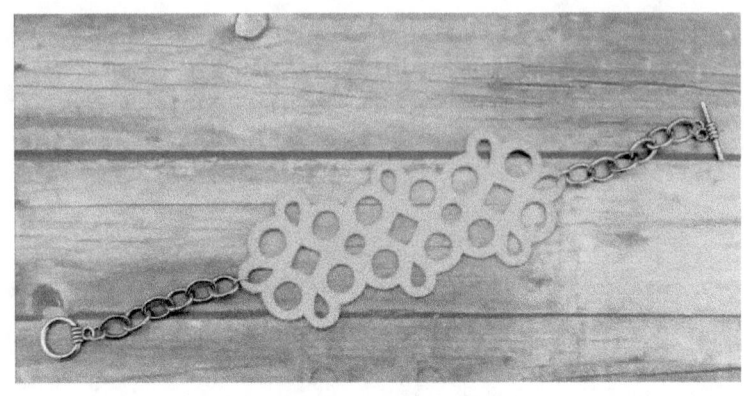

YOU CAN DO THIS NOW!

Medium Level

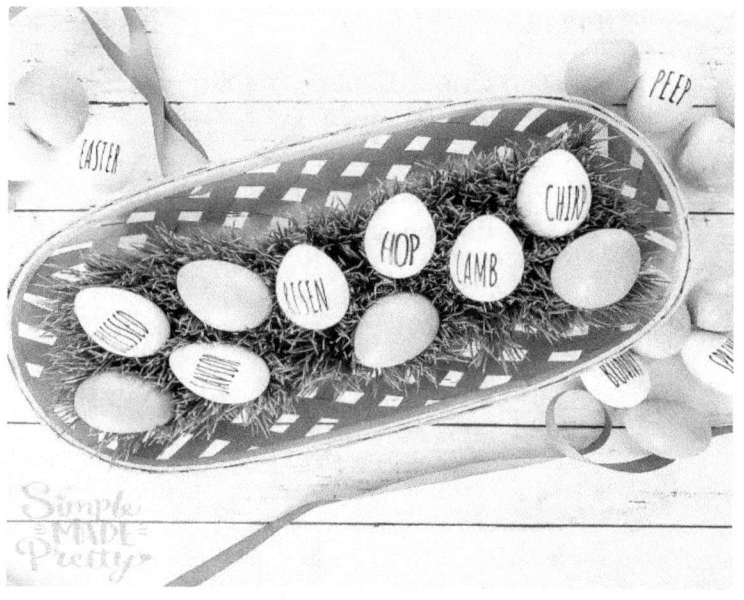

CREDIT- SIMPLE MADE PRETTY

You may have a Rae Dunn obsession like me. So, I have been able to create these Rea Dunn inspired Easter Eggs. Because we are aware that the Rae Dunn products have become increasingly popular over the years on the blown-up craft blogs and websites. You would need the Cricut machine to do these, and it is easy. This is a very useful project during a festive period like Easter.

SUPPLIES YOU NEED

- The Cricut Explore machine
- Contact Papers
- The White Craft Eggs
- Vinyl (The Easter eggs are white, so I used black)

STEP 1

Get a free SVG, PNG, DXF file online, or you just create one yourself. Upload to the Cricut Design space. And gather your supplies. I got these Easter eggs for just $2

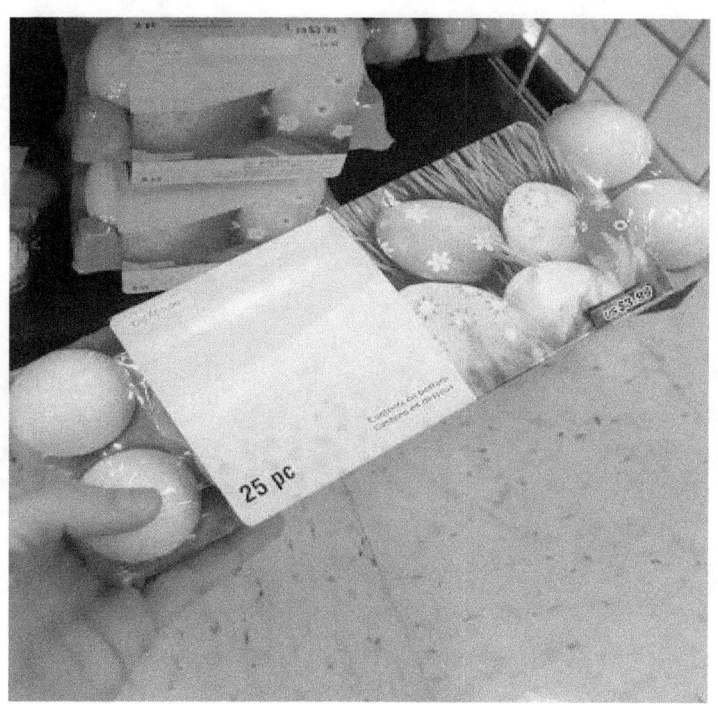

STEP 2

Make some little tweaks to the design
on the design space. You should
remember that the design measurement
should be very small to match the size
of the egg. I made use of 1 x 1 inch for
all the eggs. Then you weed out the cut
images too.

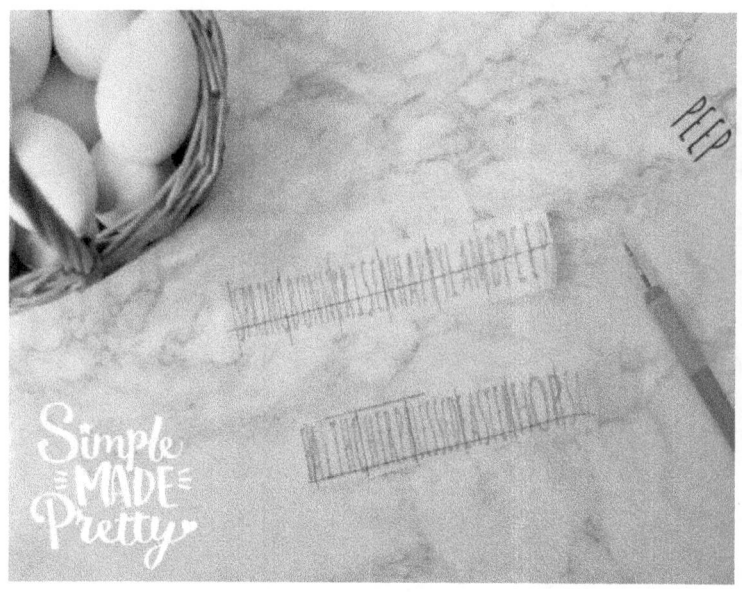

STEP 3

Spread over your contact paper and
adhere them to the eggs.

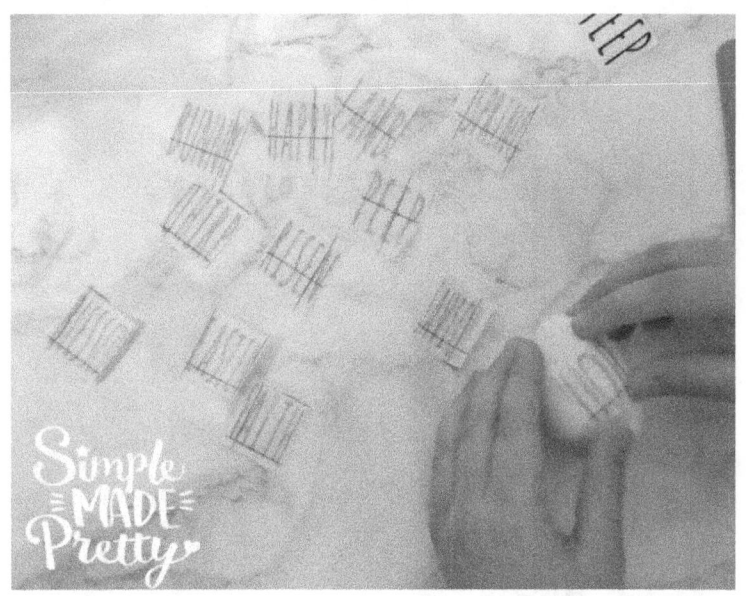

STEP 4

Peel off the contact paper to expose the egg.

Repeat the same process for the remaining eggs.

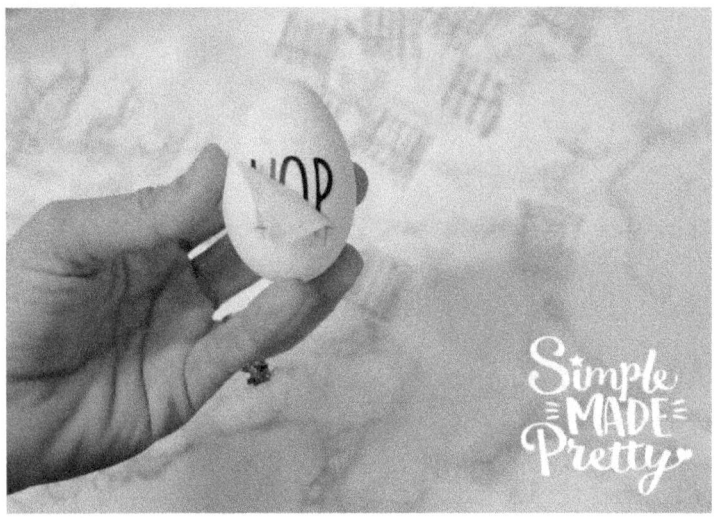

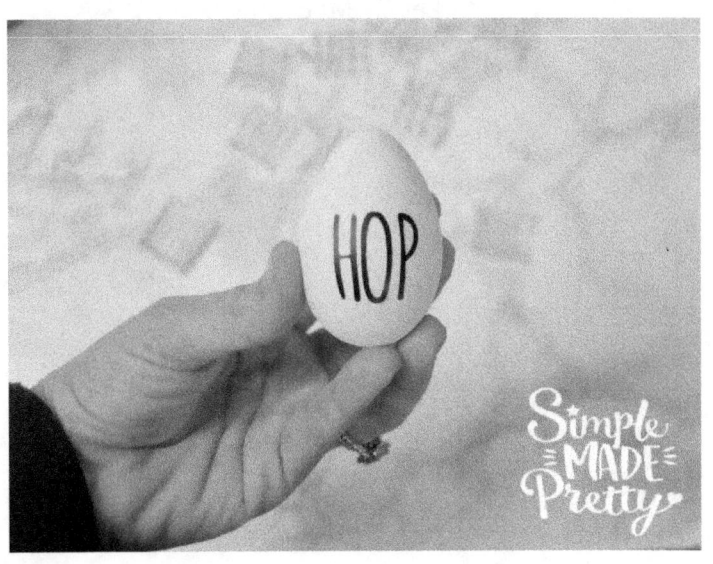

YOU CAN DO THIS NOW!

Level- Medium

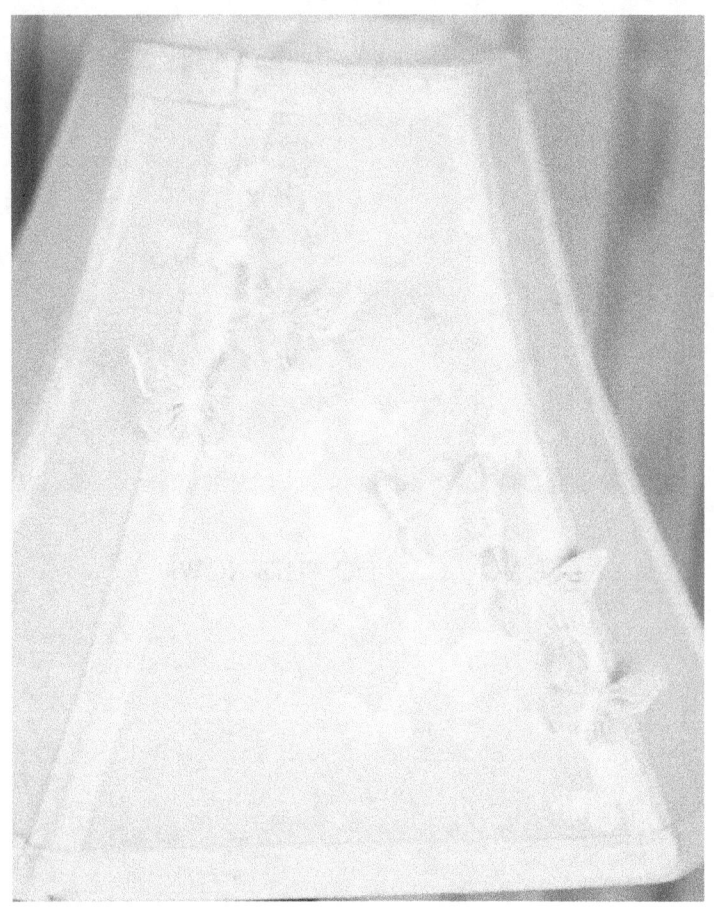

CREDIT- LAURASCRAFTYLIFE.COM

You may decide to get that unique lamp shade which would light up your room with so much beauty. We all love butterflies, so I have an instant way to create that 3-D butterfly effect on this lampshade. The butterfly effect would be very subtle and so elegant.

SUPPLIES NEEDED:

- A White Lampshade.
- Cricut Explore machine
- Iron-on vinyl, the white glitter
- Iron and ironing board
- White cardstock
- Vellum
- Hot glue gun and glue stick too.
- We should not forget the Cricut mat.

STEP 1

First, you would measure the height of the lamp. Mine was 7.5 tall, so I had the design to be 7.5 inches tall. This would have to do with working on the design space. But you have to mirror the image. Then set the custom dial to iron-on and cut the design.

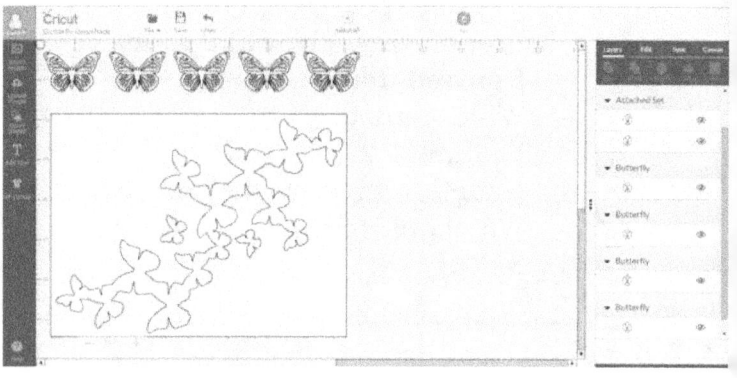

STEP 2

After printing, you weed out all the excess iron-on material from that clear backing and iron-on to your lampshade.

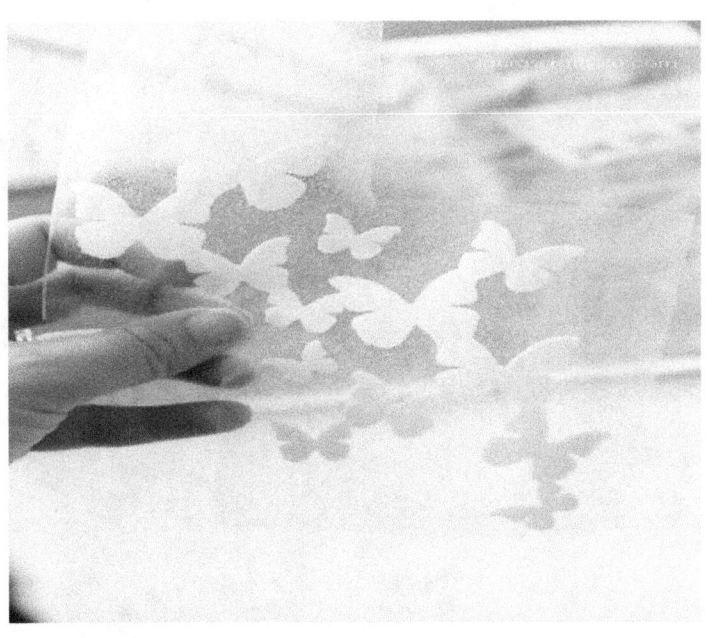

At this point, you should note that when cutting the vinyl, you can place that rectangle around the image. This would allow you to easily weed the vinyl and cut it well.

STEP 3

Add two pieces of the iron-on vinyl on opposite sides of the lampshade. Then you wrap the butterflies around the lampshade.

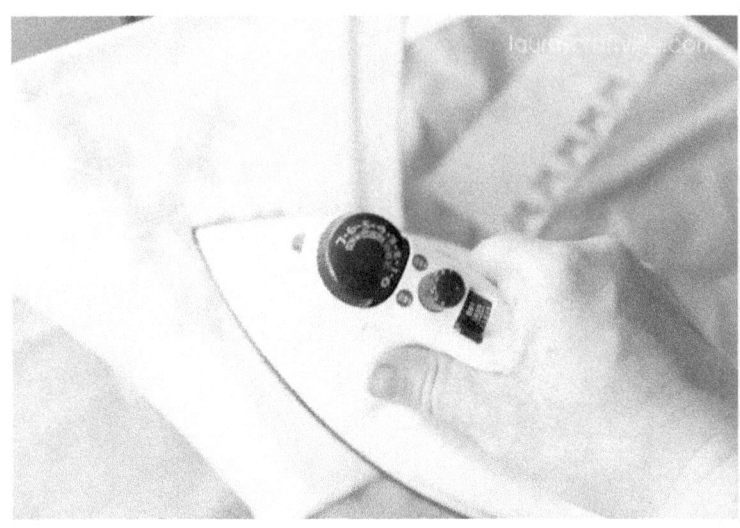

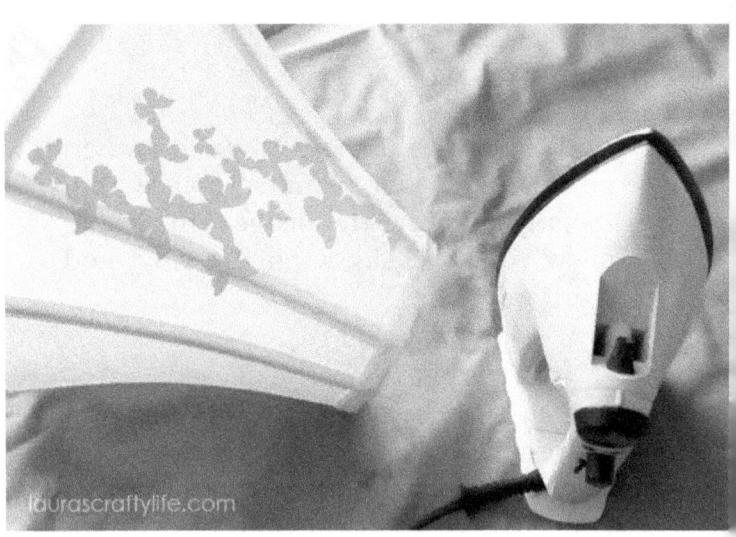

STEP 4

The next step is to cut the intricate butterfly shape that I really like. Then you would match the size of that single butterfly with that larger butterflies from the iron-on design, and then you cut out five butterflies from the different plain white cardstock as well as vellum for each side of the lampshade. That would be about twenty butterflies in all. Next, you would cut out those butterflies then bend the wings up a little for it to have that 3-D effect.

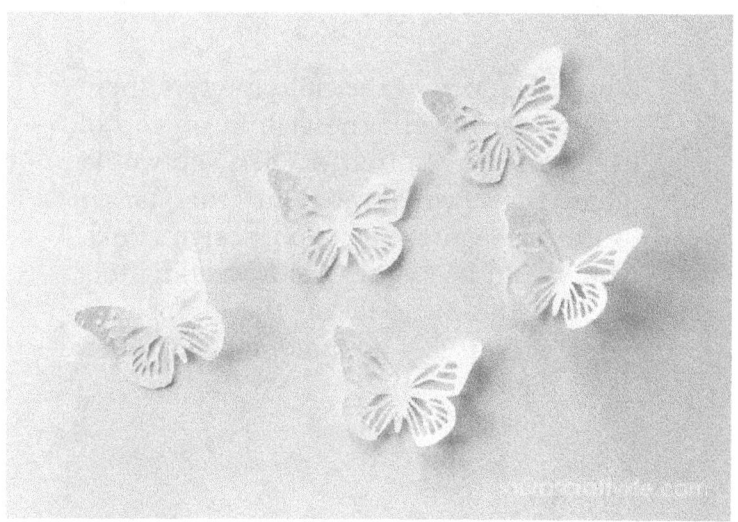

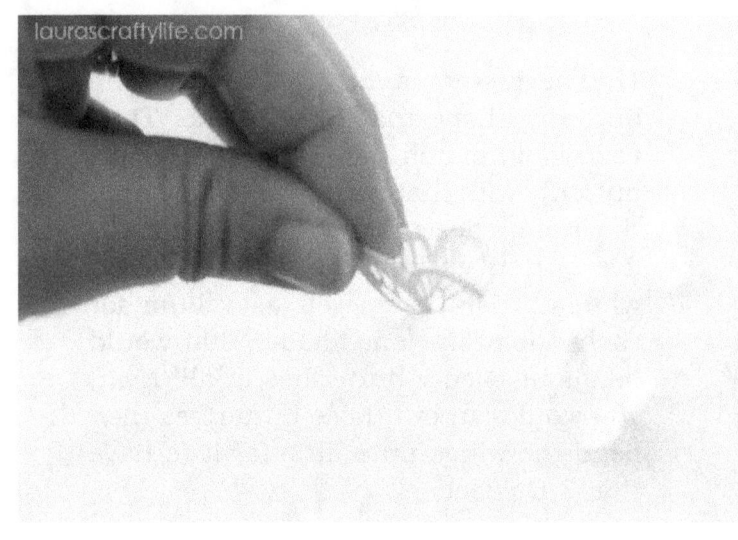

STAGE 5

You make use of the hot glue to adhere the butterfly with the vellum on top of the cardstock butterfly. Then you would glue the two layers on the larger butterflies on the iron-on design. Next, you would use your Cricut weeding tool to hold the butterfly on the lampshade while it is drying so that you don't burn your fingers.

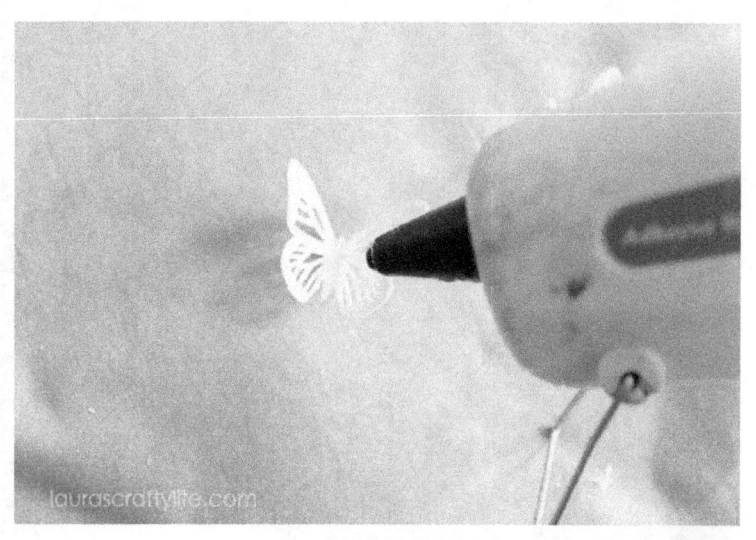

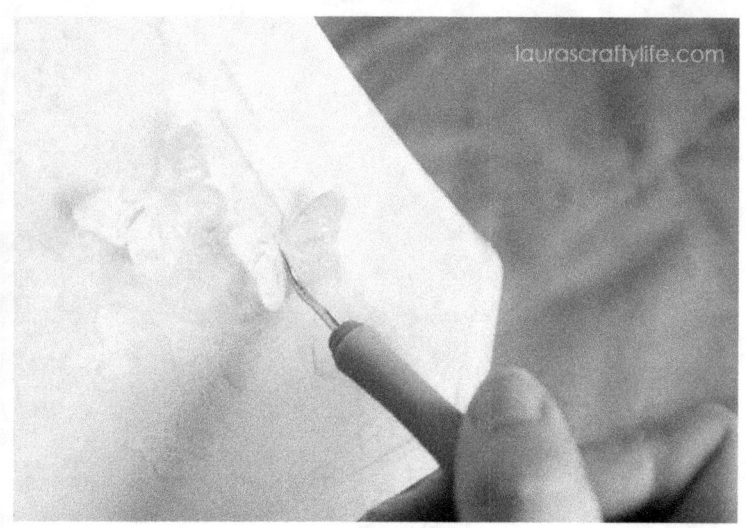

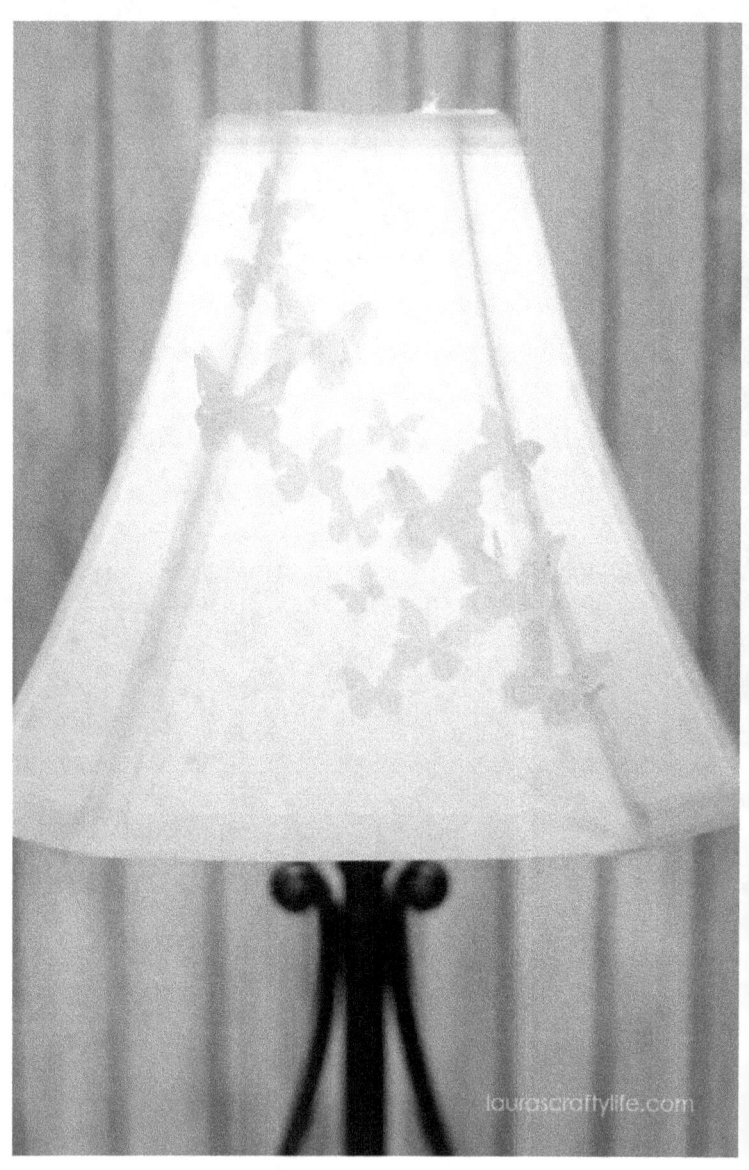

laurascraftylife.com

122

The lampshade would surely turn out beautiful when you work on it very well. Then you can move to the bedroom lamps and even the sitting room. With that silhouette of the iron-on butterflies, your lampshade cannot be ignored.

YOU CAN DO THIS NOW!

PROJECT 15- "MOMMY IS ON BREAK" SOCKS

Level-Medium

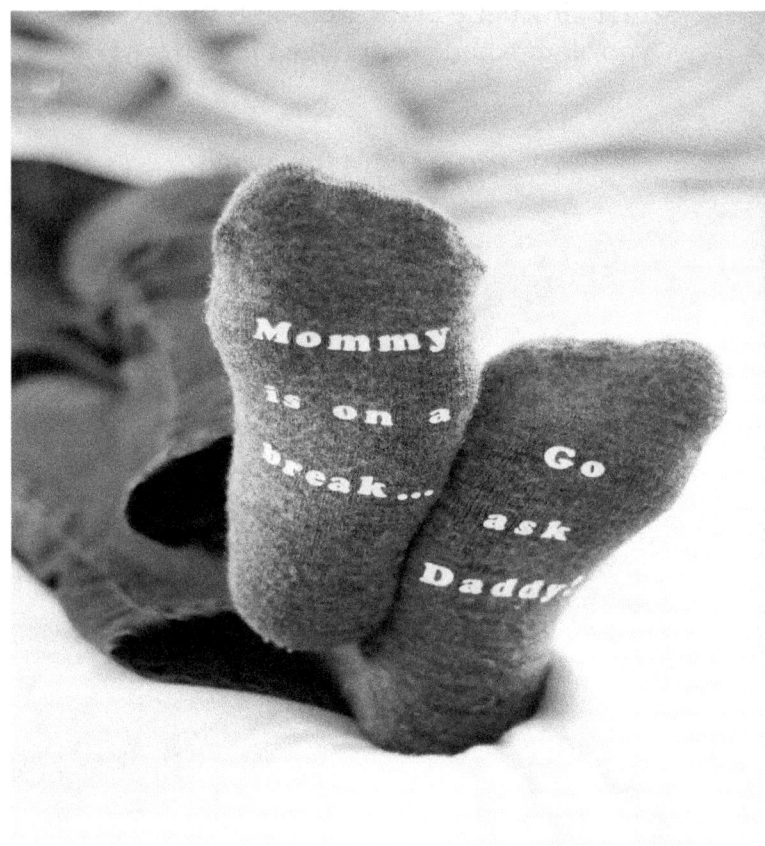

CREDIT- JESSI WOHLWEND OF PRACTICALLY FUNCTIONAL

We all need time to ourselves at times. Sometimes we just need to stay sane for a while without any disturbance, and mothers are no exception. The truth is that most times, the kids always have a kind of innate alarm which tells them that *mom is about to have her me time.* then they would come *disturbing.* You need this project so that when they come disturbing, you can raise up your feet up to your kids. They would know exactly what's up. With a Cricut, you can easily make socks like the one above for yourself. All you need to do is to iron in that vinyl onto the soles of the comfy pair of socks. This project is machine washable and dryer safe!

SUPPLIES YOU NEED

- A Cricut Machine (explore air especially)
- Iron or Heat press
- Scissors
- Heat transfer vinyl
- Thick paper
- Your favorite pair of comfy socks

STEP 1

I made use of the Cricut Explore Air to make these. So, you would start by opening up the Cricut Design Space. Then you type in those words. Spacing and sizing must be taken into consideration to make sure it would fit on the sole of your socks.

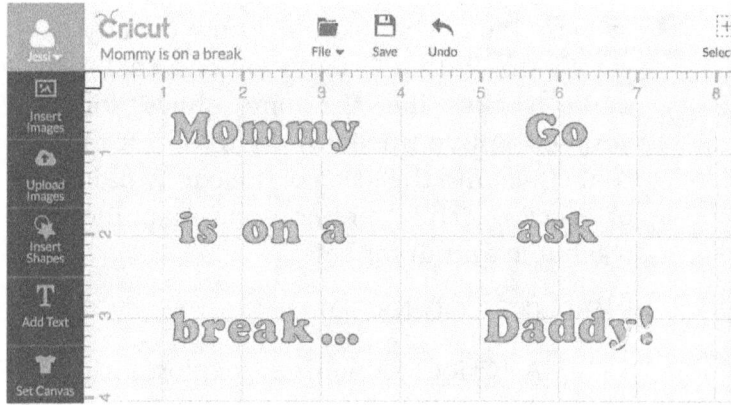

STEP 2

Then you load the white heat transfer vinyl into the Cricut machine and sent the design to the Cricut for cutting. But you should not forget to mirror the design for the iron-on images so that the text wouldn't be backward when you are through with it.

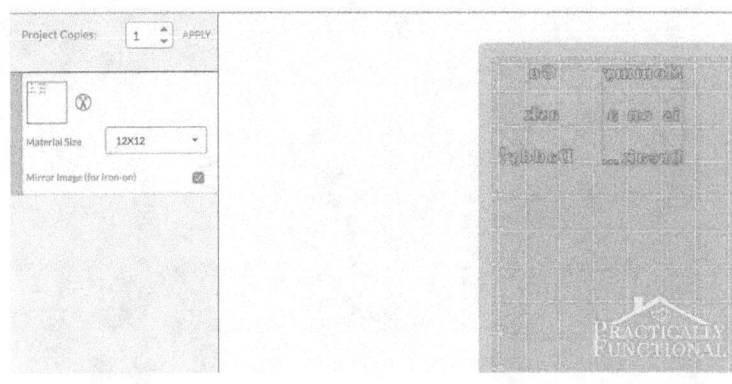

STEP 3

While cutting, you should put thick paper to make inserts for the socks to help *spread them out* and keep the flat before ironing. After cutting the vinyl, you would weed away the background vinyl then position the vinyl words on the socks.

STEP 4

After the vinyl has been pressed on the socks, you allow it to cool for a minute before pulling it off.

And there you have it.

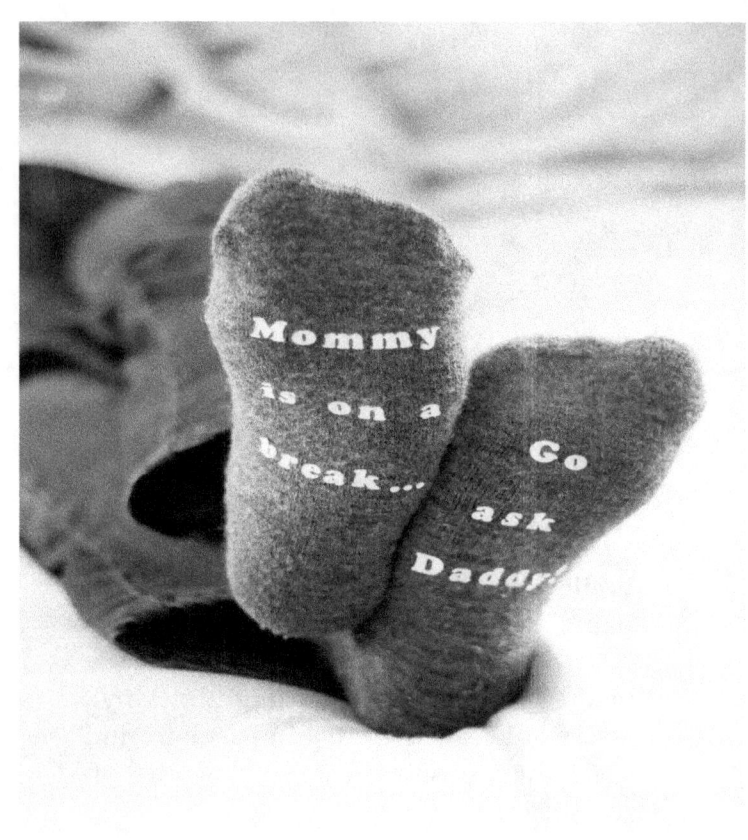

YOU CAN DO THIS NOW!

Level- Medium

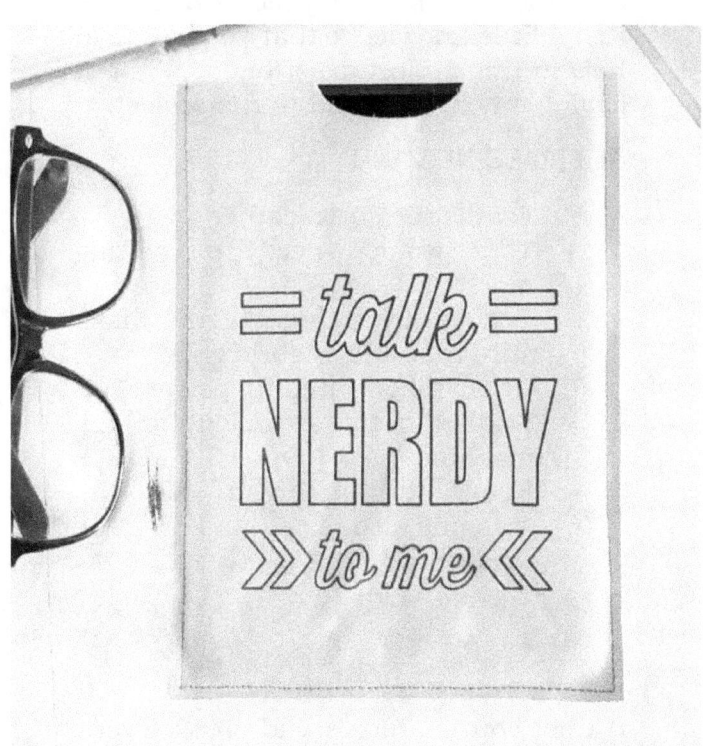

CREDIT- THE CRAFTEDSPARROW.COM

Geek Chic is now hot fashion right now. So, I know you are happy that I have something for you here. You can create this leather for your tablet. I created it for my kindle. It is something that is very easy but would require a little knowledge of fabrics and how they feel. But that is just a little knowledge that you can read now in this project description. Without saying much, let us get to the project.

SUPPLIES NEEDED

- Leather or Faux leather
- You would need a sewing machine
- Cricut cutting mat. You make sure that it is a fabric grip.
- Cricut color antiquity pen set
- Leather needle especially for the machine
- Heavy duty thread for the machine also.
- Scissors.

STEP 1

Gather your materials and prepare your leather. When I was doing this project, I yanked out a leather material from my big box of leather. This leather was so rumpled that even if you see it, it wouldn't be so much attractive. What was I able to do? I put on the iron to a low heat setting (no steam) then I took the butcher paper or a brown Kraft paper and completely covered it. I spread the surface of the iron over this paper. While doing this, I did not stop the iron at one spot because it can discolor the leather. But if you have a smooth leather, you have nothing to worry about.

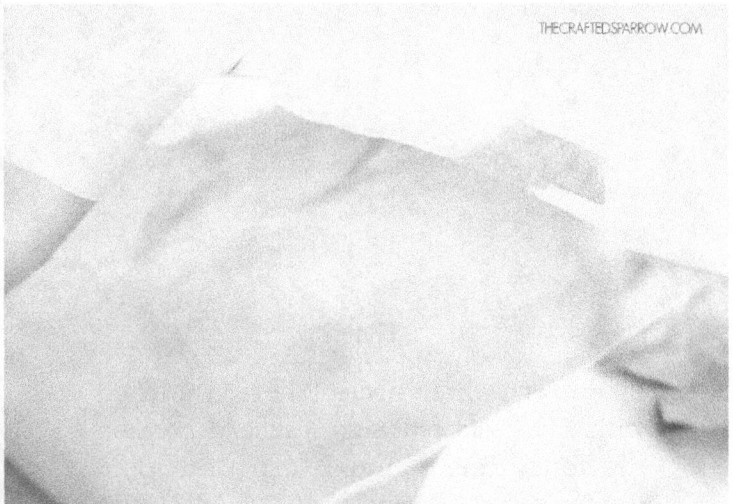

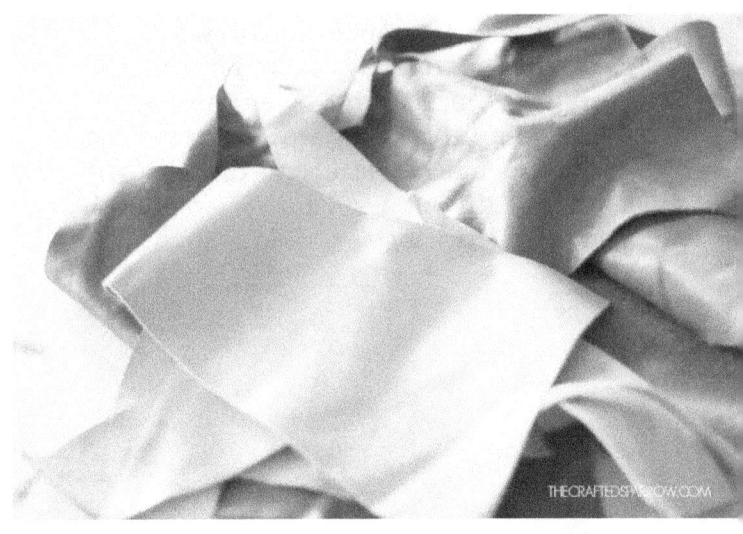

THECRAFTEDSPARROW.COM

STEP 2

Like every other project here, I started with my Cricut design space. I created the font design, and I also wanted to photoshop some images on it. After doing that on the photoshop platform, I was able to upload it on the Cricut design and turned it into a cuttable design.

You should make sure that the canvas is based on the tablet's measurements, and you should also add little spaces at the sides for the sewing purposes. You can give it a short oval cut out above like mine.

You can also make use of the graphics/letting writing feature. This design, which was made into tablet size, measured 0.5 inches each to the side and the bottom of the design for the sewing space.

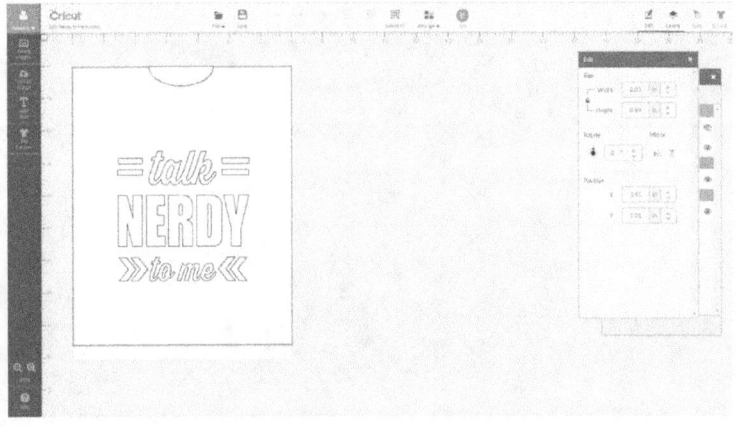

After making your design, you hit the GO button.

STEP 3

You would cut a piece of leather which should possibly fit the design a little bit larger and place it by the side of the cutting mat. You should make use of a strong grip mat with the leather. Even though I made use of a regular grip mat here, I still had that good result.

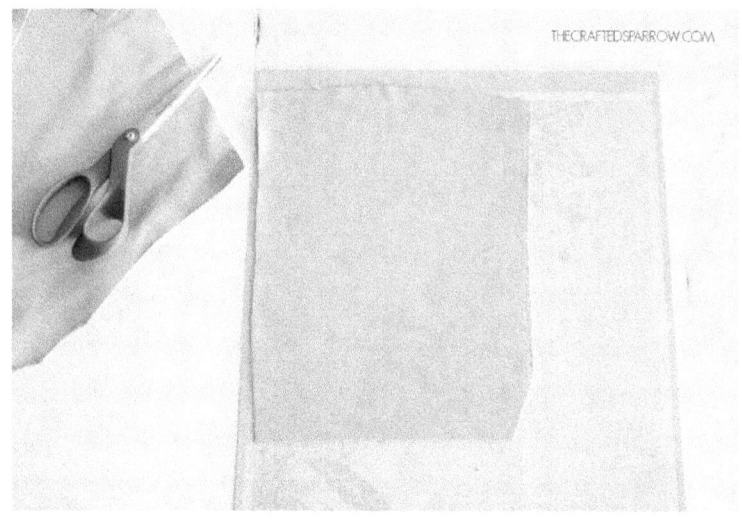

STEP 4

After loading it into the machine, you turn up your dial to CUSTOM. Then in your list of materials, you would choose leather 1.4mm Deep Cut. This should be based on the leather thickness because you might decide to use something thicker than that. Remember that regular blade is needed for this. Next, you would load the black pen into the A slot and press Go

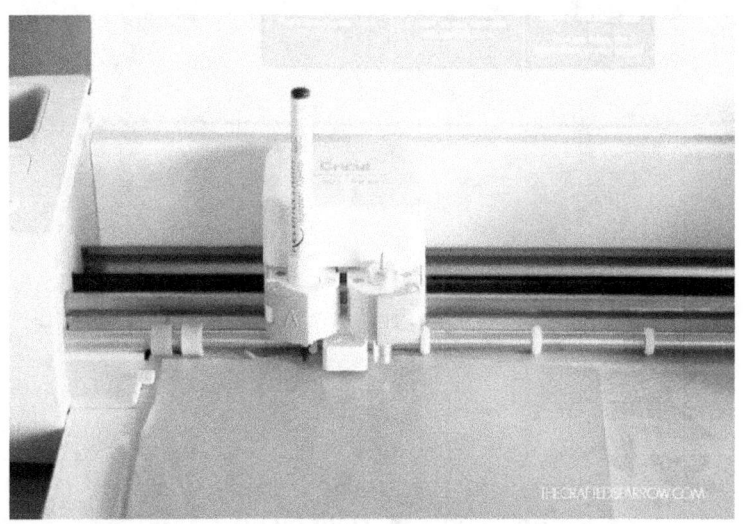

STEP 5

The machine would sketch out the design with a pen first. Isn't that cool? Then the Cricut explore would cut the design.

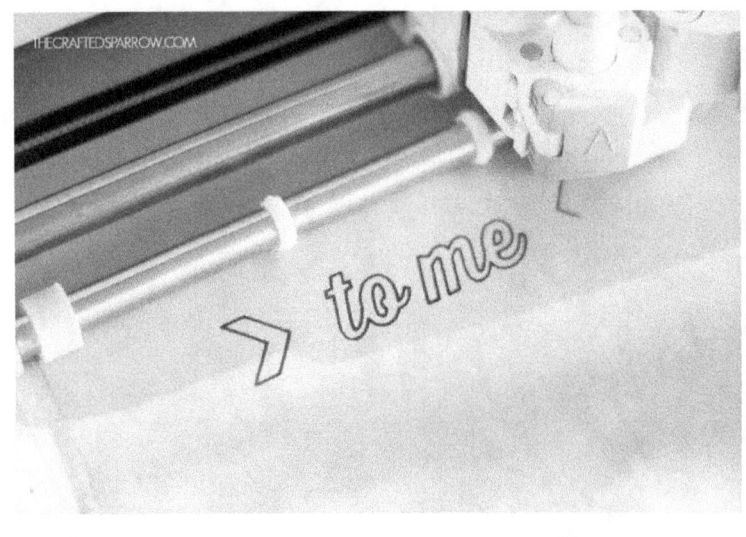

THECRAFTEDSPARROW.COM

STEP 6

When it is through, you can peel the leather from the mat carefully. You are expected to have perfect clean-cut edges. Let me give you a little tip here; I make use of a lint roller to go over the mat at first so that I would be able to remove those leather leftovers fibers easily. Then I would use a little dish soap to give it that gentle wash with my hands so that I can clean the mat. If you do it like this, your mat will not be sticky as a brand-new mat even after using it for long as most leather does.

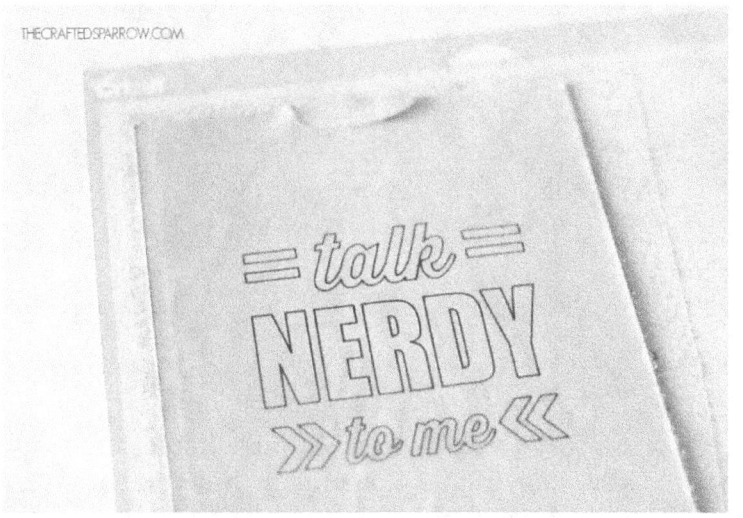

STEP 7

Line up all the edges and start from the top right corner when sewing. Make sure you sew a straight seam around the right side, bottom and left side too. For this project, I was using a heavy-duty thread and leather needle. You must do the same.

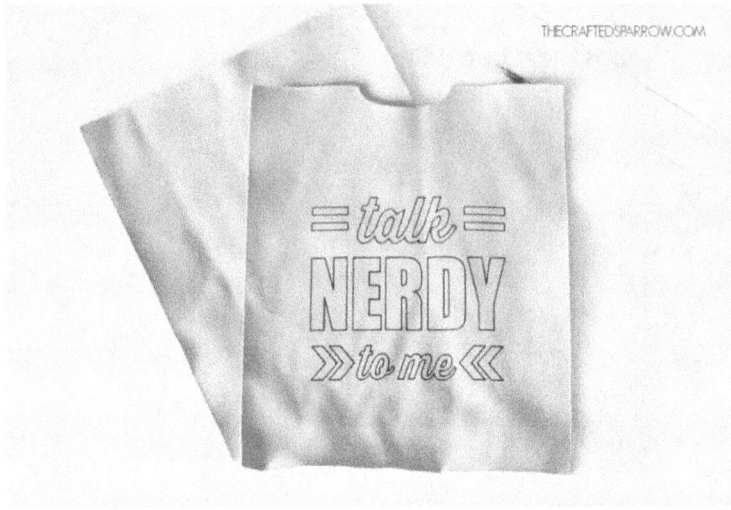

So, here you have it. Super simple and very easy right? Remember that you can customize anything you want on it. Have fun and be creative with it. Every Cricut project requires you to do so. I made a plain gray sleeve also.

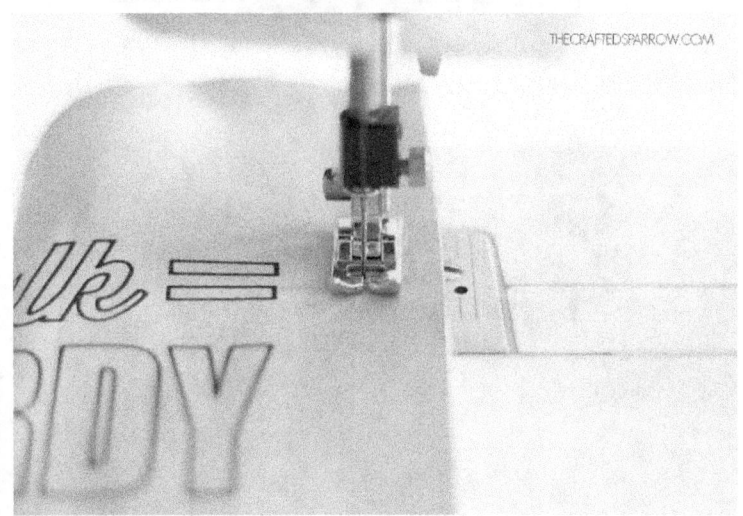

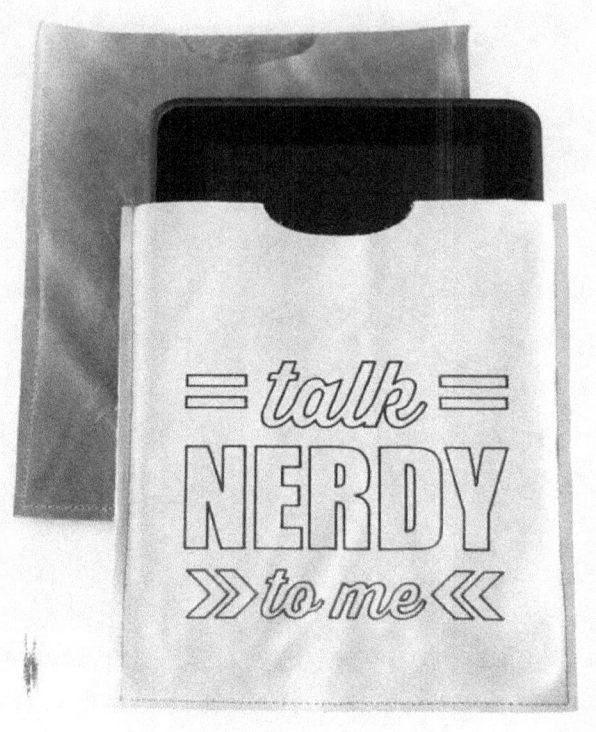

YOU CAN DO THIS NOW!

PROJECT 17- DIY ELF STOCKING WITH A CURLY TOE
Level- Medium

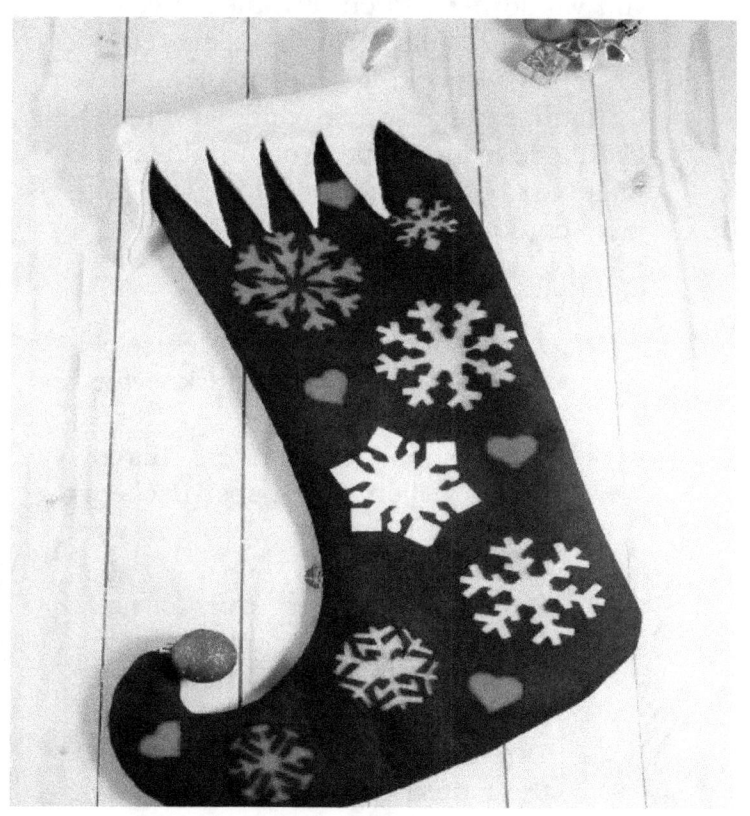

CREDIT- JENNIFER MAKER

This stocking is easy to make, and the Cricut Maker is also involved here. The Cricut maker would cut out all those all intricate snowflakes excellently. Then you would need to cut out all the color blocks as well. This super easy Christmas stocking meant for the Christmas folks would add so much beauty to your home. You would also make use of the sewing machine also, so you should get that prepared.

SUPPLIES NEEDED

- ½ yard of black felt. I made use of wool felt blend because I knew it would look very nice.
- ½ yard of *Wonder Under.* This is like a pellon 805 paper-backed fusible web that would work as an underlay.
- Felt or fleece. Feel free to use several colors. Turquoise, green, yellow, orange, and white is used here.
- Thread or other means to attach the material like liquid glue. But the thread is preferred here.
- A little red ornament which you would sew to the toe. I made use of a red ball.

- Iron Press or an Iron
- The Cricut maker for cutting the tag
- 12 by 12 inches Fabric Cutting Mat. You would probably be using this for your Cricut cutting.
- Free pattern or your free resource library.

STEP 1

You cut an 18″ by 12″ piece of Wonder-Under fusible web. This would be attached to the rough side of the back of the material that you would use in the front of your stocking. There is a need for you to iron this material also before you cut it.

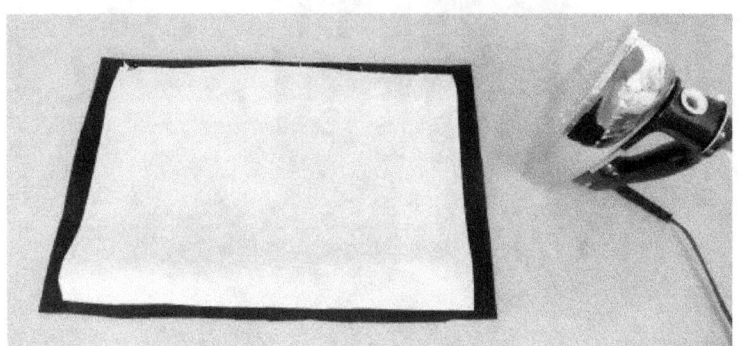

STEP 2

Then you would make use of the Cricut to cut your material. Remember to make use of the fusible web for cutting out the stocking front piece. You should remember that if you got a design online, you should upload the SVG file to your Cricut and check the measurement of the design before cutting. You can't possibly design two different stockings separately even though you are using the Cricut design space. You just design one and duplicate it. Then you flip to the right side, add all extra designs, and you are ready.

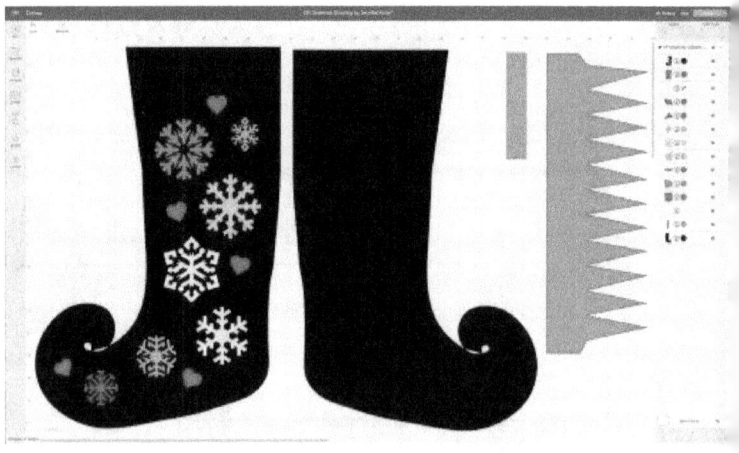

STEP 3

You may decide to cut out the stocking with the snowflakes and heart. So, you would turn over the cut-out stocking front and place it down on the table. Next, you would remove the paper backing from the Wonder-Under.

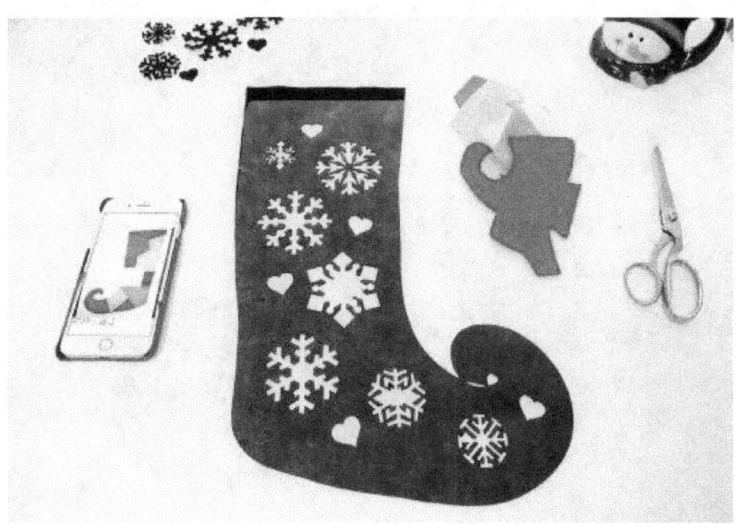

STEP 4

Place all of the color blocks that you have cut in the above step to the back of the stocking. You should be sure that the edges meet one another and they don't overlap.

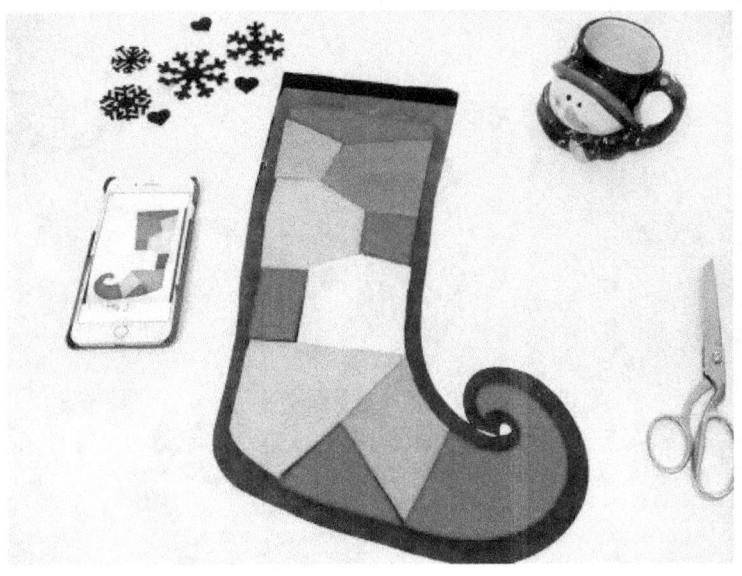

STEP 5

Iron all the color blocks onto the stocking front doing the same thing that you did with the Wonder-Under package. I was able to press mine for 5-

8 seconds with a damp clothing and then iron on with the wool setting in place.

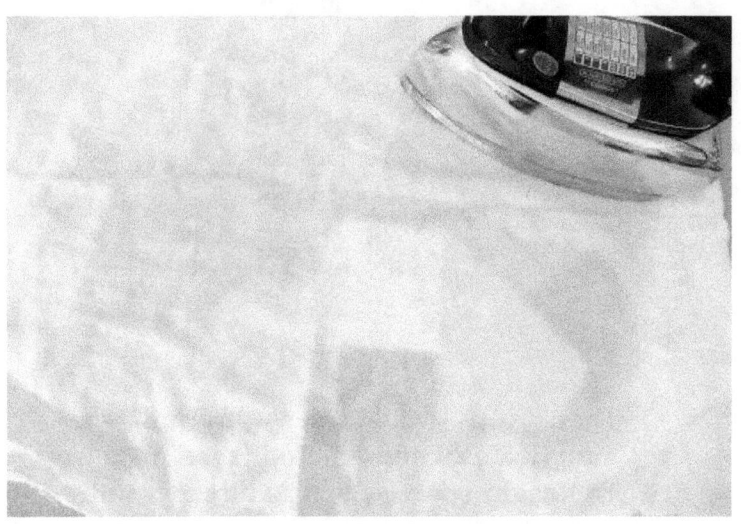

STEP 6

Place those stocking back to the top of your stocking front right side together. You should pin both of them together.

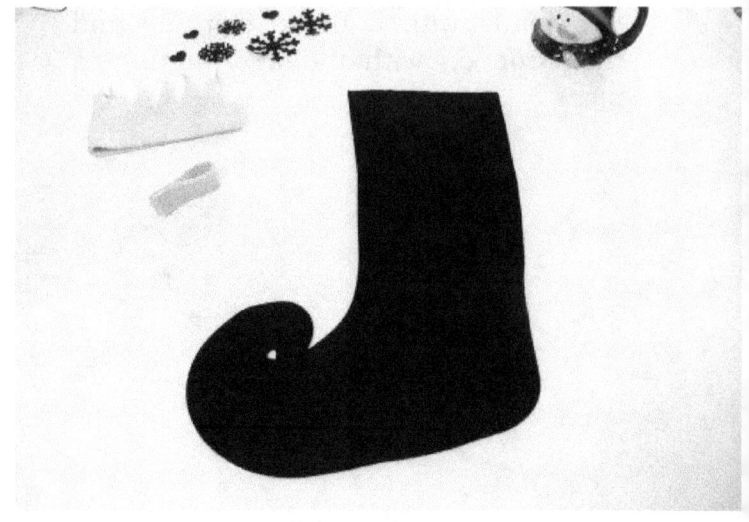

Then you would sew around the material. But this shouldn't be on top. The seam space which is already built-in (1/2 inch) space is where your thread would go. I made use of a pink thread below so that you can see those stitches. But you should use a matching thread to make the stitches invincible.

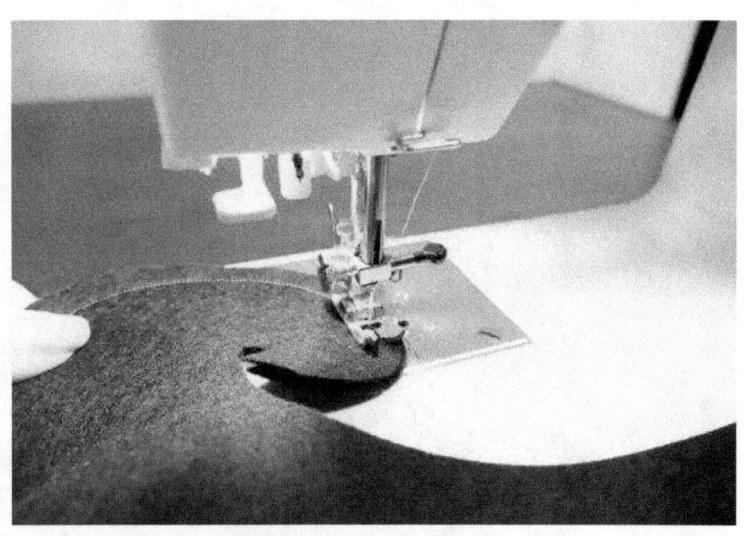

STEP 7

You clip the corner of that curly toe just like I have done below. Be careful here so that you wouldn't cut into the stitching.

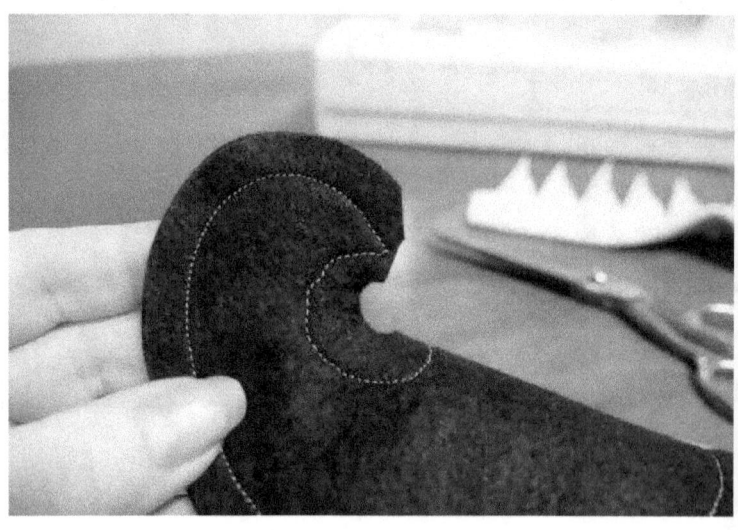

Then you would clip the curves of your stockings just as I have been able to do below. But be careful not to cut into the stitching. Doing this would allow the seams curve to be fluid.

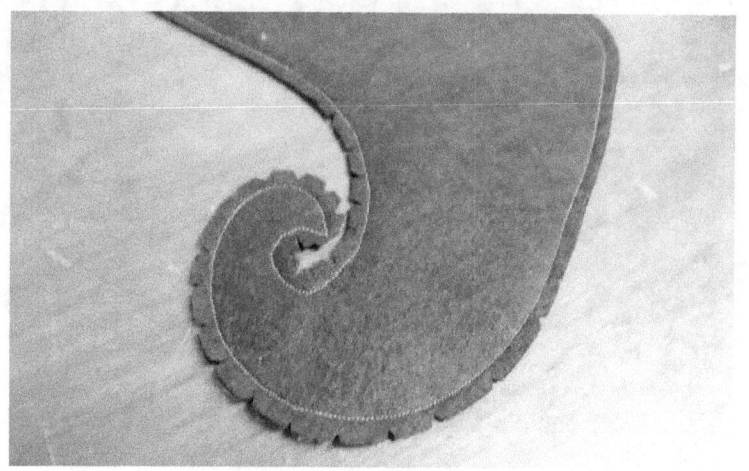

Don't forget to turn the stocking to the
right side out. It would take some time
to get the curly toe out. So, you need to
be patient.

STEP 8

Sew the fingered top which would be
closed at the side, forming that tube.
Make sure that you leave a half-inch
seam space.

Place the top inside the stocking. Making
sure that the fringe is side down and the

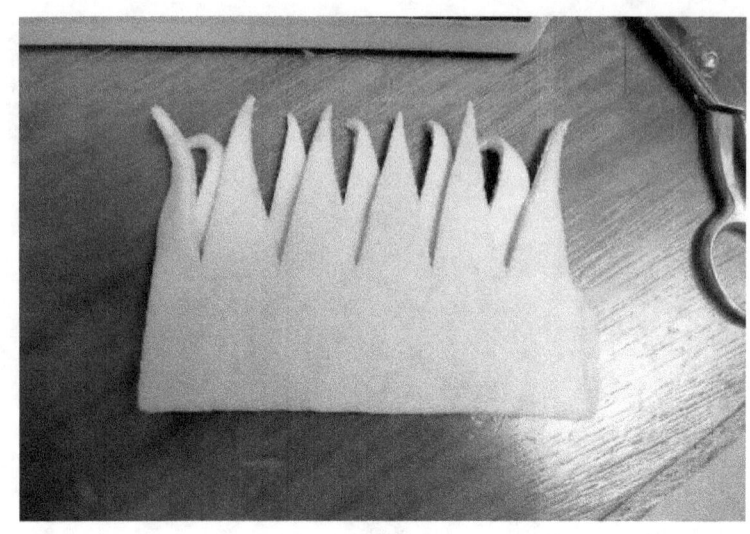

wrong side is against the side of the stocking. You should not sew it yet.

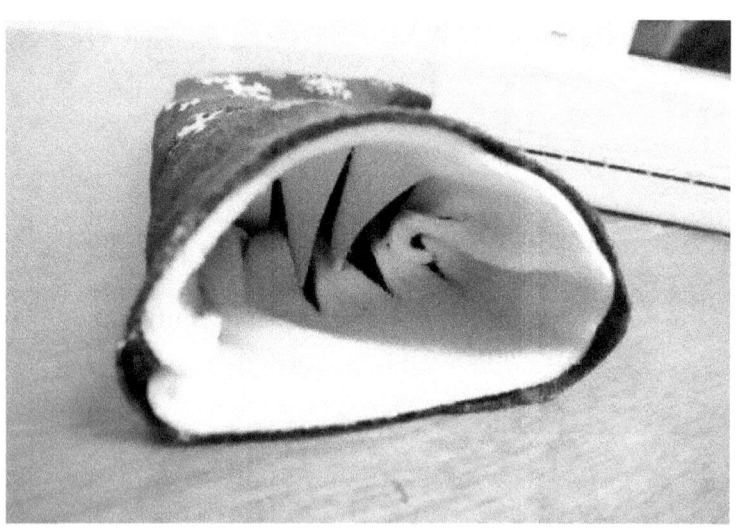

STEP 9

Fold the long rectangle cloth in half. This would become the hanging loop that you need and place it by the back seat of the stocking and that of the fringe top so that it's edging would be in line with the edges of the stocking top and fringe top also.

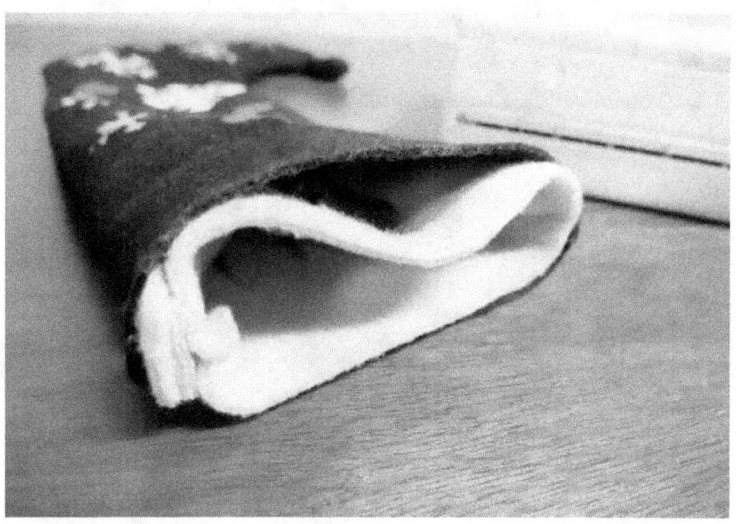

Next, you sew the fringe and the loop into the stocking with that simple stitch that would go all round that top of the edge.

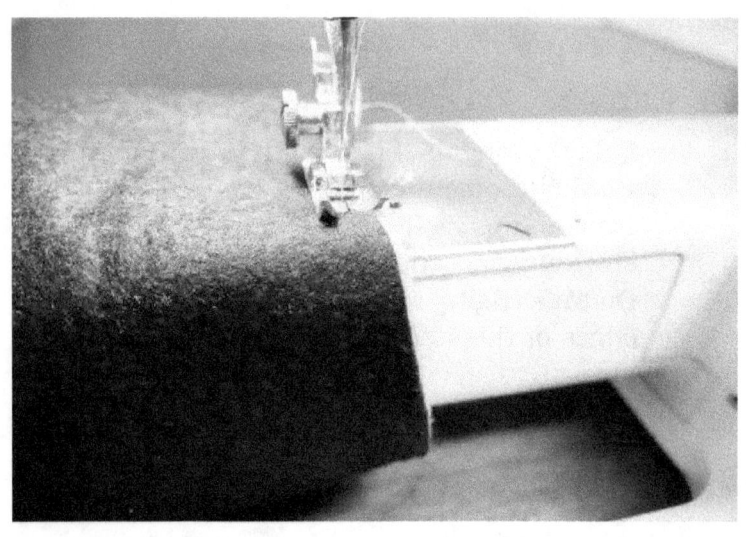

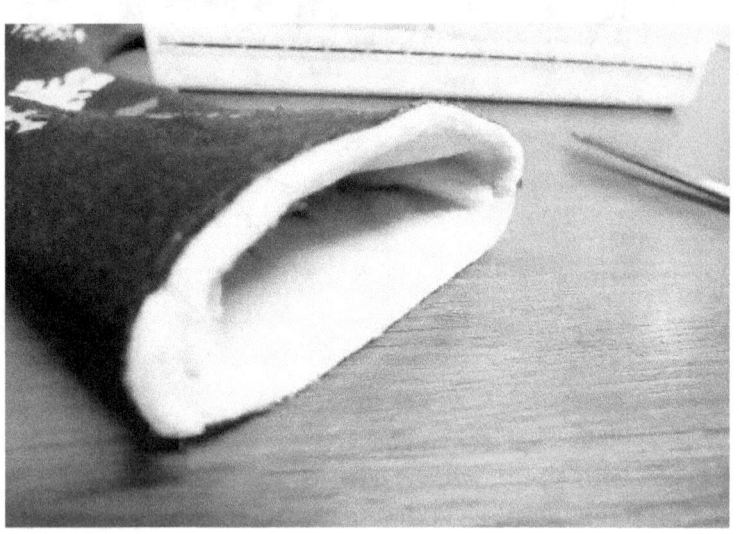

STEP 10

Flip that fringe up and over the edge of the stocking to get that perfect top that you require.

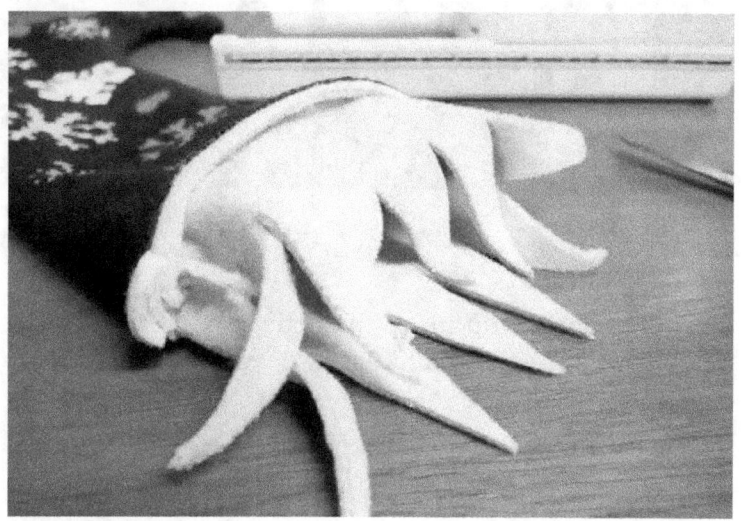

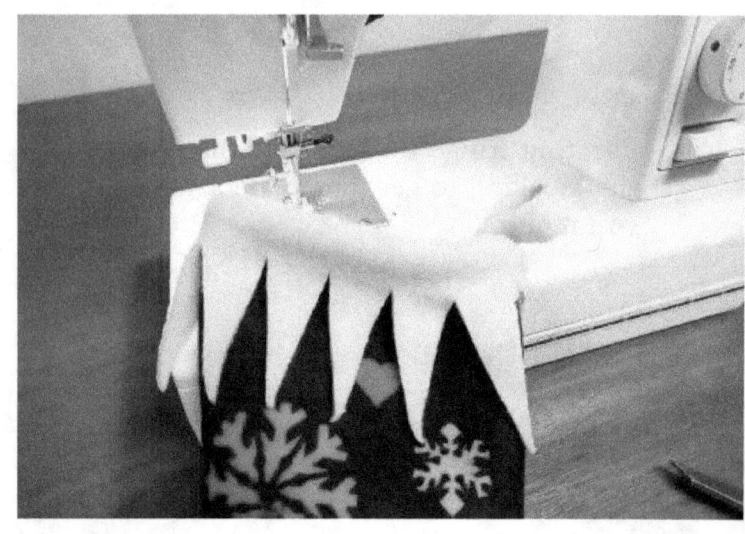

Lastly, you place the little ornamental ball at the toe like it is below

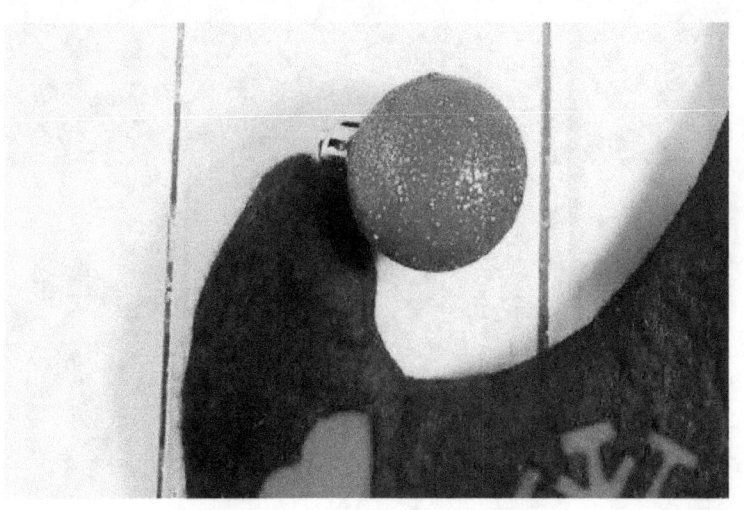

And that is how the project is completed
all within an hour.

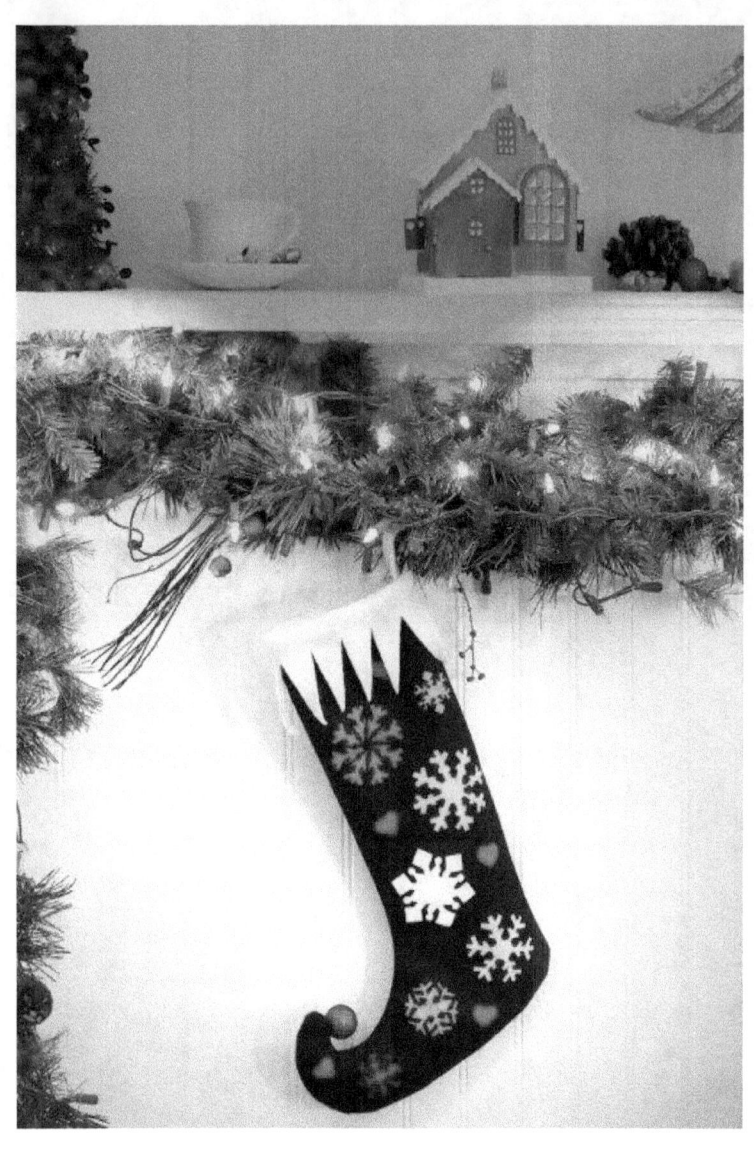

YOU CAN DO THIS NOW!

Level- Medium

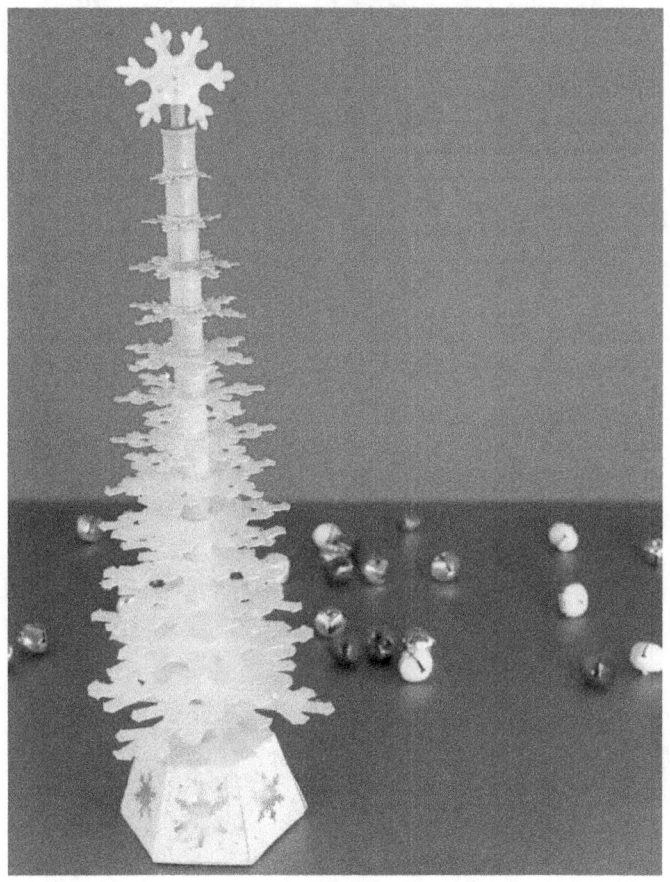

CREDIT- JENNIFER MAKER

This paper tree is 15″ tall. You should surely have a lot of fun making this. But there are some things you really need to know about this beauty. First, it is not like your regular Christmas tree. It has so much snowflakes design that would make your Christmas decoration unique. Furthermore, the Christmas tree base, which is a special kind of a paper would hold three LED tealights, so you know that this beauty would always glow in the dark. Basically, the Christmas tree is just a wooden dowel, and the snowflakes are separated with just that little wooden spools. The use of beads is allowed, but for this project, I made use of spools due to the fact that they keep the snowflakes parallel to one another. I make this tree Luminary. I am sure you would love it after it has been completed.

SUPPLIES NEEDED

- You need two sheets of white 12″ by 12″ Kraft board. For this project, Kraft board would be better than cardstock, especially if you are planning to hang some ornaments over the branches.

- ¼ " round wooden dowel which should be 14″ long
- Some 16 small wooden spools which should be ¾ high
- Some Tacky glue
- Hot glue and hot glue gun also.
- Glitter Spray or glitters. This is optional though
- Some 3 LED tealights which you would put in the base of the tree.
- Your Amazing Cricut
- TrueControl Knife or X-to knife
- Your intuition for your personal design or free SVG/DXF/PDF file pattern online

STEP 1

For the first step, you download the paper snowflake Christmas pattern from any source, or you design yours. You upload the design on the software, reduce or increase the sizes.

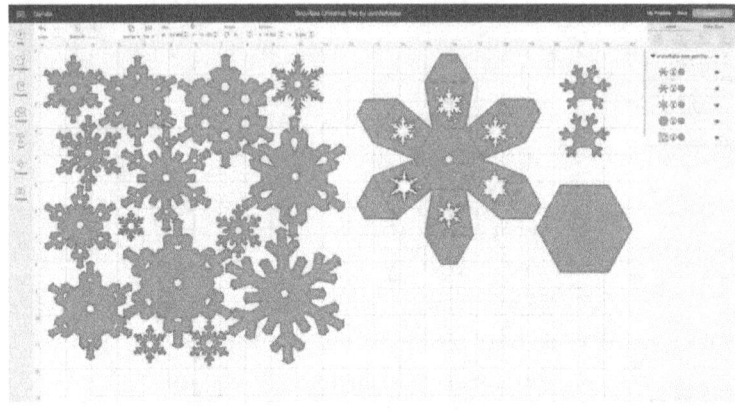

If you noticed above that, I grouped all the paper snowflakes into a single layer in that optimal configuration. This would allow them to fit perfectly into 1 piece of 12" by 12" paper. You should do the same you click the green button immediately, and it would fit onto the mats.

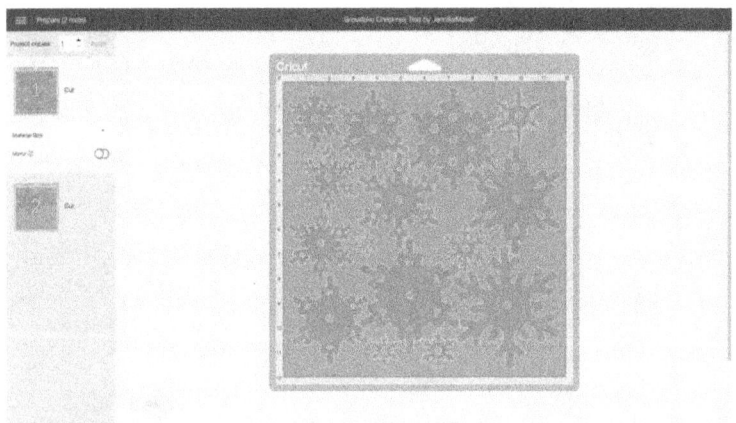

JENNIFERMAKER

STEP 2

After cutting all, you would sort the paper snowflakes from the largest to that smallest. Pile them up.

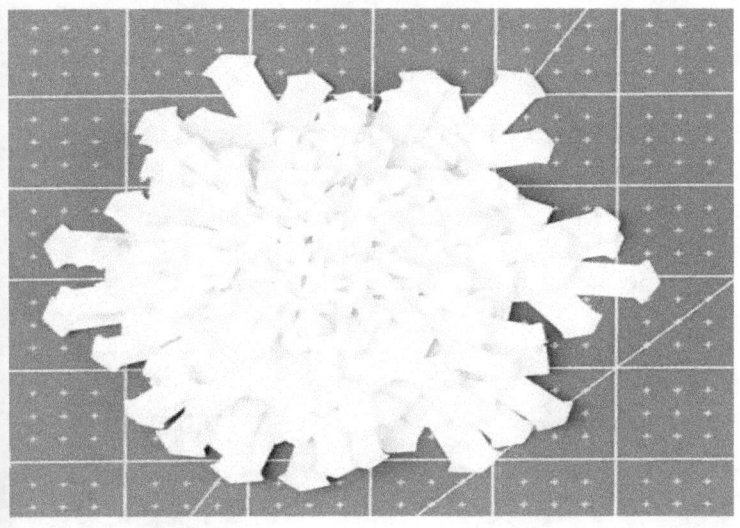

Next, you would cut the dowel to 14″. I made use of my Cricut TrueControl Knife. However, you can make use of the X-Acto knife.

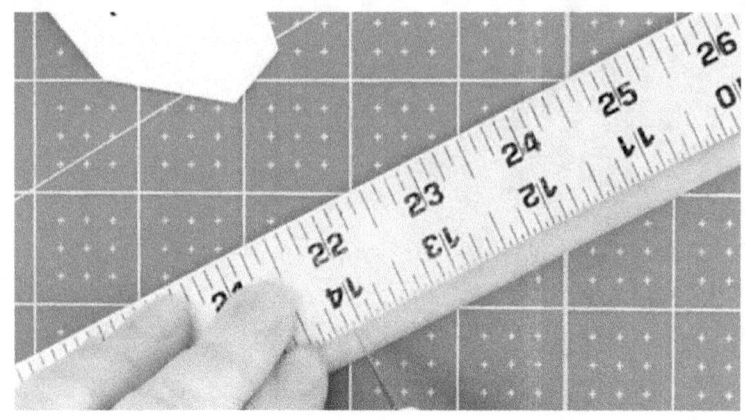

STEP 3

Place the dowel on one side and pick up the base top which is obviously a six-sided piece having those snowflake cut-outs. You fold them in all six sides and the flaps too.

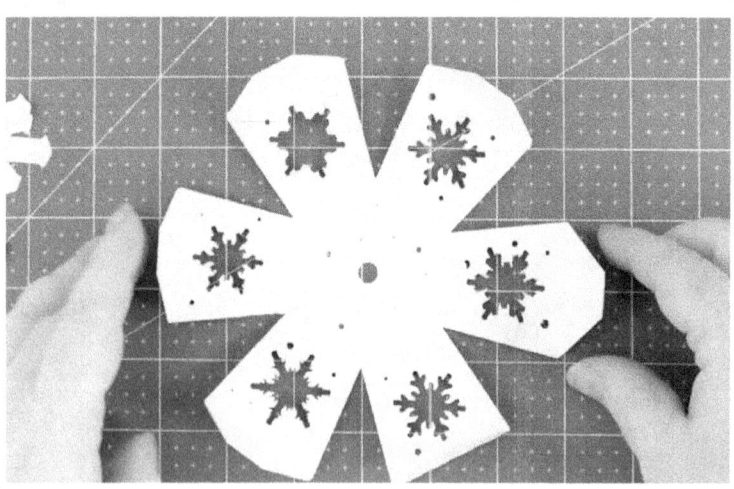

Then you would glue all the flaps from the base top to the base bottom. What this means is that you would glue three flaps, and some other three would not be left the way they are. In the picture below, I glued the flaps to the interior of the base.

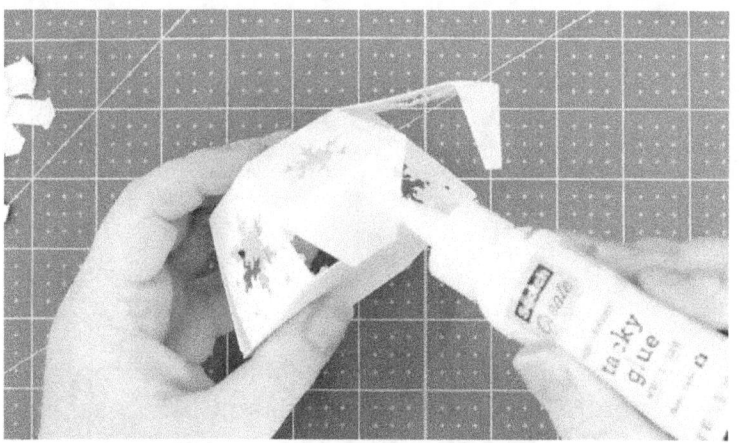

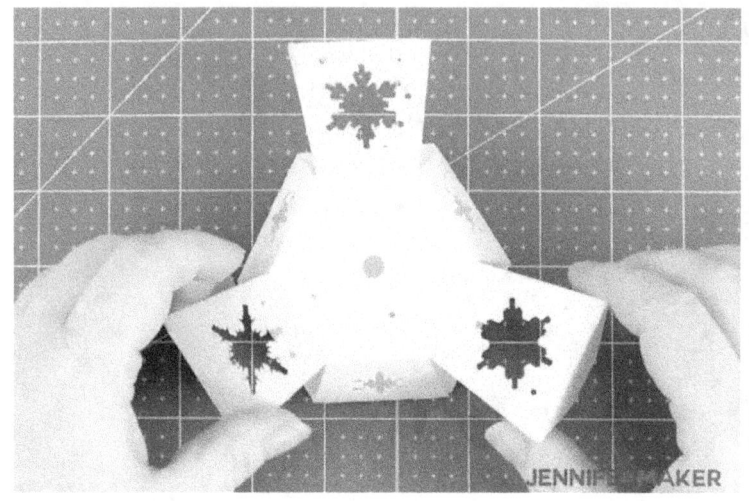

STEP 4

Put your dowel into the hole on the top of the base of your snowflake Christmas tree. Make sure you hold it firm to the interior of the bottom with the hot glue.

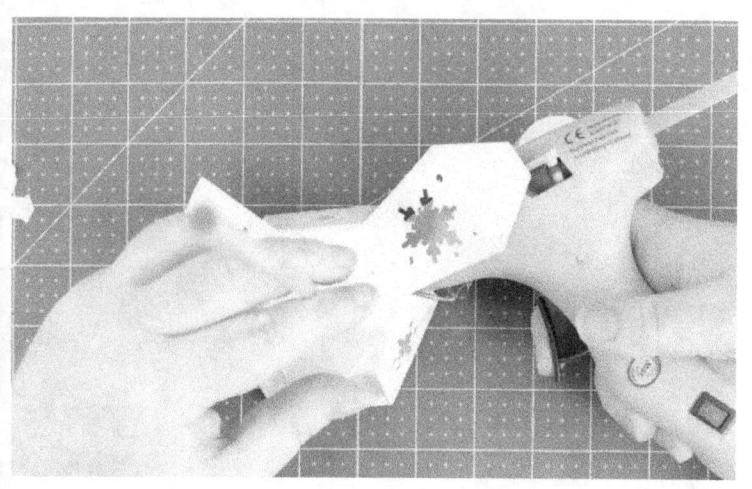

STEP 5

The Next thing to do is to put your three LED tealights inside the base. You should snug them up close to the dowel. When it is inside you would fold the sides down and then tuck the flaps under those tealights also. This would keep everything in place all at once. Remember that it is not all flaps that you would glue so there would be this particular one that you can open and close to put on put on the LED tealights on and off.

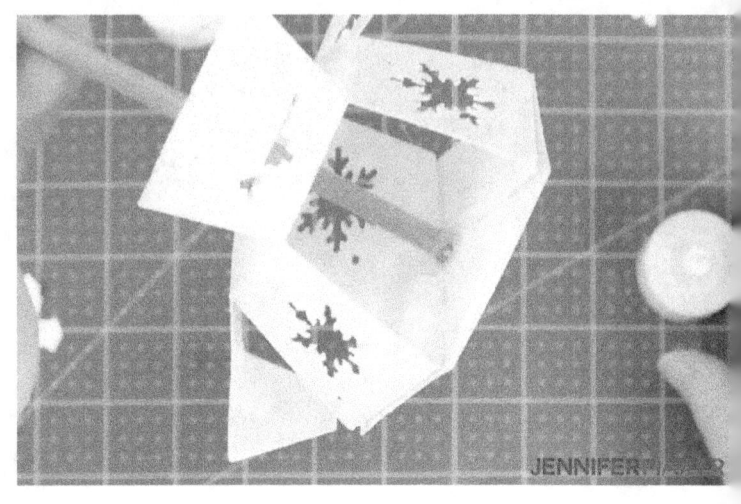

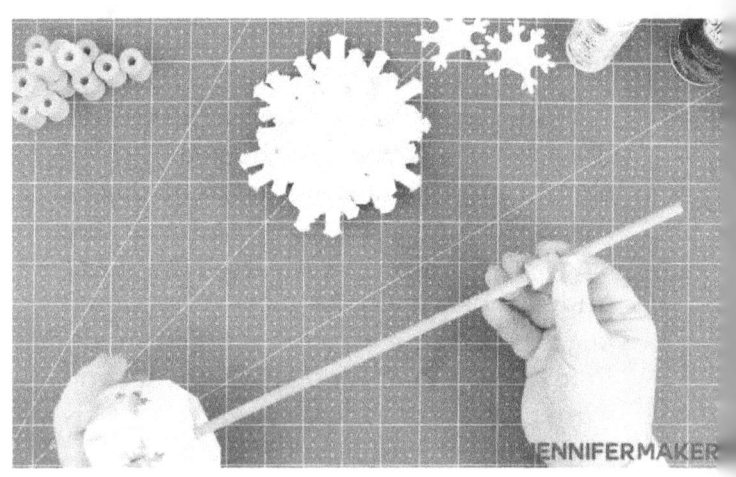

STEP 6

You would slide the wood spool over that end of the wood dowel and let it go all the way to the base. Now, this is where the best moment of this project begins. You'll start by sliding the largest paper snowflake first onto the dowel, down to the spool.

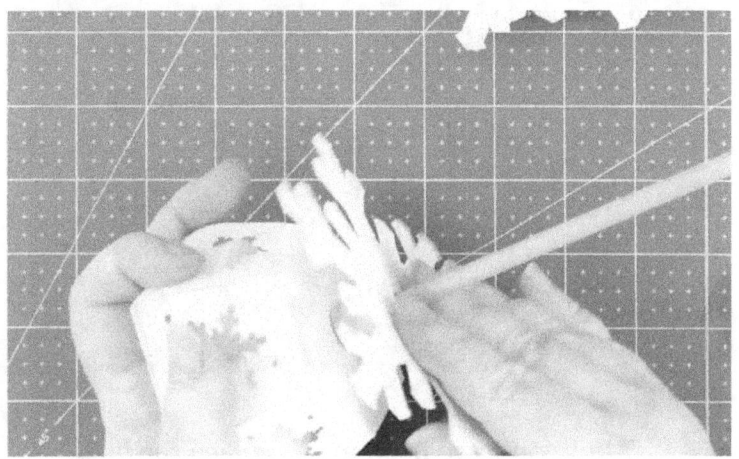

STEP 7

Repeat the process over and over again with another spool and another snowflake. This would be from the largest to the smallest, till the dowel is entirely filled with your paper snowflakes.

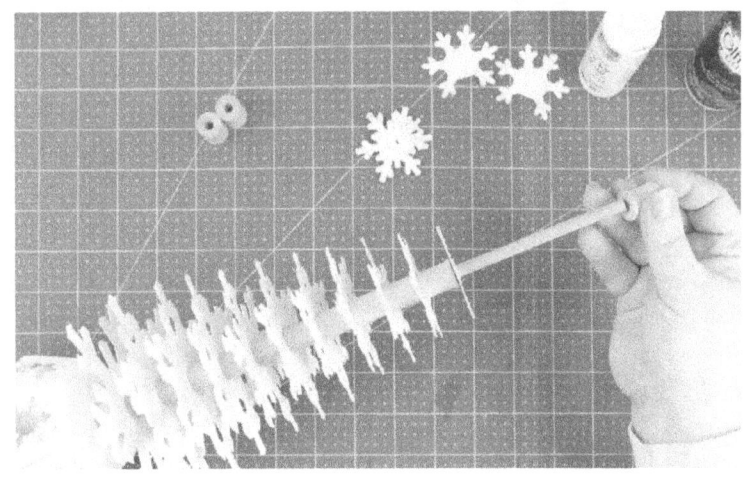

After you have been able to place the last snowflake on that last slide of your wooden spool, you begin to make the snowflake topper. How can you do this? You would glue the two topper pieces together at that points alone. It should not be in the center. After it dries, you open up the center then you would slide it onto the top of that paper snowflake Christmas tree.

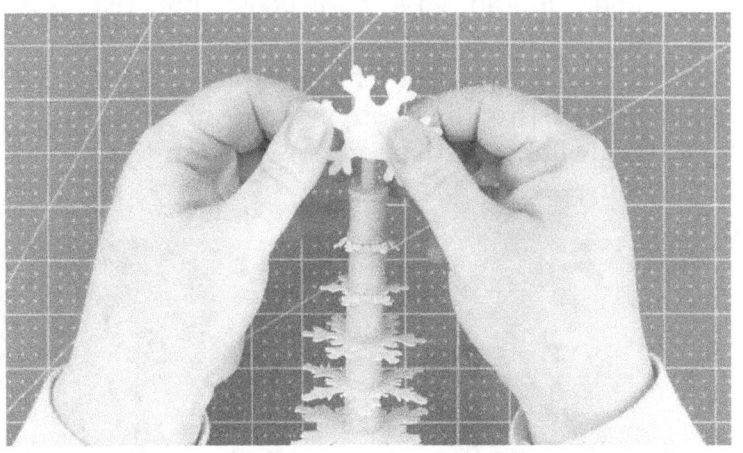

And there you have it. Your snowflake Christmas Tree is ready! Recall that I listed glitters as one of the tools to be used. You can decide to fancy it up with that glitter spray, or you can just pour some glitter on it. In the picture below, I did both. And I know you're probably thinking, what about ornaments? Well, I designed some little paper ornaments which you can put on the paper snowflake Christmas tree. It is quite easy. Just make use of the flower knowledge and all other paperwork we have been able to talk about in this book. Like every other Cricut project, you need to open up your mind. Add something unique and different. This book should serve as a boost, not just some word for word guideline (even though it can be that). However, just make sure that you make your Paper Snowflake Christmas Tree better than mine.

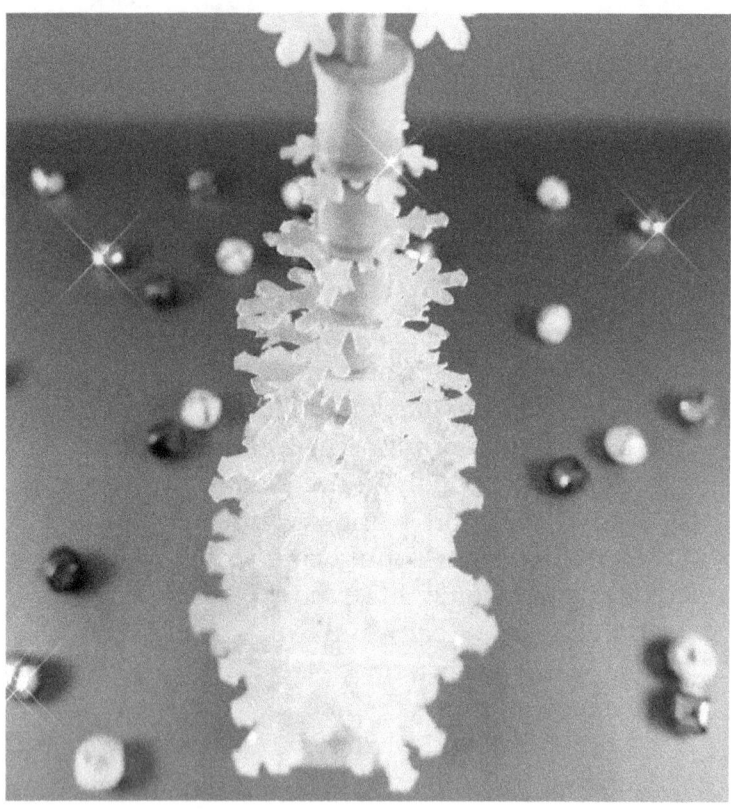

Allow these Cricut projects to bring out the creativity in you. With that, you would be able to do beautiful and unique things that are not even in this book. In fact, that is the point of all these. Yes, you can do these projects, but you should also be inspired to do something different from what you have here, you should be able to sit down, think of a project and execute it perfectly.

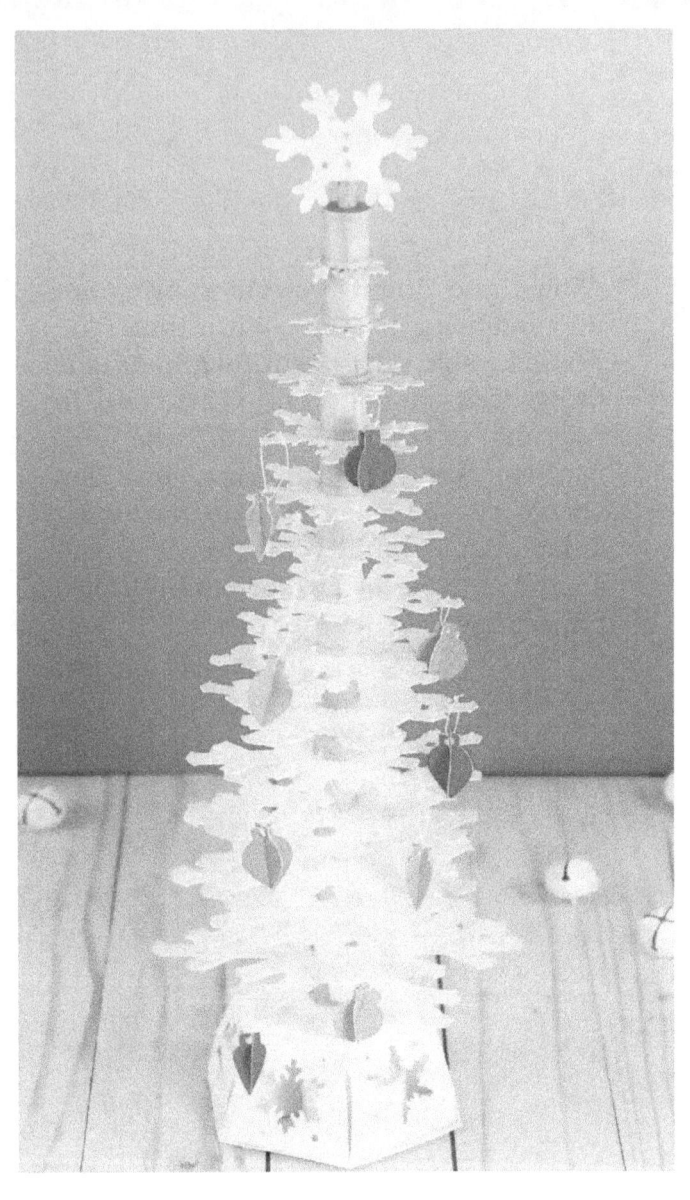

YOU CAN DO THIS NOW!

PROJECT 19- DIY LEATHER KEY FAB GIFT
Level-Hard

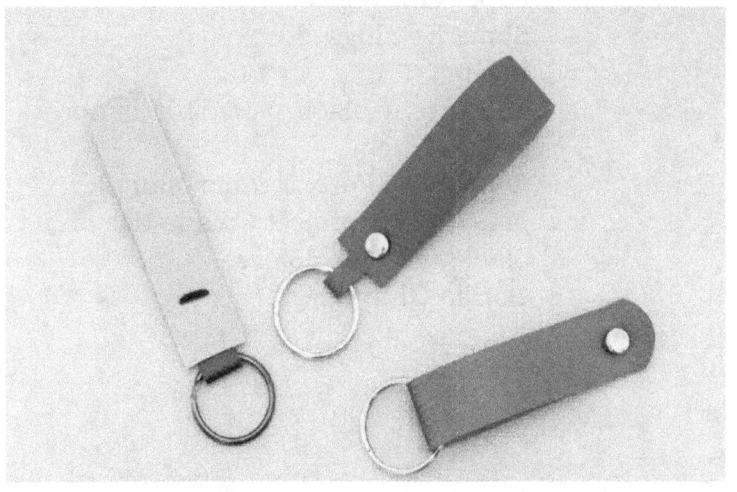

CREDIT- JENNIFFER MAKER

Key holders are perfect gifts for men, especially Dad's. It spreads that affection, especially when it is customized. This is a leather project which shows that Cricut cut through several materials easily.

SUPPLIES YOU NEED

- Key fab templates
- The standard grip cutting mat
- Faux leather. Feel free to pick any color. I'll be using brown, silver and beige
- Cricut Explore Air 2
- Paper crafting set
- Some Keyrings
- Rivets
- The Cricut black pen. This is an optional item.
- A pebbled Faux leather sampler pack in this project I made use of black and blue colors.
- Gorilla Glue

STEP 1

You know the first process, right? The design spaces. You chose your design, and you set the dial to Custom while you chose faux leather. If you're thinking of personalizing your leather Key fob, you can go ahead to load a Cricut pen into that machine. It would look like the image below.

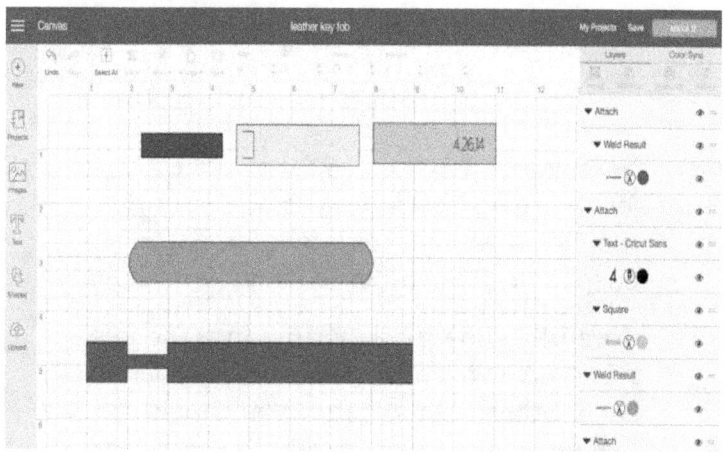

After cutting we have something like these:

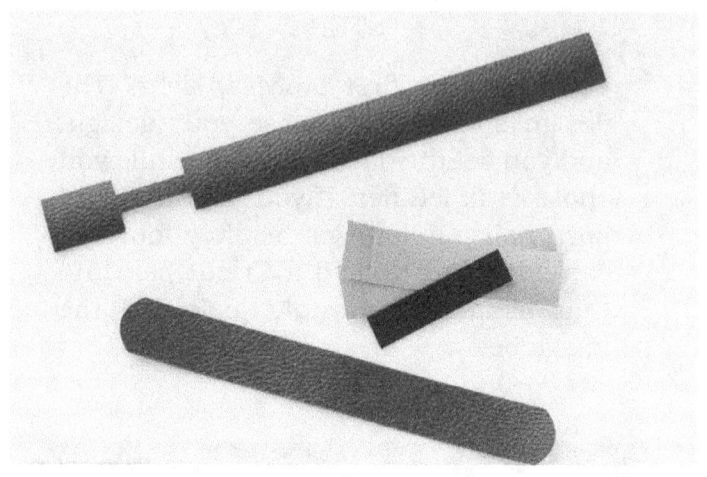

STEP 2

Next, you'll use the piercer to poke holes for the rivet. You should make sure that the holes are big enough for the rivet base to fit. Remember, it must fit closely.

Carefully slide the key ring onto the key fob. The two ends must be parallel to each other. Make sure you push the longer end of the rivet through the leather layers from the back.

Put the rivet tip over the rivet base then you use a rivet mallet immediately on top of the rivet. Strike gently because you wouldn't want to spoil the rivet but make sure it is very firm. I made use of the rubber handle of a hammer to strike because we need that gentle but firm touch. That is the final process. But you can make use of your Cricut pen to personalize it. Write your husband initials on it. However, there are several designs for this project.

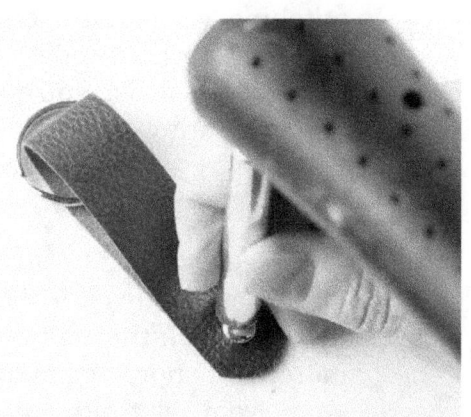

STEP 3

The next style would be very different. You would be making use of 3 pieces of faux leather, and you would use a stitch to secure the keychain instead of the rivet.

You'll start from the design space with the template which we have from the first project. You would insert the small black faux leather piece into a slot in front of the DIY leather Key fob. You would secure both pieces together with some glue. You should make sure to leave it to dry overnight. Next, you'll make holes marking the positions for stitching with that piercing tool. Then with a large needle plus a black embroidery floss, you should begin to start the stitch from the inside so that you can be able to conceal the knot at the back of the key fob.

The needle should be placed through the other hole then you'll slide the key ring, and you stick through on the back once more. You should complete the stitch by going from the front, especially from the top of the key fob to the inside. Next, you would tie the knot and then you'll trim off the excess embroidery floss away. The picture below would help that sink.

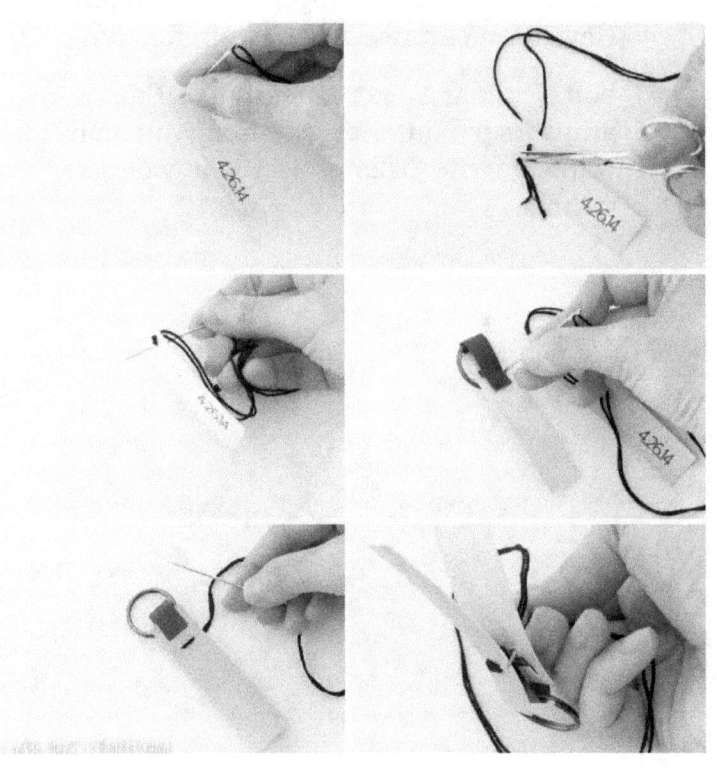

181

STEP 4

Place some glue between the front and the back of your DIY leather key fob, and you'll hold them together overnight. How? You can use a bobby pin for that.

You can personalize. Names, anniversary date, or anything you may want to write. This project is a good gift for men.

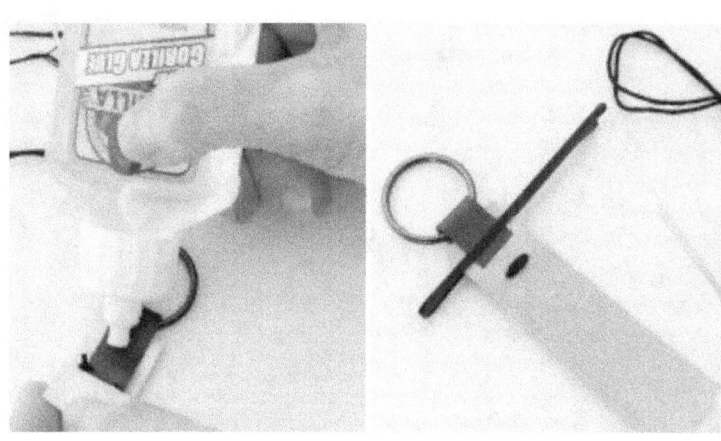

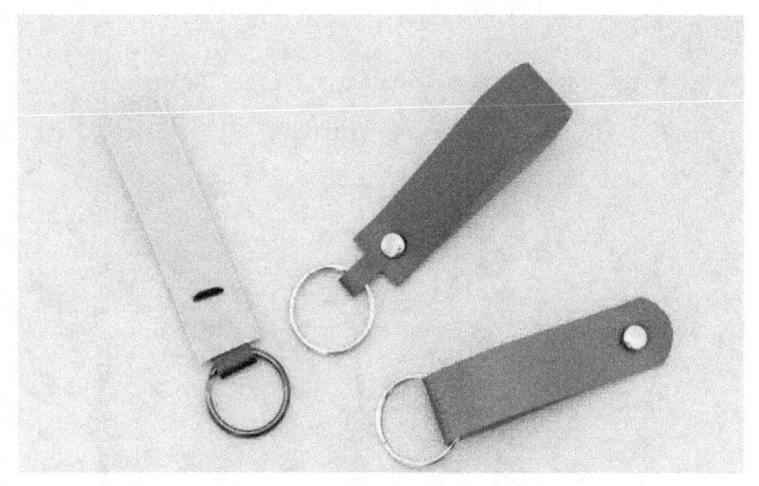

YOU CAN DO THIS NOW!

Level- Hard

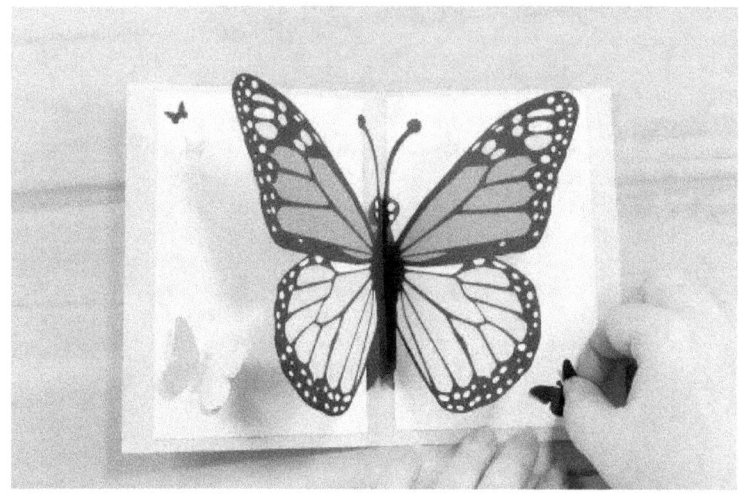

CREDIT- JENNIFER MAKER

This project is *a Pop-up butterfly card* which is good for a Mother's Day celebration, summer birthdays, and anyone who loves butterflies. There are several versions of this card because obviously there are several, countless number of butterflies.

SUPPLIES YOU NEED

- A 65 Ib. cardstock which should be in the complementary or opposing colors. You should have 1-3 sheets of the wings; a sheet meant for the outside of the card while the other sheet is meant for the inner part.
- Cricut machine for cutting out your butterfly.
- Adhesive spray. The 3M spray mount is preferred here.

The first thing here, unlike other, is that you should cut out your cardstock. And the only way you can do this is to work on it from your design space. Working on a butterfly is not easy. I must confess, but there are over 50,000 patterns, shapes, and objects to guide you into making that perfect shape. The beautiful thing is that you can check online, understand how it is constructed or you download the file online and work on it. Any way you choose, just make sure you have that butterfly ready. Mine was something like this;

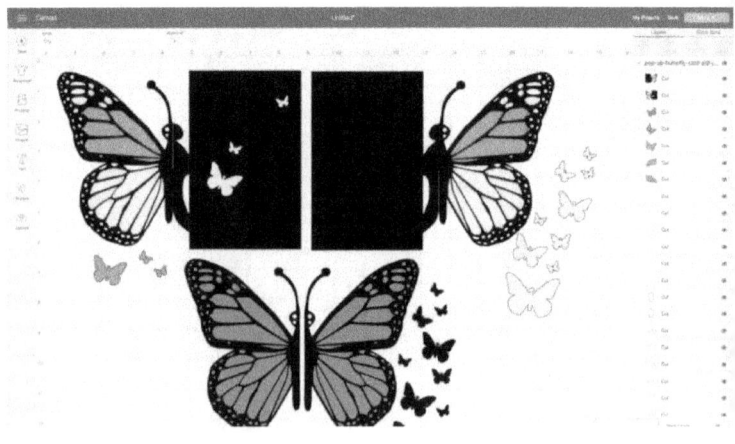

STEP 2

After cutting these intricate pieces.
They would look so much like the
picture below:

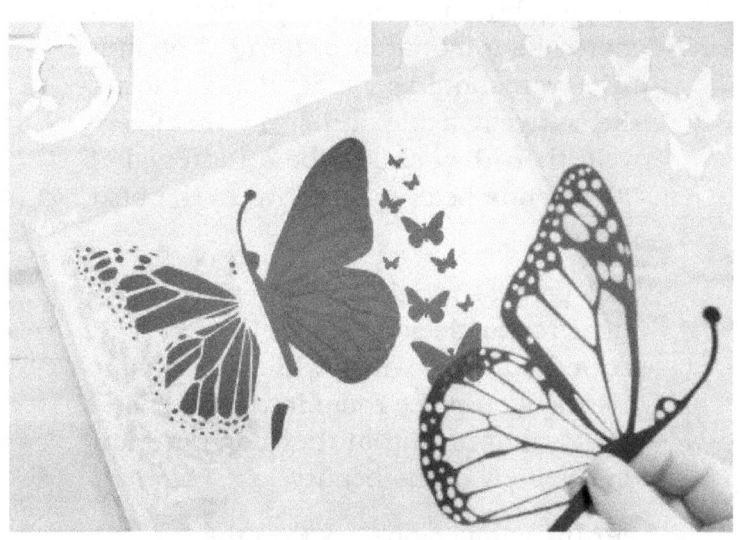

STEP 4

I know you're probably thinking, how
would I be able to do this? First, you can
start with the simple versions. Just get
two halves of the butterfly together then
you can wrap that outer card all around
them. Make sure you make use of an
adhesive spray to stick the rectangle

sections from the slotted butterflies to that outer car but be careful as you do so because you wouldn't want to get any glue on the wings.

You may be thinking of assembling the fantasy butterfly or something looking more like a monarch butterfly. The first thing you should consider doing is to set the butterfly aside and spray them very well; then they should be an interval of 30 seconds before you move to the next process.

This process requires you to place the inner rectangle sections on those slotted butterfly wings while watching the way you place them in the middle top-to-bottom so that they don't overlap on the body of the beauty.

Put the wing color pieces on the butterfly wing. You may decide to choose the fantasy rainbow butterfly you would use one full wing piece.

For the monarch butterfly, you would use six butterfly pieces which would all fit in together like that puzzle. Just note the way you place these pieces so that you'll position them well perfectly. Keep covering those areas and do the same for the second wing.

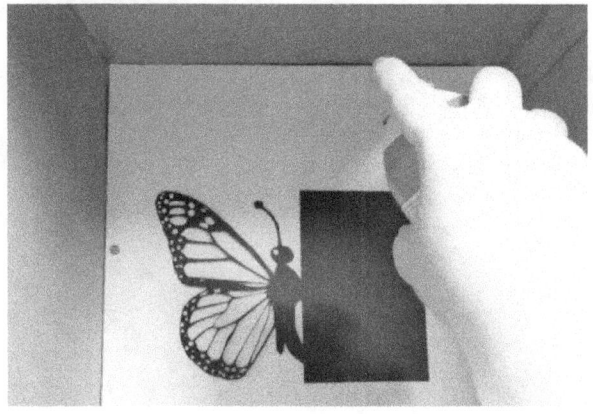

STEP 5

When you have the wing color in place, you should spray the back-wing pieces also with the adhesive which you've been using right from time to cover the colored wing. Make sure that you line up the back wing so that it would sync with your pattern. You'll be required to fold the assembled wings where the body of the butterfly meets the rectangle. Each part should be slotted together side by side from one side, then to the other from top to bottom.

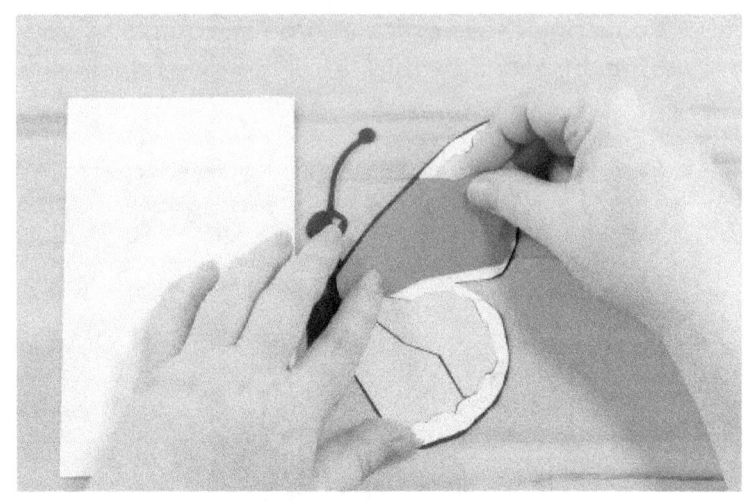

STEP 6

What is followed next? You place that outer card. How can you do this? First, you fold the butterfly and put the small black butterfly cuts you have gotten from the Cricut back into their positions. Doing this would allow you to protect the inner cardstock, especially when the next step comes on.

Protect the wings with some of your scrap paper. I made use of blue scrap paper in the picture below. So, you'll spray both the front and back of that your folded piece.

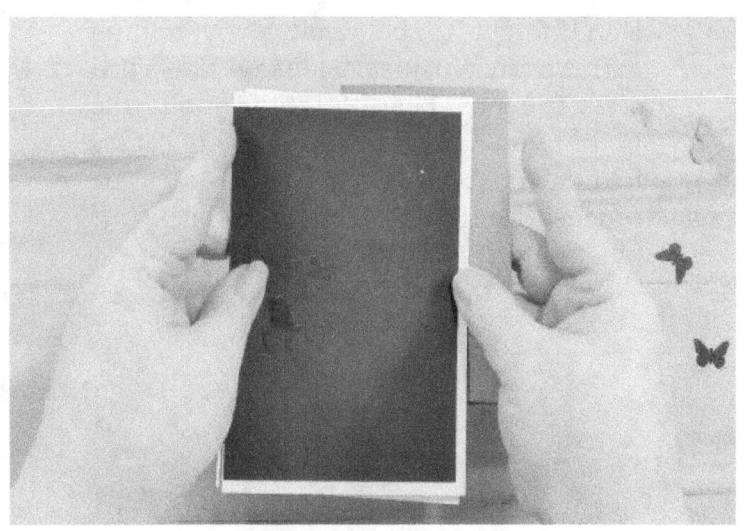

The next process if for you to remove the black butterfly inserts that would show some white butterflies also. Then you would line up the outside card with those pretty looking butterflies so that all the butterfly's images are all lined up perfectly. Place the black and orange butterfly into those empty spaces that are present on the front of the card so that it would cover the adhesive card beneath it.

Don't forget to be creative by adding extra butterfly inserts inside the card also. The most beautiful thing about this is that you can create that 3 D effect by folding the butterfly up a little bit. The process seems to be very complex but trusts m; it's worth your time.

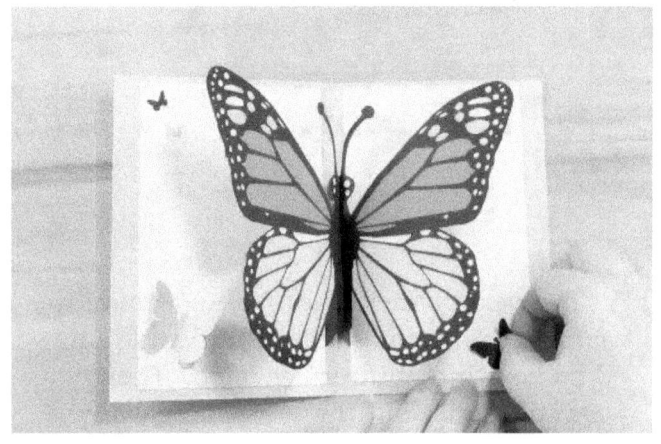

YOU CAN DO THIS NOW!

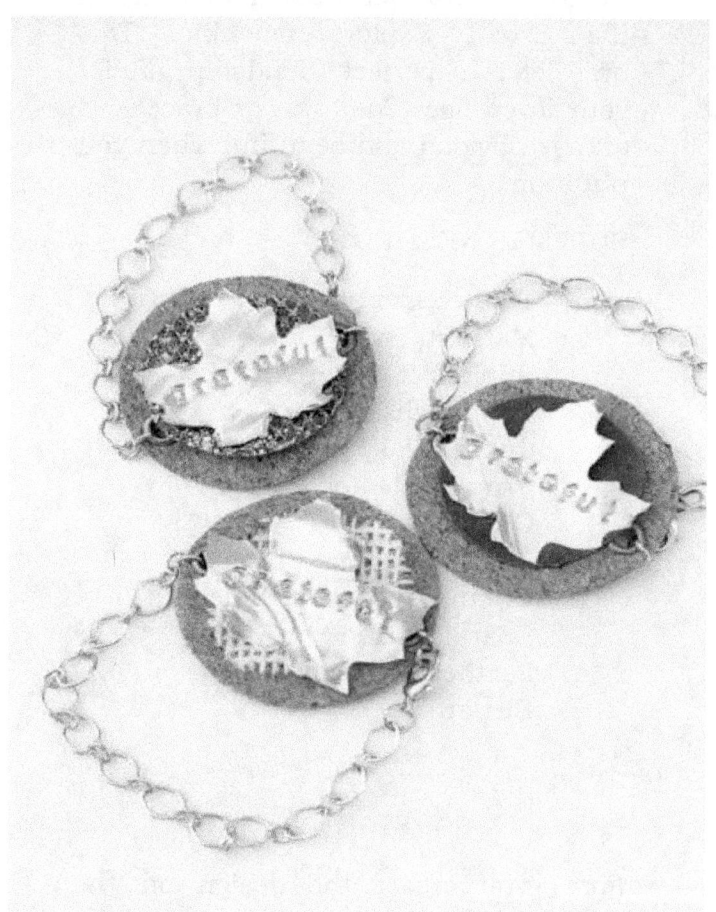

PROJECT 21- RUSTIC FRIENDSHIP BRACELET
Level- Hard

CREDIT- AMONGTHESEYOUNG.COM

The Cricut Explore can cut Metal. Do you know? It can work on those sheets effortlessly and fabulously. So, this friendship bracelet was created using the Cricut Explore machine. This bracelet is a perfect friendship gift for your loved one. That sparky bracelet is always obvious and beautiful when you put it on.

SUPPLIES NEEDED

- Thin copper sheet
- Metal stamps
- thin sheet of Corkboard
- Copper chain
- Copper clasps
- Crop-o-Dile and Eyelets
- Glue Dots
- E-600 glue
- Cricut Explore machine
- Sparkle fabric
- Leather or suede
- Burlap

STAGE 1

First, you create the design on the design space. You can make use of the leaf design or several others. I found a leaf design for this project.

194

STAGE 2

Make use of the thin metal and load the Cricut machine. Then make use of the handstamps to punch out whatever letters you want to choose. For this project, I made use of GRATEFUL because of the Thanksgiving theme.

STAGE 3

Get the Thin cork board and cut out 2 ½ - which is 3 inches circle using the Cricut Explore. The cork board was adhesive, so for this project, I made use of two cutting circles and stuck them together to make one.

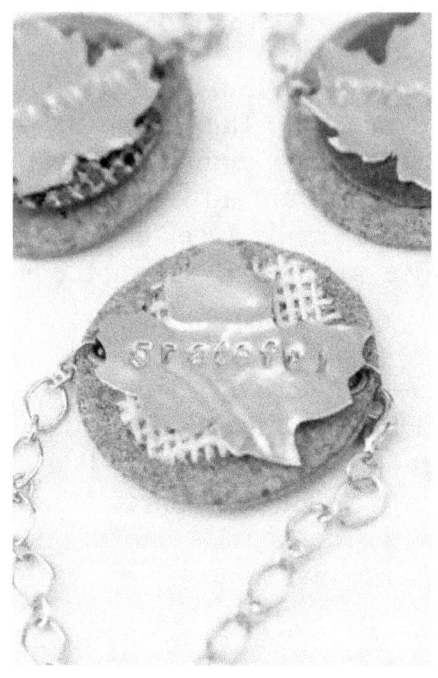

STAGE 4

Cut out 2-inch circle of burlap, sparkle fabric leather. Next, you can make use of the E-6000, assemble the bracelet which includes the first cork, the sparkle, burlap, leather then the leaf. Then you glue it together and allow it to dry for at least 12 hours.

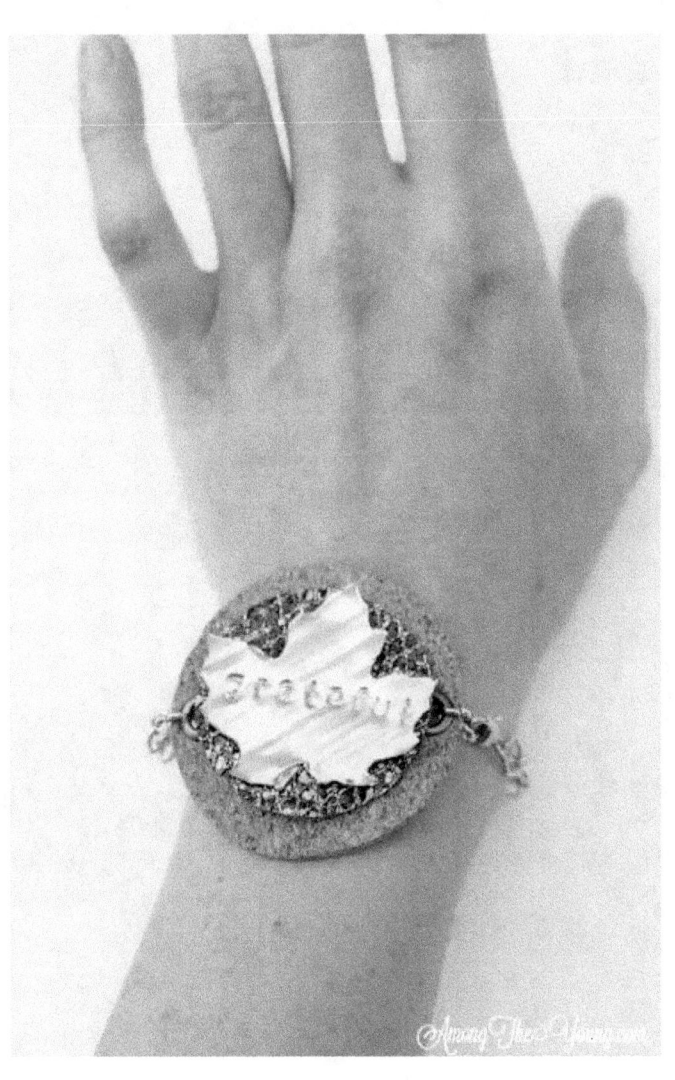

YOU CAN DO THIS NOW!

Level – Hard

DIY
Wedding Invitations

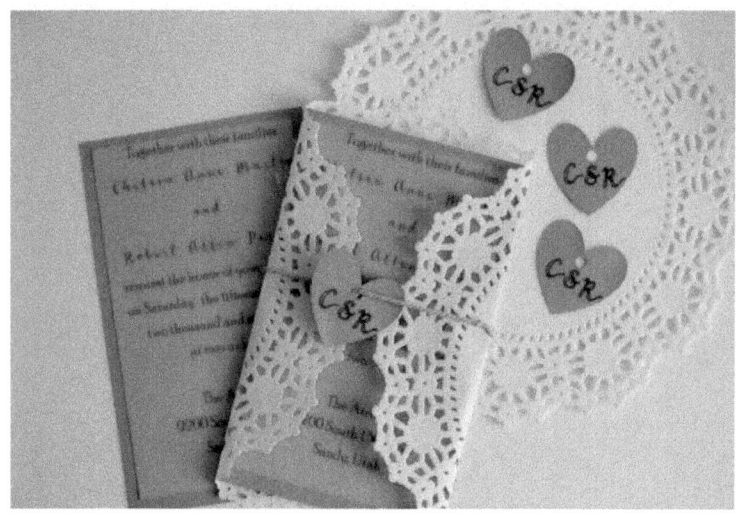

CREDIT-JENNIFER MAKER

This next project should come as a surprise for you. We are using a Cricut machine to make wedding cards.

Wedding cards? *Isn't that too risky?* Not at all. In fact, it is quite easy and simple. And I am sure with this information you would be able to save some money. I know that wedding cards are always expensive. Just imagine each card cost $3 and you are sending 200+ invitations that are a whopping $600 for invitations alone. So, we would call these projects DIY wedding invitations. Making your wedding card would just cost you a little over $40 because that is the amount for the supplies meant for 200+ invitations. You'll be spending $40 instead of $600! We all know that wedding cards are not like your regular cards; they would have to carry the theme of the event, which includes the color. My favorite is the coral and turquoise combination. After that, you need to choose the wordings of your invitations. The host? The venue? Is the invite meant for both the ceremony and the reception? You should be able to provide answers to these questions. If you have no idea on the wordings, go online, or you probably have one wedding card with you. Make the necessary changes and carve out your own words. Once you have been able to get all these ready. We can proceed.

SUPPLIES NEEDED

- Cardstock: The cardstock I used here; coral, turquoise, and grey.
- 10″ Paper Doilies
- Different Cricut Pen but the 4 Fine Tip Black one.
- Cricut Explore air machine
- Ribbon, string, or twine. The turquoise ribbon is used here.
- A Turnbow Adhesive Roller. If you can't get that you can use the double-sided tape.

STAGE 1

The measurement for the invitations here is 5″ by 8″. The invites were in two different tones. So, the first thing to do is to design a rectangle 5″ by 8″ in the design space. Creating a rectangle is quite easy. You click on the *insert shape* button, and you pick the square that you require. Next, you press the lock button so that the length and the width wouldn't be the same. You would have to click on the Edit Tab to change its size to 5″ width and 8″ height. Make use of the duplicate button to make another similar rectangle. I hope you've forgotten the duplicate process. Remember we have two different colors so you should copy and paste. This would make it two invitations for one page.

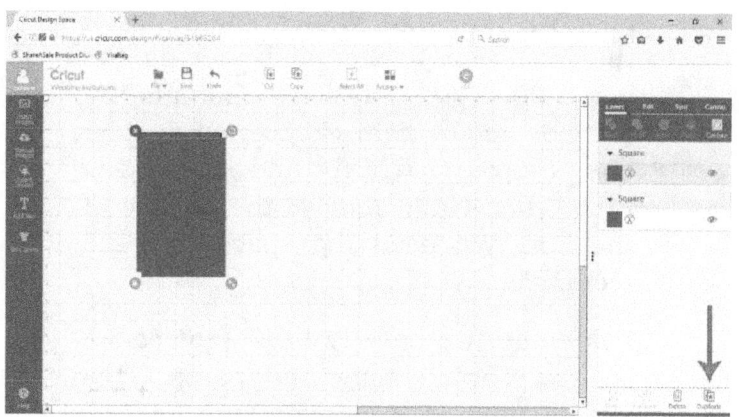

STAGE 2

The next process here is quite different from what we've been doing. Notice that most times when we are working on a project, we just talk about designing, cutting, and then finishing but this time we would have to make part of the designing process on another application. The actual invitation would be in Microsoft Word. It is quite easy. Make sure the ruler is on the screen, and you can make this possible by clicking on the VIEW TAB. Draw a text box which should measure 7.5″ tall by 4.5″ wide.

Compose your invitation in the text box. Make sure you use the appropriate fonts and sizes. For this project, I used the Poor Richard and Wilder Fonts. Make the invitation horizontal by giving the box a 90-degree rotation. Eliminate the text box line by right-clicking on the text box. Select OUTLINE and chose NO FILL. This would remove the outline of the box. We need the space, not the rectangle.

Remember we have two different colors so you should copy and paste. This would make it two invitations for one page.

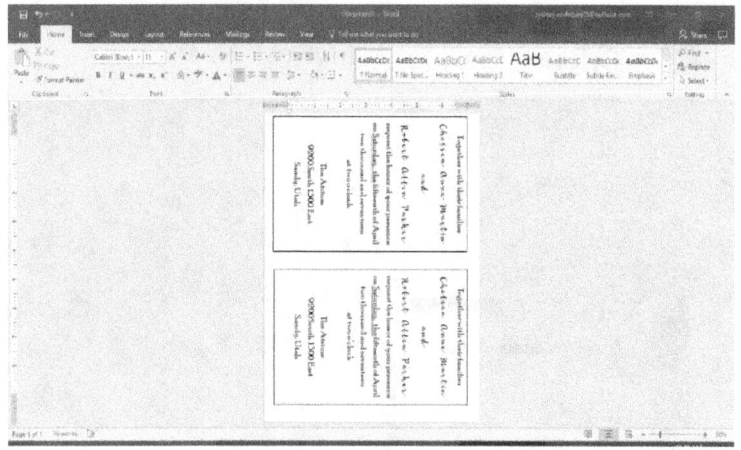

STAGE 3

You go back to the Cricut design space, and you'll create an 8.5″ by an 11″ rectangle. You input another rectangle, but that one would be 7.5″ by 4.5″ (that is the same size as your textbox on Microsoft Word) Duplicate the second rectangle so that there would be two similar rectangles. Place the two smaller rectangles into the bigger ones just close to where the text boxes are in the word document. Pick all three rectangles by dragging around the largest rectangle and click on ATTACH, then allow the 8.5″ by 11″ rectangle surface by clicking on the eye icon. Send the design to the Cricut.

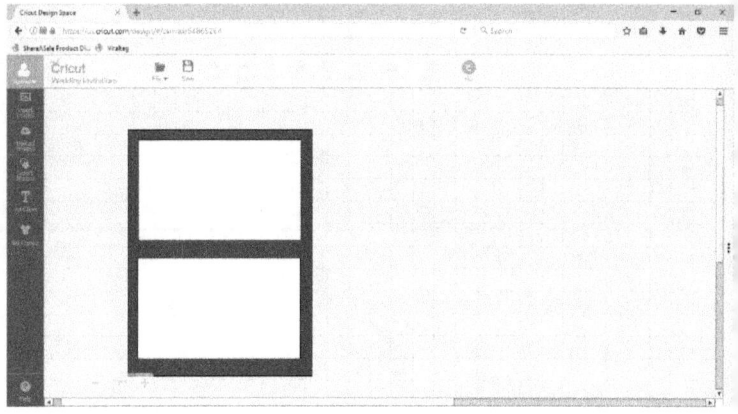

STAGE 4

The next process requires you to put invitations together

Make use of a Tombow adhesive roller or your double-sided tape to apply the teal invitation on that grey backdrop. In the Cricut design space. Create a new page. And add a heart which should be 2″ wide. Type in the bride and groom's initial into the heart. Make sure it is centralized. During this, the initials should be in WRITE not cut. Place a circle above the initials then blend circle and heart. Blend in the sense that you should put the circle inside the heart that is where the hole would be. Next, you would cut and write hearts. Get a 10″ paper doilie around the invite and fold it. Make use of the ribbon, string, or twine to fasten the heart to the invite and tie at the back.

DIY
Wedding Invitations

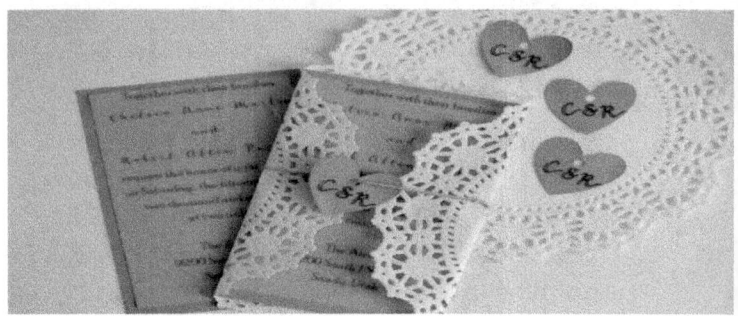

YOU CAN DO THIS NOW!

Level- Hard

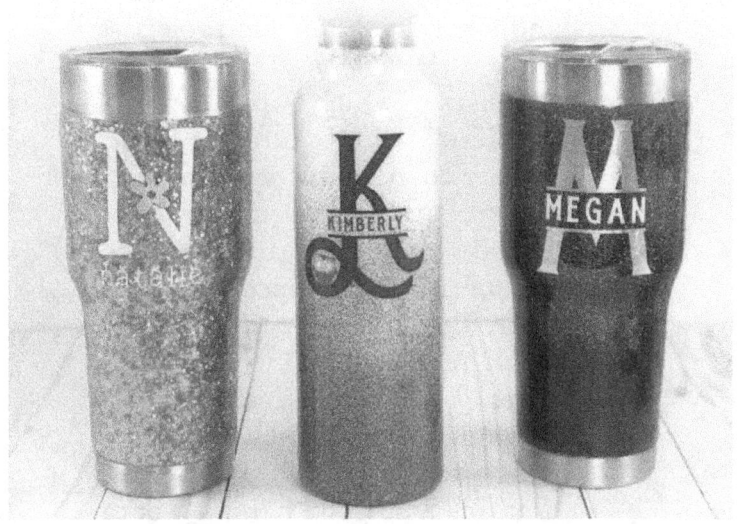

CREDIT- JENNIFER MAKER

Have you ever seen a tumbler so beautiful that you want to get it at that very instant? The beauty of any Cricut project is that it allows you to express yourself in a way that only you can achieve. The Cricut glitter tumbler is one object that you would want to have with you. You shouldn't be afraid of the difficulty level of this project. It is quite easy.

SUPPLIES NEEDED

- Stainless steel tumblers, cups, and/ or mugs. For this project, I made use of Mossy Oak 30 oz. tumblers which include; a stemless wine tumbler and powder coated pink water bottle.
- Glitter, extra fine or chunky ones. I made use of chunky glitters having the teal, copper, and pink color. I also included purple, black, red, pink and white
- Epoxy resin. For this, I would recommend the EXACT brand.
- Spray adhesive. The EXACT brand is also good here; it works like a charm.
- Spray Sealer. The EXACT brand is very good. Pls. Note that this is not to discredit other brands; I am just telling you what works for me.
- Painter or electrical tape.
- 91% isopropyl alcohol
- Disposable gloves
- Respirator which would be used when sanding epoxy resin

- Extra plastic cups for mixing
- Extra popsicle sticks meant for mixing
- Freezer paper which can be used to capture your glitter as well as drips.
- Adhesive vinyl with transfer tape.
- Any mechanism to make the glitter tumblers rotate. I was able to use both cardboard box with PVC pipes and those homemade tumbler turners.
- Cricut Machine
- Free SVG/DXF/PDF cut files/ patterns or your own peculiar design.

STEP 1

Make your tumblers for the glitter ready. Take off all the labels and wash your tumblers. You can decide to sand the outside of the tumbler. This would help any paint which you would apply on it stick better. Once the labels are off, you can tape the tumbler in any way you choose. But make sure that when you tape it, you can make use of a continuous piece of tape that would go around the circumference of the tumbler. Make it very thick because you wouldn't want the paint to touch those sides.

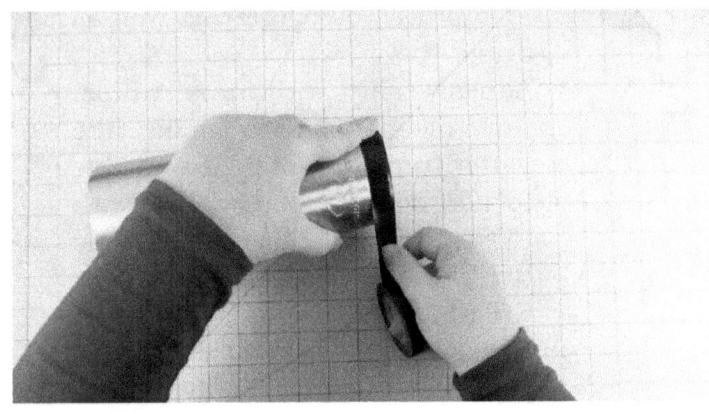

STEP 2

I taped the two bottoms of the tumblers. You can decide to put the glitter all over the bottom also. But this isn't compulsory. When you tape the tumblers, fold over the edge of your tape so that you can remove it later very easily. After taping you wipe the surface of the tumbler with alcohol. This would allow you to remove all the dust and impurities. Especially those residual adhesive form of labels. The cleaner the surface, the better it becomes for the sticky paint.

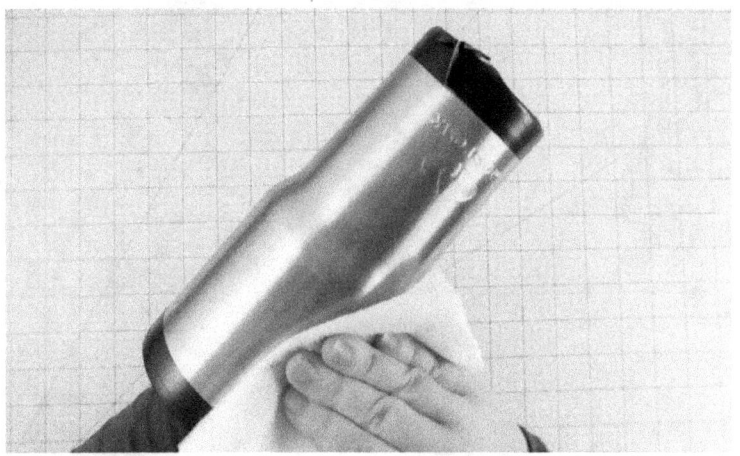

STEP 3

Paint the tumblers. I was able to do this with three kinds of paint. There is no need to spray the paint in the first instance if you are going to use so much glitter or that extra chunky glitter. But if you are making use of that transparent or translucent glitter, you would want to paint it first.

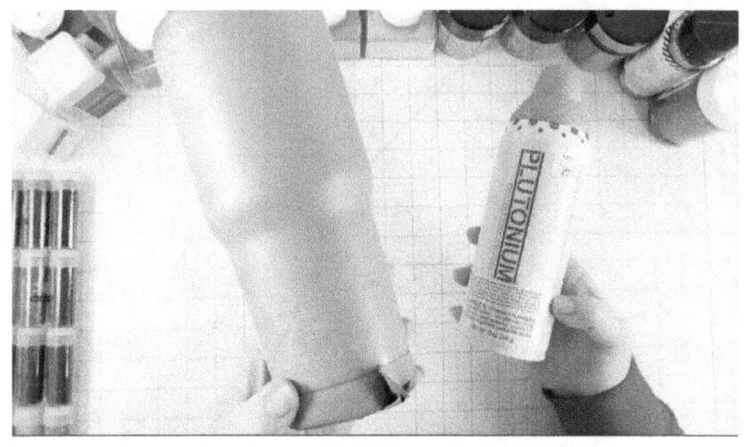

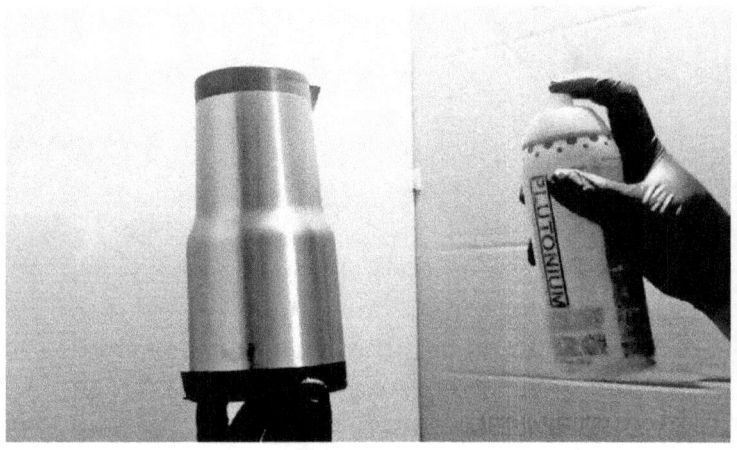

When spraying makes sure you make use of short burst instead of that regular going all out while holding the button. The short burst is always good and goes a long way. Like above. If you noticed first, I used Plutonium spray paint. I was able to try Krylon Color Maxx too, and they worked perfectly. I also painted another tumbler with the Rustoleum powder-coated paint which had a primer in it.

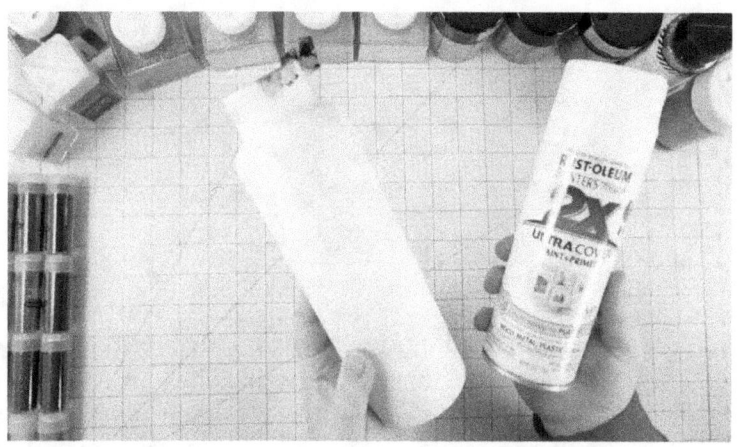

STEP 4

Place the adhesive on the tumbler then you glitter them. You have two choices here. first, you may decide to go with the mod podge or the spray adhesive which is my preference.

You can apply the mod podge by getting a brush and put the mod podge on your tumbler in that nice equal strokes. You should be careful not to allow too much glob on in one section or the other.

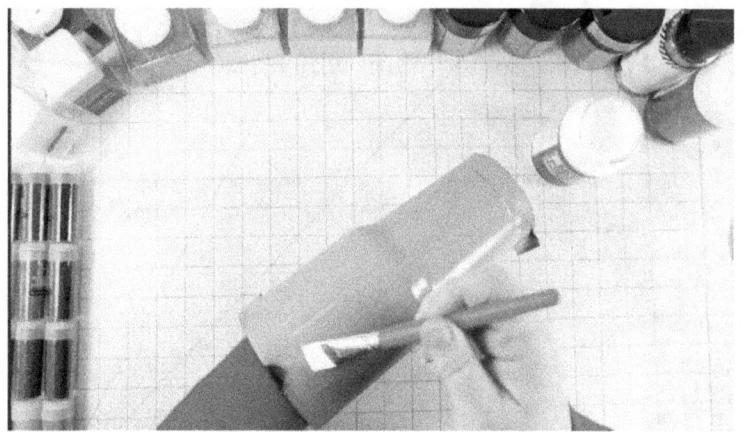

After the mod podge is applied evenly, you must glitter it immediately, or it would dry. It is advisable that you put something on the surface to collect the falling glitter. For this project, freezer paper and that little plastic bowl you see above was used.

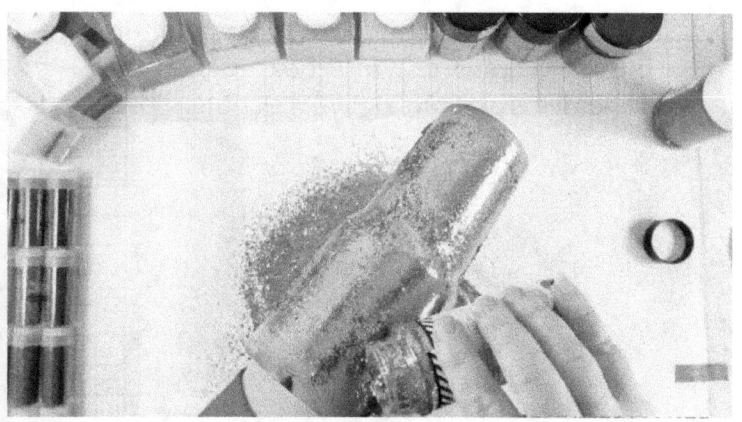

Sprinkle the glitter onto the tumbler on as evenly as you can. Just like you can see above. You should recall that the Mod Podge doesn't adhere with the experiment very well there are sections with no glitter so it would require a second coating. When you are through glittering you can pick up the freezer paper or whatever you are using underneath then you would pour part of the glitter back into the container. This would allow you to use it again.

STEP 5

Spray the adhesive 100 Loctite spray adhesive, not the 300 Loctite spray adhesive. Make sure you spray in a well-ventilated space, preferably not in your craft room. Remember to use short bursts. I made use of a box to keep the adhesive from getting where it shouldn't go.

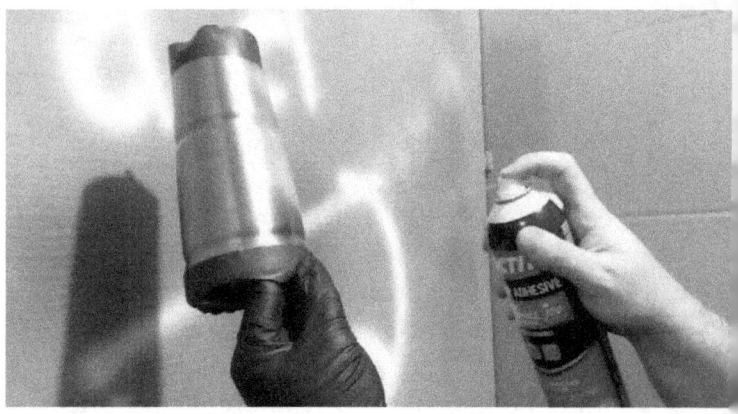

After you have been able to apply the spray adhesive on the tumbler, you should glitter it immediately just as we have said earlier. Get the glitter around the surface of the tumbler without leaving spaces or uneven spots.

Let us make a quick comparison of tumblers that required Mod Podge and Loctite. I compared all three below.

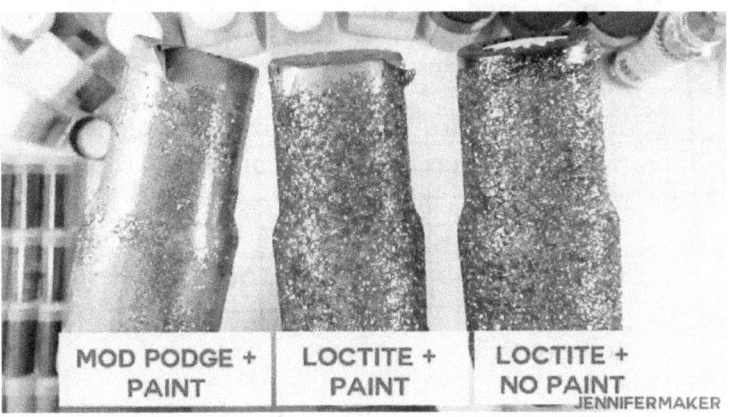

MOD PODGE + PAINT | LOCTITE + PAINT | LOCTITE + NO PAINT

JENNIFERMAKER

The Loctite and paint combo seems to be the best option. There is no need to spray paint if you don't want to. If that tiny bit of aluminum peeking through doesn't disturb you, you can go with no paint at all.

STEP 6

Seal the glitter on the tumblers with that clear coat. This must be done in a well-ventilated area. Why should you do this? Because there is still that tendency of your glitter flaking off even after you have applied adhesive. Furthermore, when you apply that epoxy, there is a need to keep things under control. Wait for about 30 minutes before applying the sealer to your glitter tumbler then you can proceed to step 7.

STEP 7

While you are waiting for it to blend perfectly, you should prepare that mechanism you can use to rotate the tumbler. You can set this in advance. That would be better. I would present you with two methods you can use to achieve this.

First is the manual turning method which can be structured with a cardboard box and some PVC tubes. You would attach tapes at the end of the PVC tubes. They would fit right in. Those soft little footballs would fit perfectly with the glitter tumblers. They would smoosh in, and they would become stable. This method is very cheap and effective, but you can decide to manually turn it frequently right from the beginning to keep the epoxy from dripping away. This would require you to sit several hours to babysit your glitter tumblers.

The second method is a power turning method which would require you to build that rotisserie turner. Something like the picture below

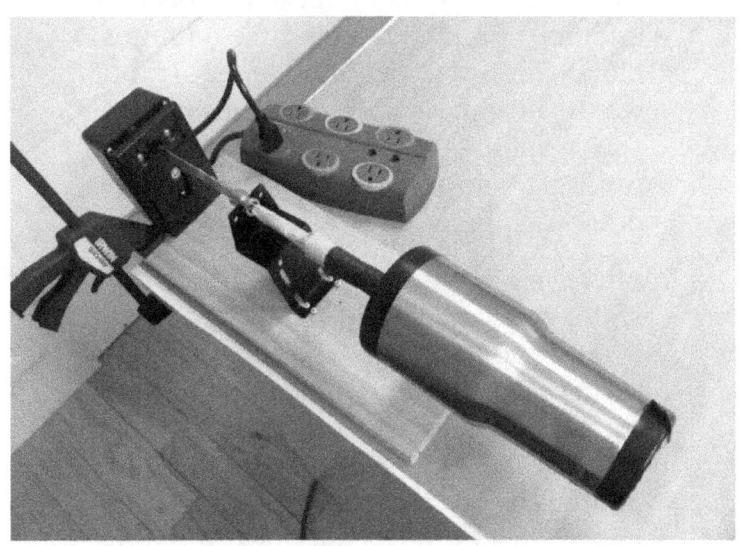

STEP 8

Put on your gloves and mix and apply high gloss resin to your glitter tumbler. When I was doing this, I made use of 25 milliliters of the A bottle and B bottle of that resin. You may have smaller ones, and this would require you to do less. However, you would notice that the A bottle is quite thicker than the B. Be sure to have enough supply of plastic cups and Popsicle sticks for mixing. There should be a proper mix of A and B individually for one minute, and above, then you would combine both together and mix for a total of three minutes. Make sure you get all the liquid out when you are combining them because you wouldn't want it to look of. You wouldn't want one to be more than the other.

After you have been able to mix the resin, you would immediately head on to where you have placed your tumbler turner and place the tumbler on it. Next, you would need to apply those epoxy resin on the mugs. For this project, I just poured it on the mug and used my gloved fingers to trace it down the mug. Make sure you are rotating the tumbler while doing this. Even after application, you should keep the tumbler rolling especially for the five minutes then you do it 10 to 15 seconds. This means that for the first half hour or so you would be tumbling the tumblers. And you can do it every few minutes.

STEP 9

Get rid of the tape after 30 minutes or before 45 minutes. If you don't do this, you wouldn't be able to clean up the edge of the glitter. Then after at least five hours you should tape them and sand them. When doing this, you should wear respirator and gloves so that there wouldn't be epoxy contact and buildup or allergic reaction.

STEP 10

Here is where you would want to make use of the Cricut machine. You apply your vinyl decal on the tumbler. Use beautiful fonts for the decals. For the project, I was able to use *mother Nature, Roland Emerald, Black Django (a mixture of both)*

STEP 11

Add another cost for the resin. You can do this by repeating everything in step 8.

STEP 12

Make sure you remove the tape after 30 minutes and before 45 minutes then you allow it solidify for 34-48 hours.

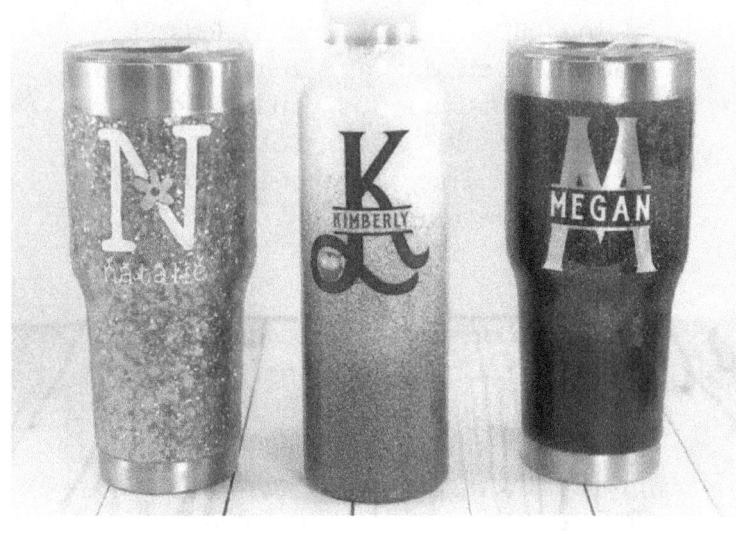

YOU CAN DO THIS NOW!

Level- Hard

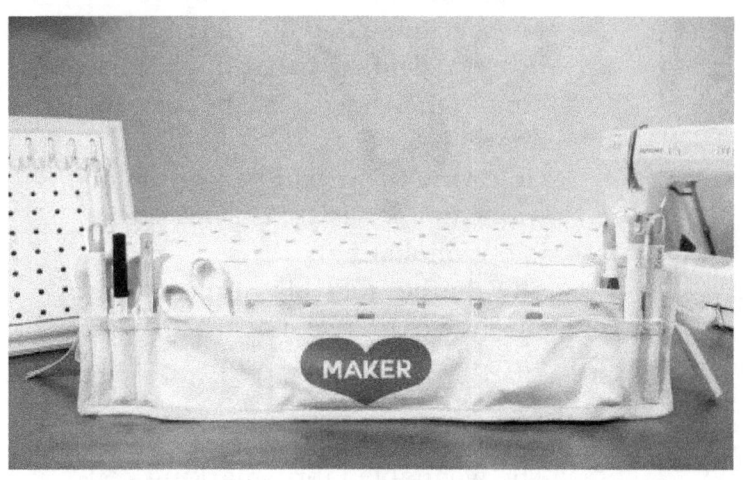

CREDIT- JENNIFER MAKER

We have always been talking about projects from the Cricut maker. How about we change things a little bit. Let us talk about a project for the Cricut machine itself. This project, known as the *Cricut maker tool,* serves as a dust cover and tool organizer also. It took me less than 1.5 hours to make this mat, and I finished it with the dimension 22″ wide by 17.5″ long.

223

SUPPLIES NEEDED

- Mint Cotton fabric, 24″ by 24″ feel free to pick a color you love.
- White cotton fabric or any other color you need also. 24″ by 36″
- Fusible (one-side) interfacing, 24″ by 24″. This is what I used to create the object in the picture above.
- Gold vinyl. This can be iron-on or the usual adhesive. However, this is optional supply.
- The double fold bias tape which would be in two packages of 3 yards each. That would be 6 yards in total.
- A matching thread.
- The washable fabric marking pen which is used from the Cricut maker.
- Scissors
- Pins
- The Cricut easy press or iron.
- The maker mat pattern which can be gotten from a resource library or you can design yours.
- Cricut maker with a rotary blade which would have 12″ by 24″ FabricGrip mat.

- A sewing machine. I made use of the Janome sewing machine here.

STEP 1

So, we would go back to the initial method. You can download several designs for this project, which can be accessed as an SVG, DXF, and a PDF in the free asset library. In case you're utilizing Cricut Design Space, transfer the SVG and spot it on your canvas. Ungroup everything, at that point change the two arrangements of lines (demonstrated by the red askew line symbol) to Write (pick a washable texture checking pen). You additionally need to join these two textures checking pen lines to their particular texture sorts, so they remain out.

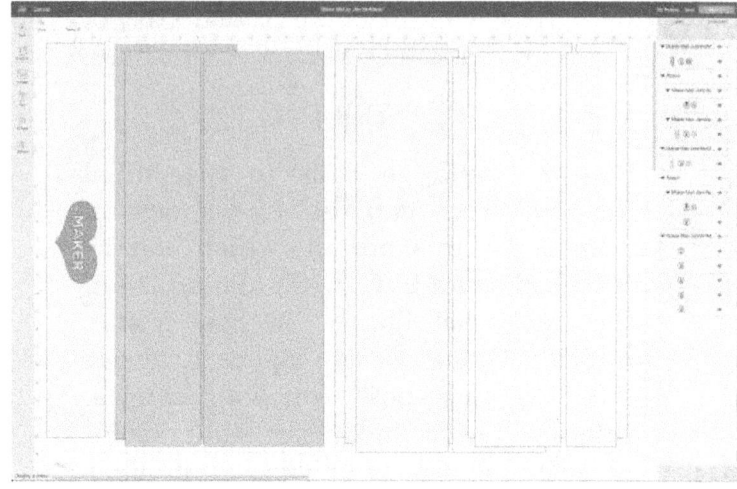

STEP 2

Iron your cotton texture, so it has no wrinkles. (Try not to press your fusible interfacing!) Iron your texture before cutting on the Cricut Maker

STEP 3

Cut out your materials (cotton texture, interfacing, and the discretionary vinyl for the heart) utilizing my example. Tip: If you're removing the example on your Cricut Maker, put a full 12″ x 24″ bit of texture on your FabricGrip cutting mat before you slice it to guarantee you have a sufficiently enormous piece. You can, obviously, simply cut the huge example pieces by hand. You'll get more exactness in the event that you utilize the Maker, in any case.

Tip #1: Don't neglect to put your Washable Fabric Marking Pen in the apparatus holder in the event that you intend to check your texture!

Tip #2: Place your mint cotton material on the FabricGrip tangle face down with the goal that the texture stamping pen shows up on the back, where you need to see it. Different layers of mint texture and the white texture can go on the tangle face up.

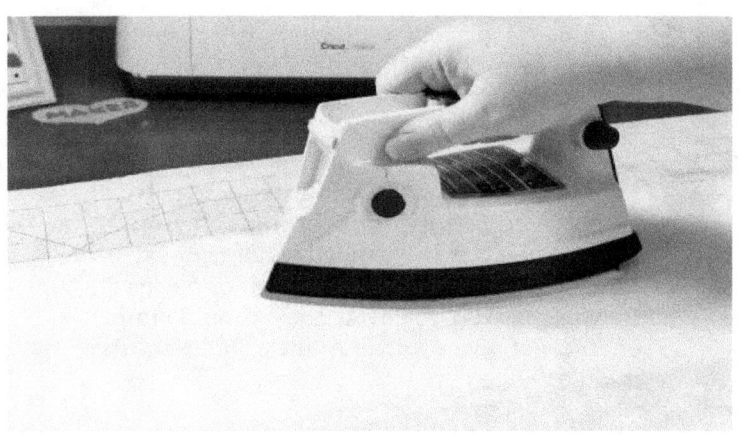

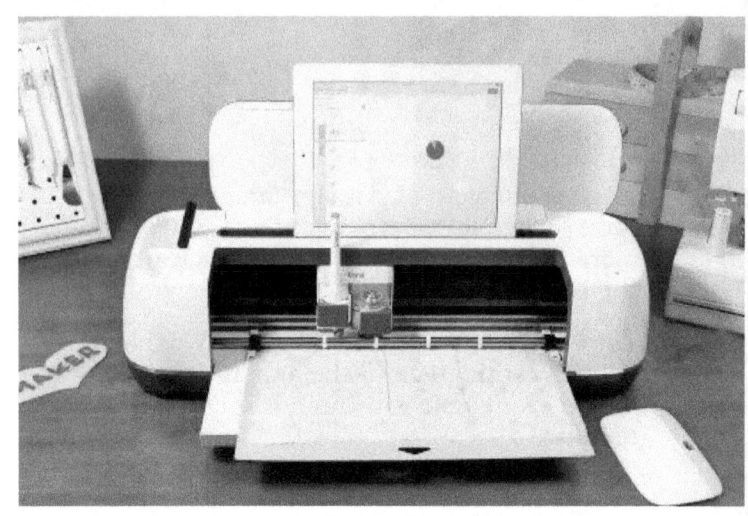

STEP 4

When the majority of your materials are cut, distinguish each piece utilizing this outline as I will allude to them by name starting now and into the foreseeable future.

Lay one (1) of piece A (backboard), one (1) of piece B (front board), and piece E (top board) on your work surface, face down. Presently lay one (1) of piece F, one (1) of piece H, and the two pieces G over pieces A, B, and E. Note that both of pieces G (interfacing strips) go on piece E (top board). Interfacing ought to be focused inside the edges of the texture pieces. What's more, on account of pieces G, they ought NOT to cover; they should simply contact of even have a little hole in the middle.

Significant note: Interfacing must go sparkling side against the texture — the gleaming side is the fusible side.

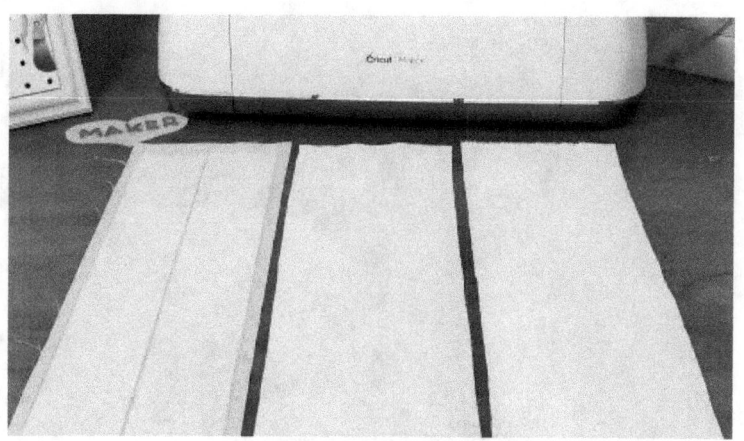

STEP 5

Presently pursue the headings on your fusible interfacing bundle to combine them to the posterior your front, top, and backboards. The headings for Craft-Fuse say to put glossy cement side of interfacing against the wrong side of texture, at that point spread with sodden press material. Utilizing a hot, dry iron, apply slight weight with a floating activity to intertwine, enabling iron to remain on texture for 8-10 seconds.

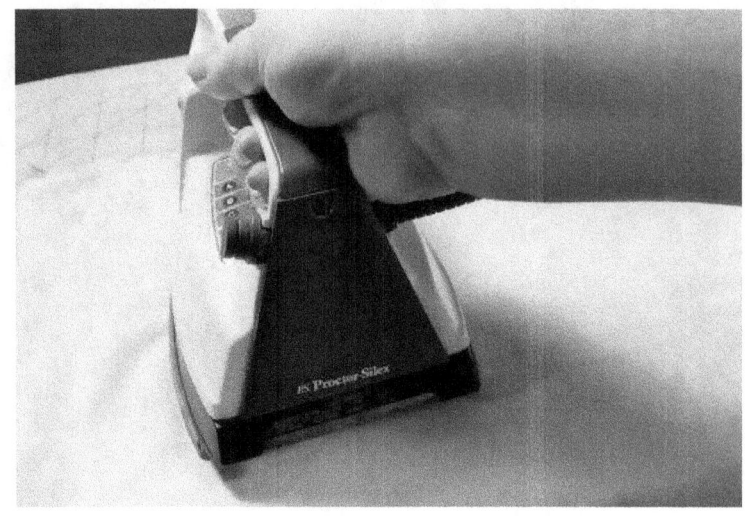

STEP 6

When you have your interfacing combined on, you can sew these three layers together in a specific order: front intertwined layer (A/F) + top melded layer (E/G) + back combined layer (B/H). Spot right sides together and sew 1/2″ from the edge (the 1/2″ crease remittance is worked into the example).

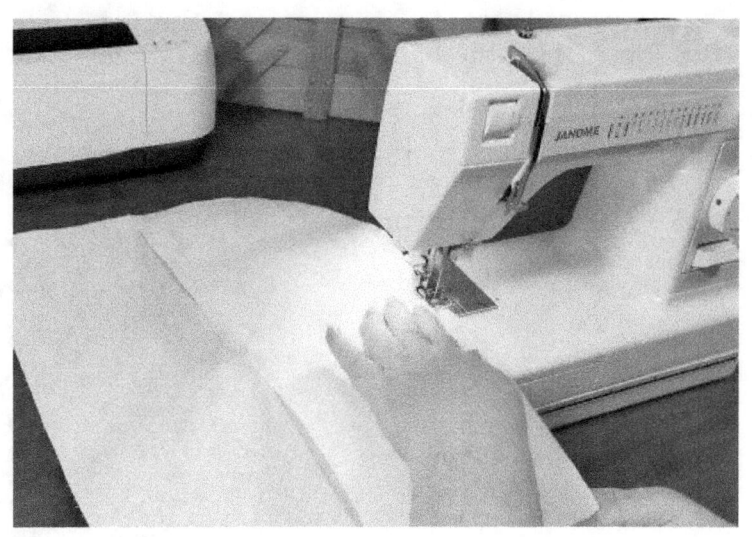

STEP 7

Sew the boards together for your Cricut Maker Mat

This is what it resembles when those pieces are sewn together.

Layers are sewn together for Cricut Maker

Presently press the creases open for perfect, fresh creases. (In case you're curious about what that implies, a squeezed crease is a crease that is opened on the back and squeezed to lie level.)

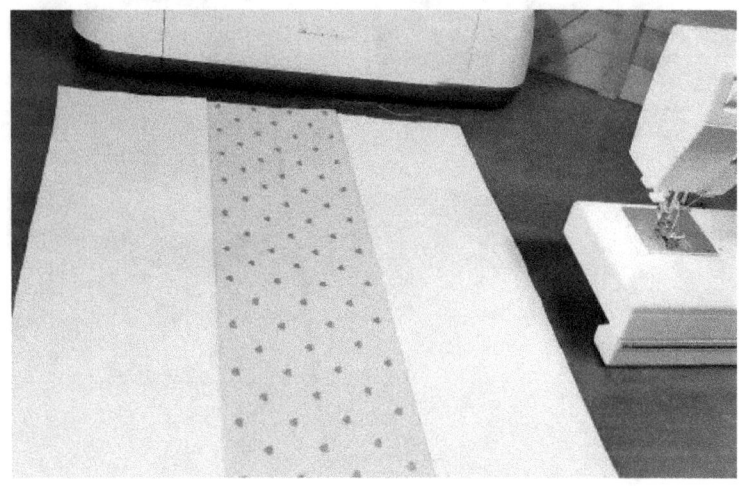

STEP 6

Presently sew together the rest of the piece A (backboard), remaining piece B (front board), and remaining piece E (top board). Spot right sides together and sew 1/2″ from the edge (the 1/2″ crease recompense is worked into the example). These three pieces are the covering of your Maker Mat and won't be seen except if you turn it over.

Sew the coating layers together for your Cricut Maker Mat

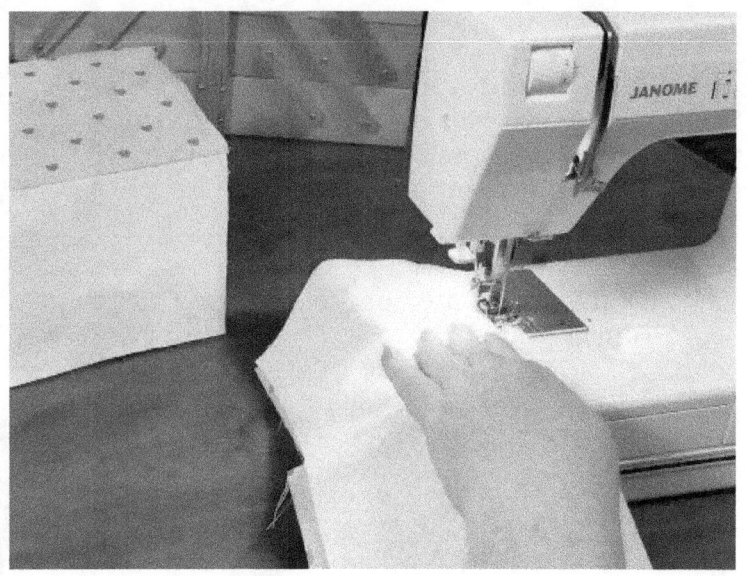

On the off chance that you need to press on the gold heart onto the front pocket (piece C), this is a decent time to do it. Simply be careful to depart enough space at the base of the pocket for the inclination tape (around 1/2″).

This is additionally an opportunity to sew the inclination tape onto the TOP edge of your two pocket pieces (C and D). The tape ought to stretch out right to the edge of each piece.

STEP 7

It's currently time to sew the pockets! Spot piece over piece D, both right sides up. Line up the checking lines with each other. Stick set up.

Front and center pockets of the Cricut Maker Mat

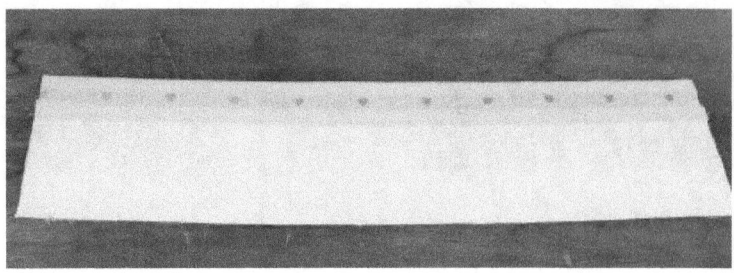

Sew along in the spots set apart with a yellow specked line in the realistic beneath. Sew from the base right to the highest point of the predisposition tape on the front pocket, yet don't sew past that first column of inclination tape.

Sew along lines on pockets for Maker Mat

Tip: You can thoroughly change the design of the pockets on your Cricut Maker Mat in the event that you wish — don't hesitate to modify this to your requirements.

When pieces C and D (front and center pockets) are sewn, place the pocket gathering on the combined layer get together (the pockets go on the little white segment, flush with the external edge). Stick set up.

STEP 8

This time, sew along the spots set apart with the orange spotted line in the realistic beneath.

Sew along spotted lines on pockets for Maker Mat

This is what it resembles when the pocket gathering is sewn to the melded layer:

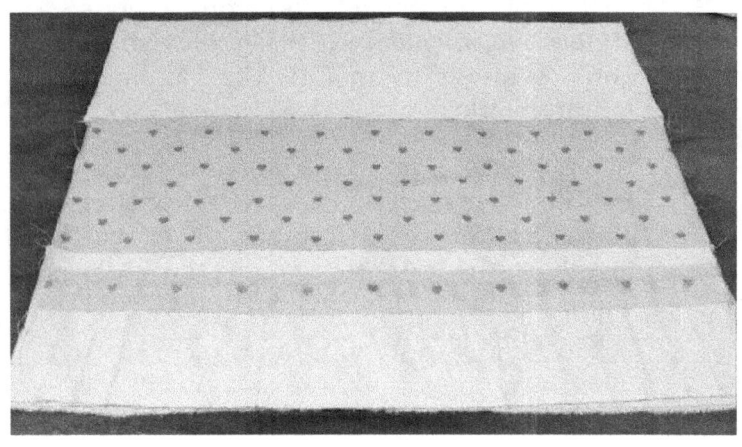

Spot the pocket gathering on the front melded layer

Spot the intertwined layer over the coating layer, wrong sides together. Ensure all creases coordinate.

236

Set up the two layers together for the Cricut Maker Mat

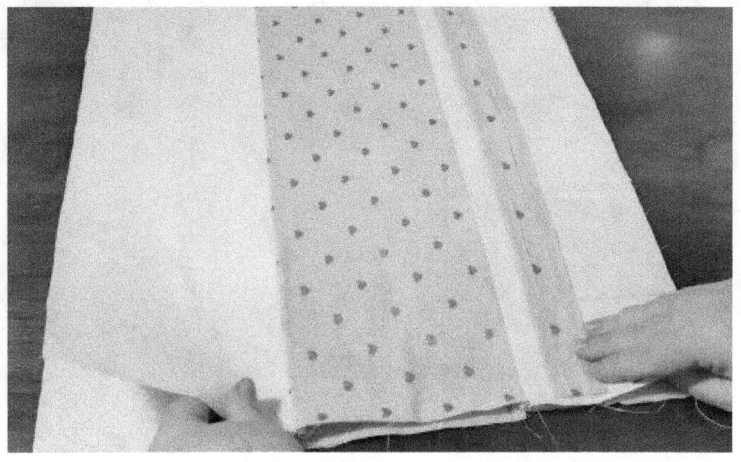

Stick set up.

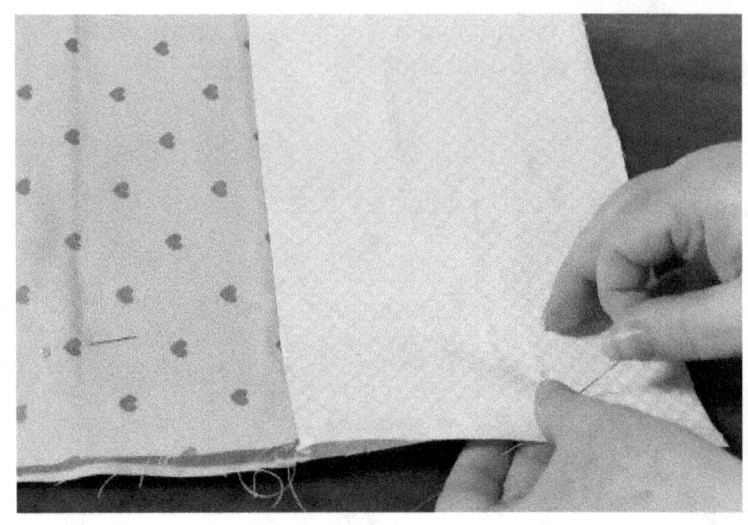

STEP 9

Stick your layers together for your Cricut Maker Mat

Cut out four ties from your inclination tape, about 12″ long each. What I did was ensure I had enough predisposition tape to circumvent the four sides of my Cricut Maker Mat, at that point, I cut the rest of the tape into four strips.

Cut out four ties for your Maker Mat

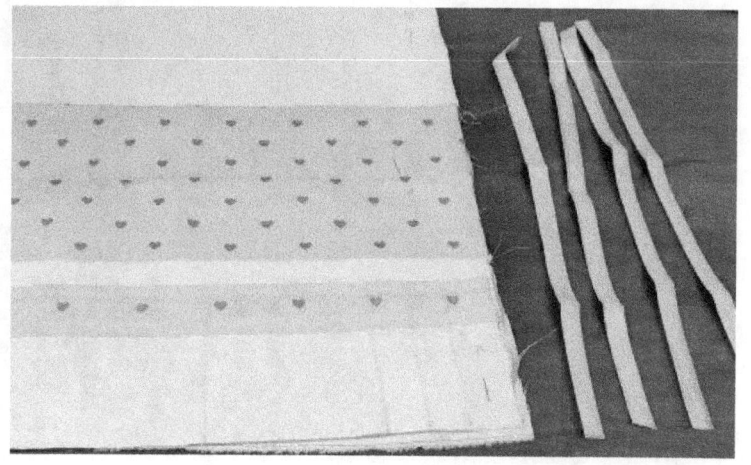

Start sticking the inclination tape onto the edge of your Maker Mat, start at the base back corner (as appeared in the photograph beneath). Ensure you're getting the inclination tape around all layers at the edge and as far over onto your texture as could be expected under the circumstances. Stick the principal 12″ crawls into spot.

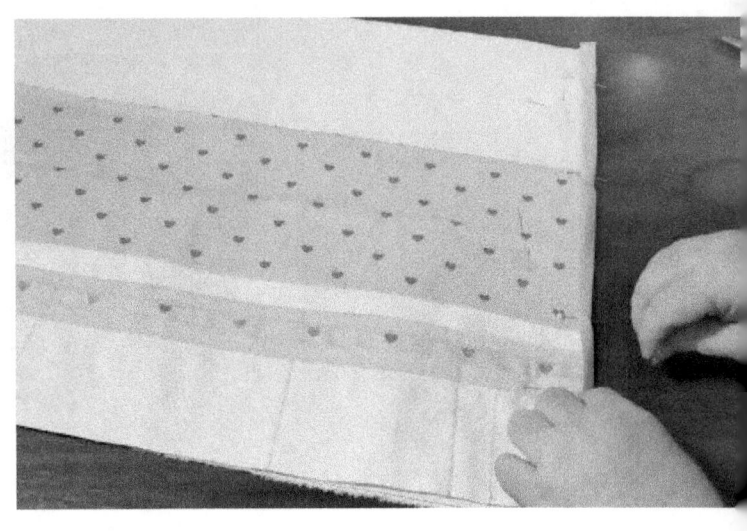

STEP 10

Spot a tie on the BACK of the front board your Cricut Maker Mat, in accordance with the highest point of your front pocket, and fold the edge under the predisposition tape. Do the same for the opposite side.

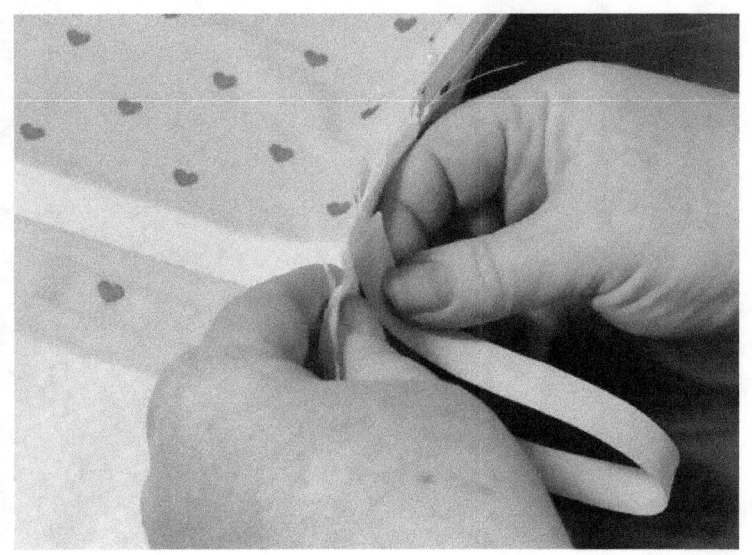

Put the ties in the correct spot on the Maker Mat

Ensure the ties are under the same level with the tape

STEP 11

Stick the other two ties onto the back of the backboard of your Cricut Maker Mat, about 2.5″ from the top board, and again fold the edge beneath the bias tape.

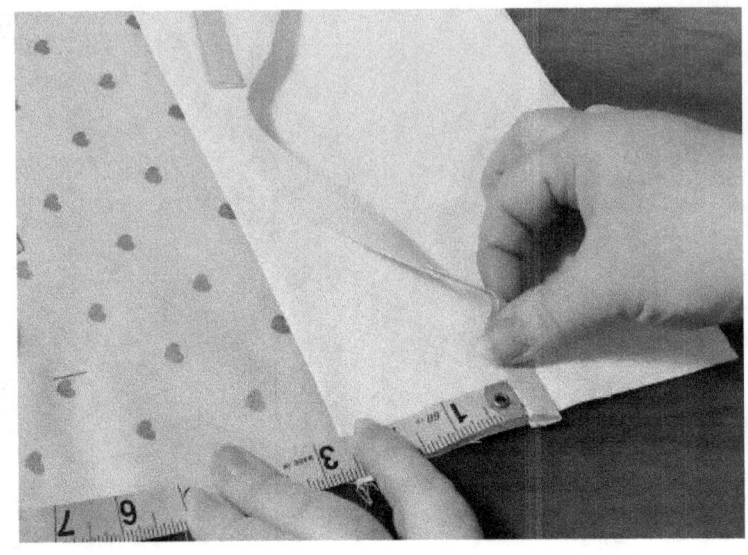

Put the ties in the correct spot on the Maker Mat

Sew down the edge of the predisposition tape, around 1/8" from the edge. Ensure you're getting all layers, including any ties and the opposite side of the inclination tape, when you sew.

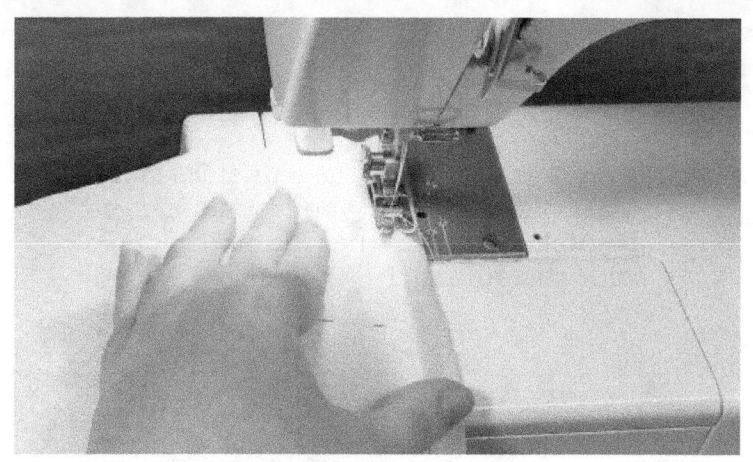

When you arrive at the corner, you'll need to crease the inclination tape into a correct edge to shape the corner.

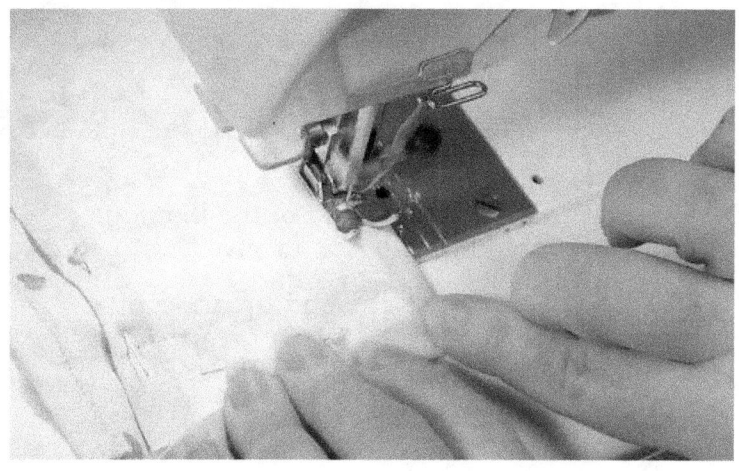

Sew the edge of the Cricut Maker Mat

Keep sewing each of the four sides of the Maker Mat. When you get as far as possible, remove the inclination tape with an additional 1/2″ to extra.

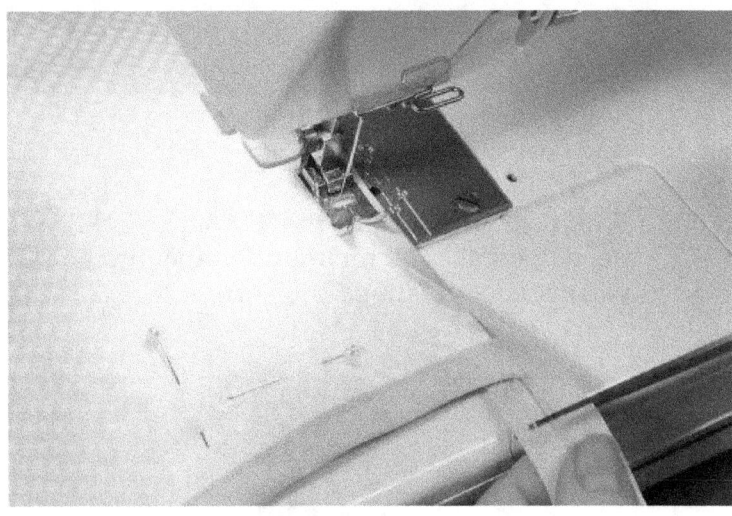

Cut that folded the end of the bias tape with an additional 1/2″ to save

Next, you crease the end up and under to be flush with the edge of your Cricut Maker Mat and get done with sewing.

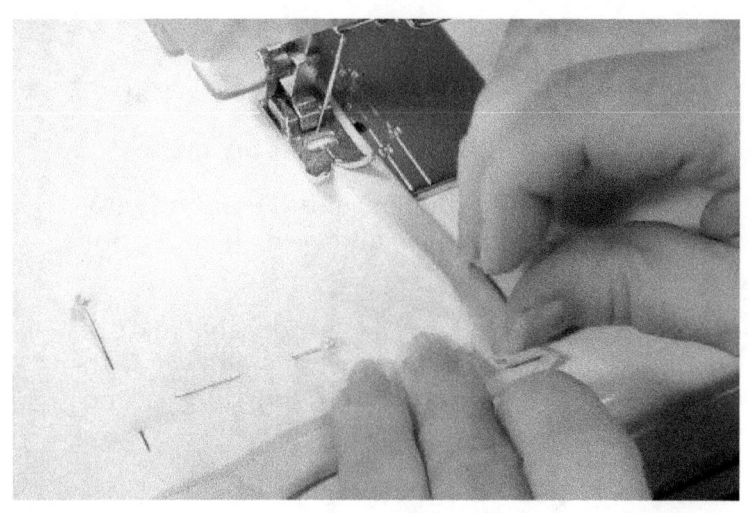

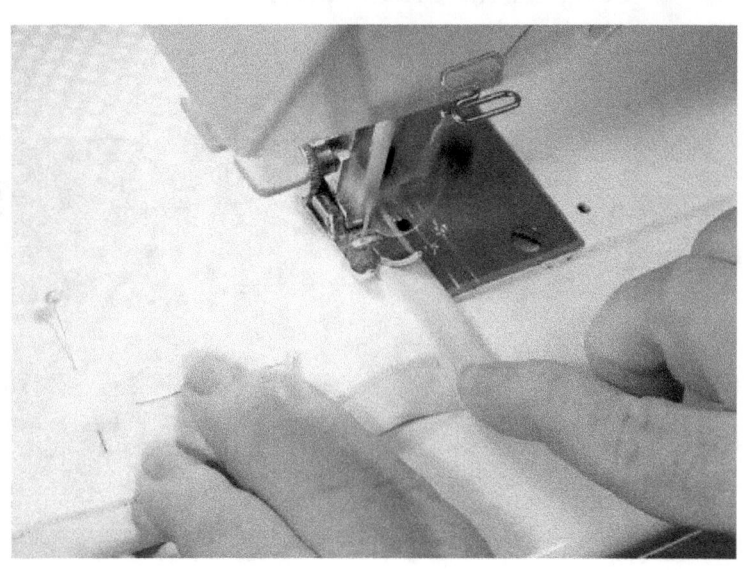

Sew the side of the Cricut Maker Mat

Turn the other side of that bias tape

And there you have it! Trim off any hanging strings and put it on your Cricut!

Tip: To evacuate the launderable texture stamping pen lines, simply shower with water, rub a little with your finger, and permit to dry.

Creator Mat Tool Organizer and Dust Cover for the Cricut Maker

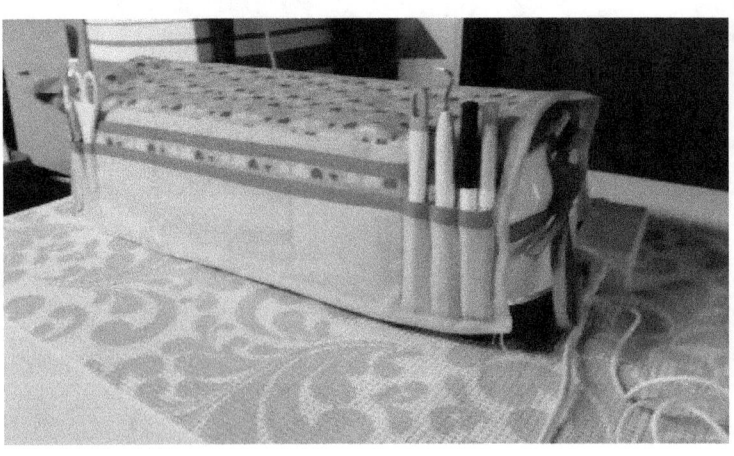

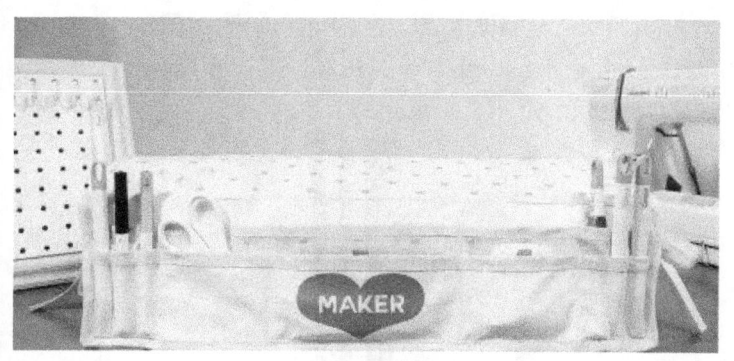

YOU CAN DO THIS NOW!

Level- Hard

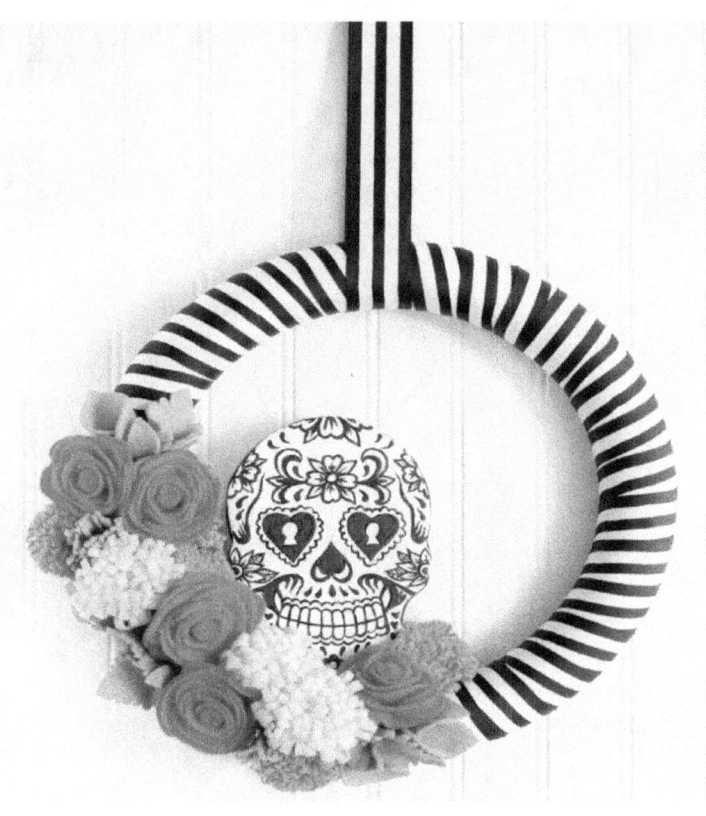

CREDIT-
THECRAFTEDSPARROW.COM

Recently, I grew an interest in sugar skulls. They are fun colors and exquisite

Halloween designs. I shop on a weekly basis, and I was inspired by this during my last shopping. This is perfect for Halloween, and it gives that dangerous but sweet touch.

SUPPLIES NEEDED

- Foam Wreath
- Small spatula
- Marker
- Pencil
- Sanding block or sandpaper
- You would also need White acrylic paint
- Some black acrylic paint too
- Small detail paintbrush as well
- Felt flowers
- Toothpicks

STEP 1

Start by getting your design. Which you can make yourself, or you can download the template online. Then get your foam disc ready.

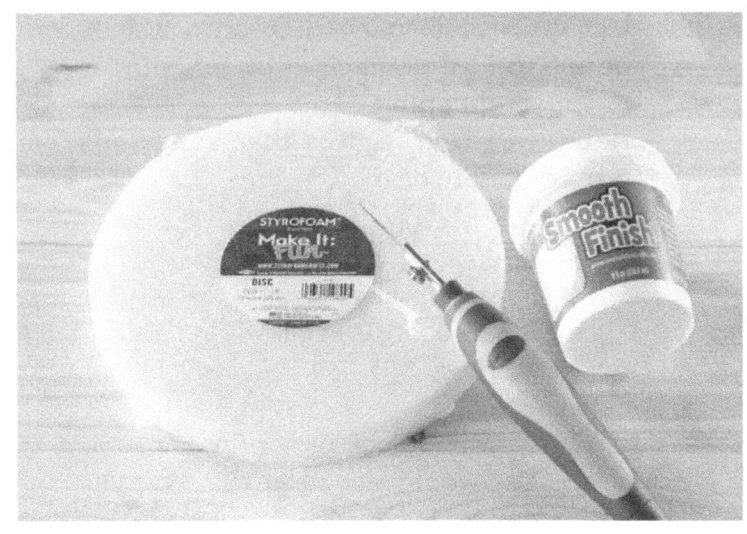

STEP 2

You make use of your black marker to trace out the shape of the template on your foam disk. And remember to keep the template disk because you would need it later.

STEP 3

You would make use of the foam cutter to cut out the shape of the sugar skull. You can make use of a Xacto knife if you don't have a foam cutter. After that, you

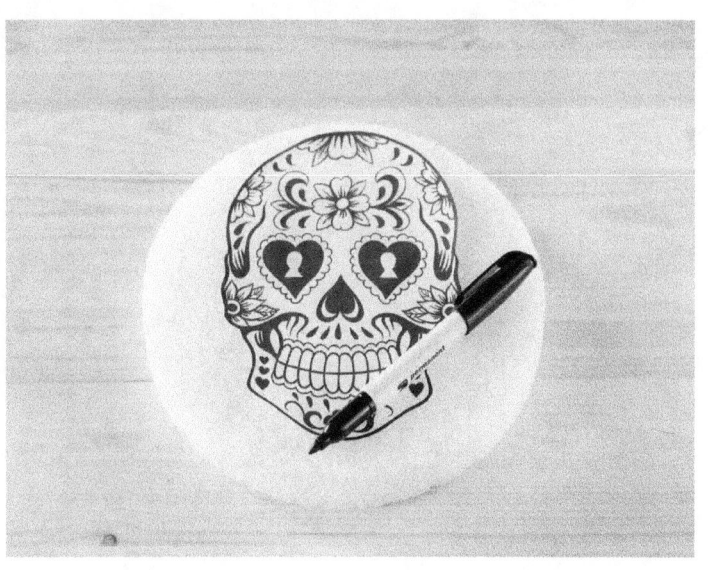

are to make the surface of the foam smooth by making use of the small spatula. Doing this would add that smooth topcoat that you need and would also create a plaster-like sensation for your foam. For this project, I made use of the smooth finish for the first coat. Allowed it to dry then applied the second coat. When applying it, the layers should be as equal as possible and very smooth too. The front and the side should be covered completely. The back is not compulsory.

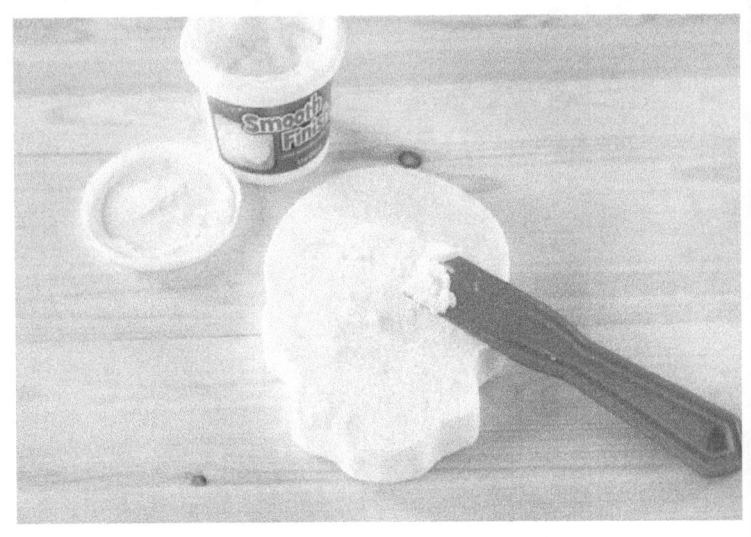

STEP 4

After both coats are smooth and dry, you should make use of your sanding block to smoothen the bumps that would affect that texture. You should make it gentle. Don't go too hard the smooth finishes sands easily. After that, you would take your white acrylic paint and give it one more last coat to prepare it for the sugar skull design and allow it to dry.

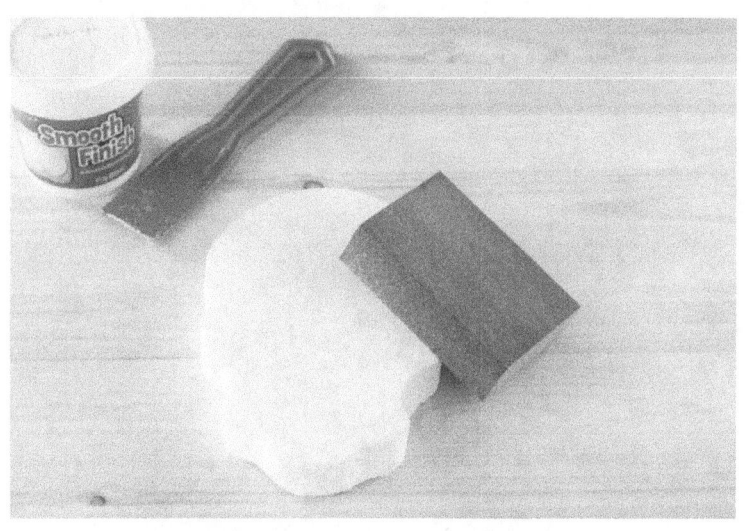

STEP 5

Get your template once more. This time you should make use of a pencil and trace over the design completely. You should make sure that you paint the solid potions. That you would be using for this transfer.

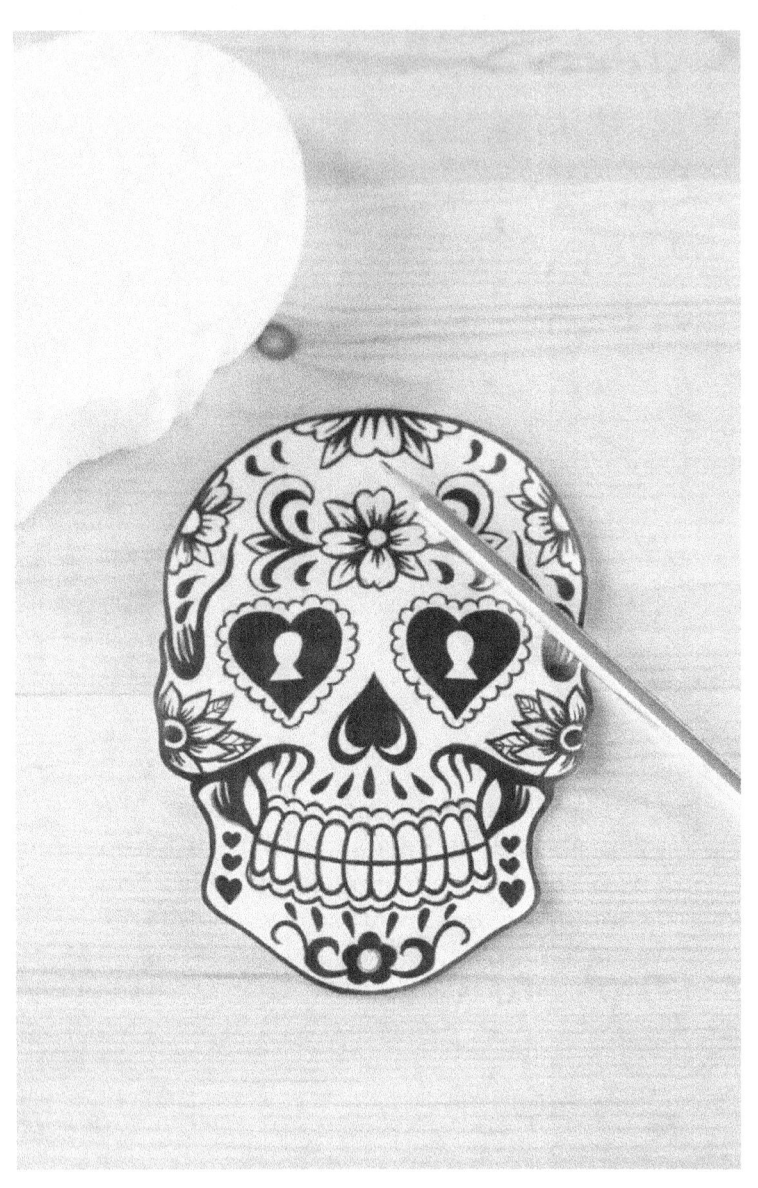

STEP 6

Turn your design over and place it on the form of the skull. Make sure that the side you painted with the pencil faces down. Next, you use your pencil to trace the complete design onto the foam. This should be very easy through the paper. You should be sure that you don't press it too hard. If not, you would imprint the foam with your pencil. It should look very much like the picture below.

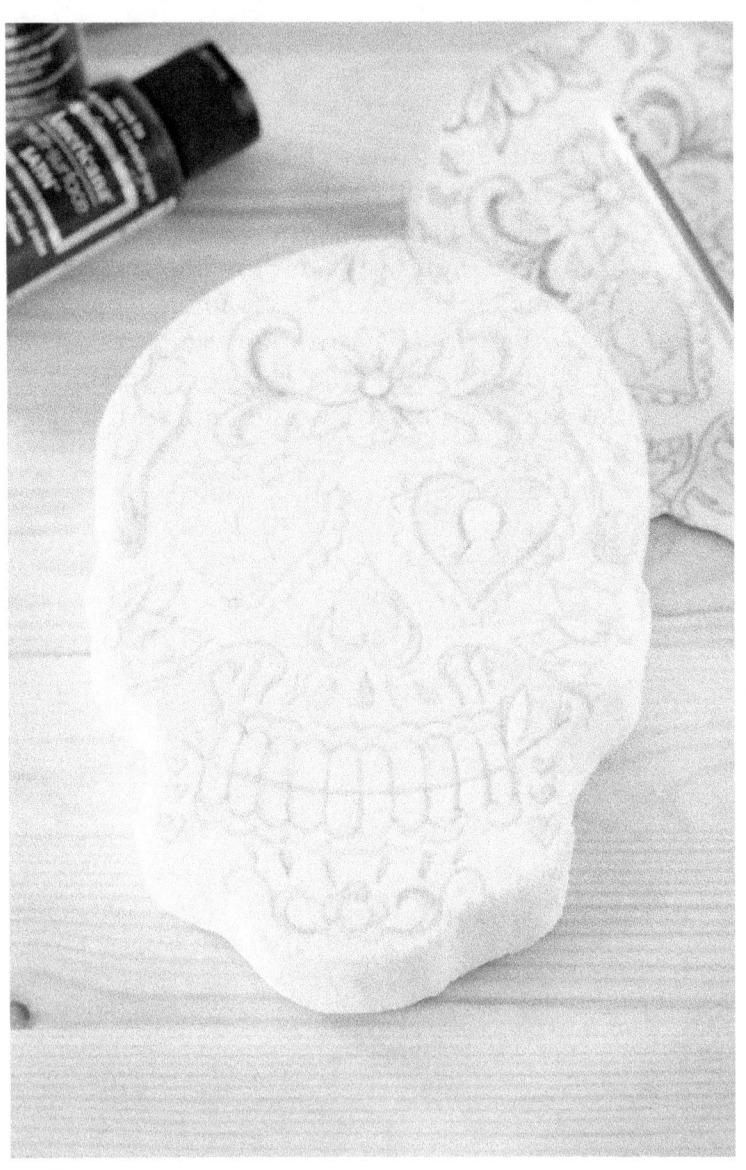

STEP 7

With that small detail paint brush of yours, you should coat them with black acrylic paint to fill in your design. You may not choose to use the black and white design so you can paint your sugar skull whatever colors you like. You can also paint the outlines black to add more details, which gives it so much beauty.

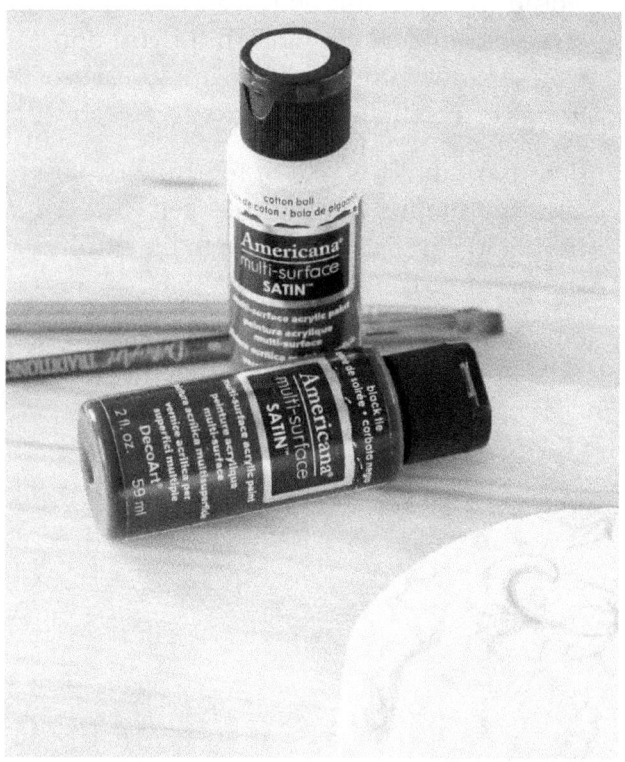

STEP 8

Next, you can wrap your wreath with your black and white straps. That is what I did here. And for the flowers, you have been taught how to make felt flowers, apply that knowledge now. The leaves are basic leaf shape which you can just cut from some edges. Then you would pin all the felt flowers to that strategic side of the wreath. IF you don't want to use pins you can make use of hot glue a well as toothpicks to attach it.

If you are making use of toothpicks, you can put some behind the felt flowers then you carefully slide the foam skull to the point of the toothpick

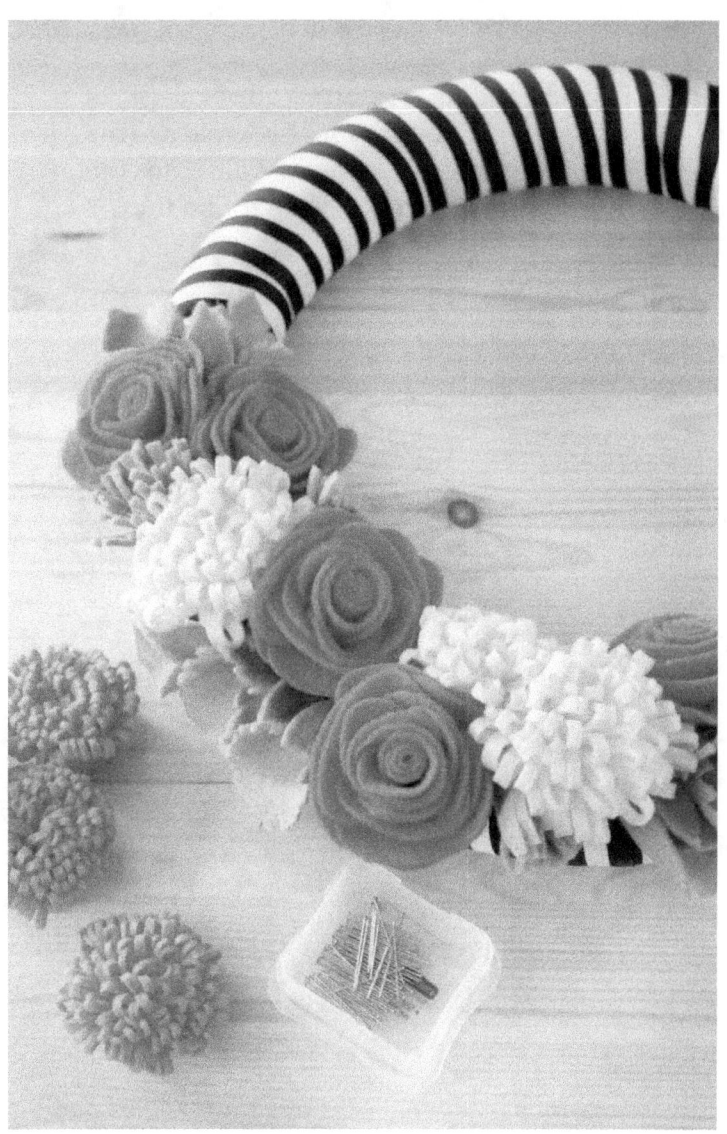

STEP 9

This is the last step. You can get a stripped felt hanger for the wreath. This also adds that aesthetic value to the project or you simply leave it like that.

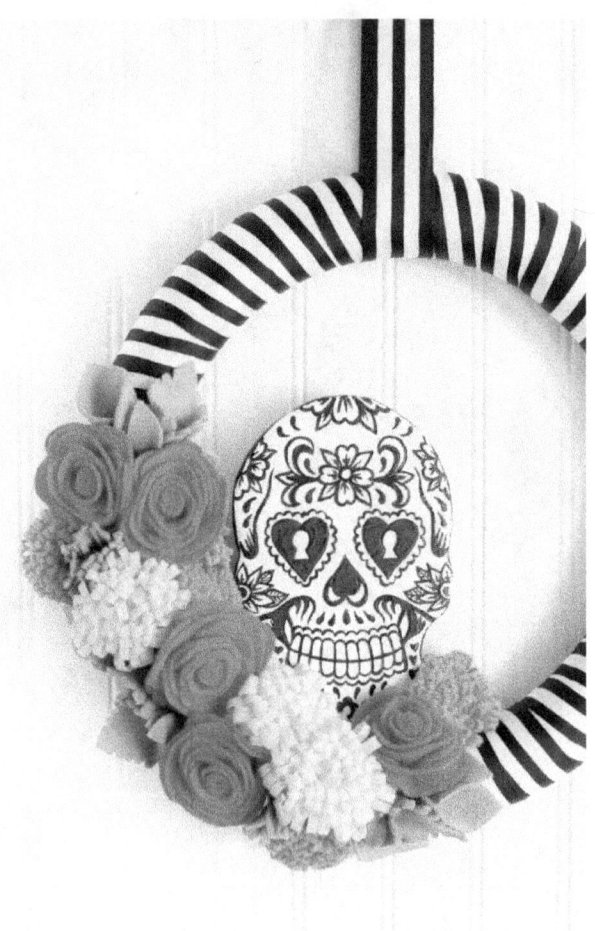

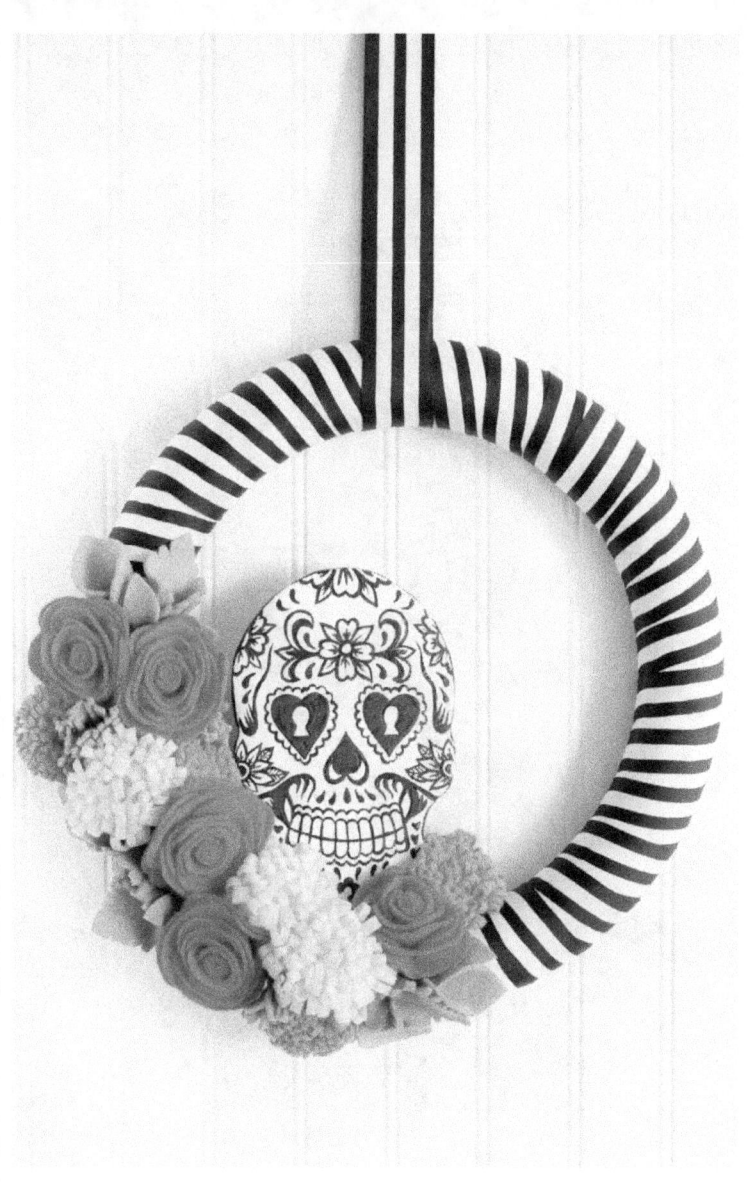

YOU CAN DO THIS NOW!

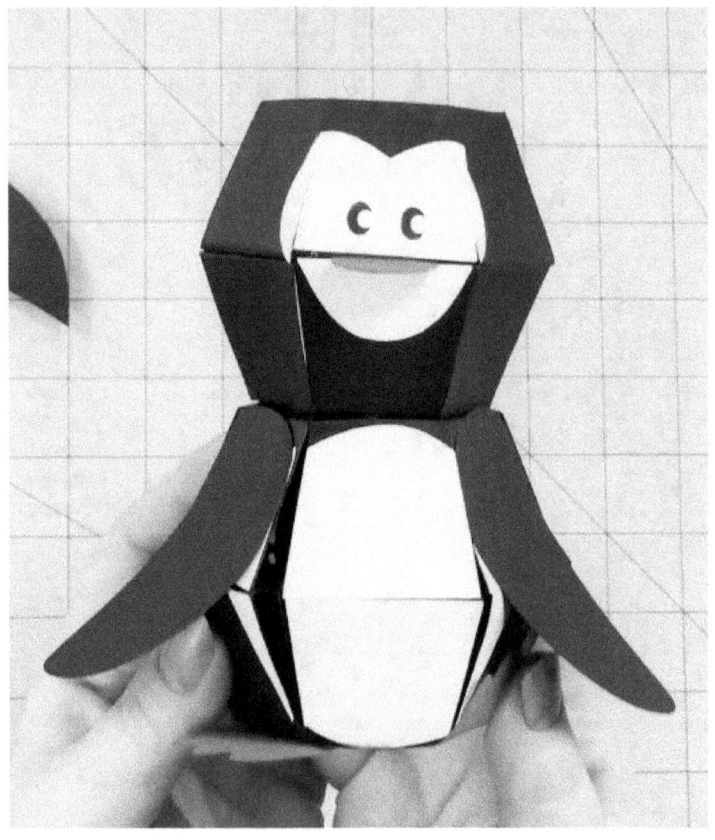

CREDIT- JENIFFER MAKER

I named this project *penguin paper bomb!* Because it is a bomb actually.

Why? You can actually make the penguin bomb. This means that when you drop it, it will pop up. But that is a challenge for you. This project is a unique and a wonderful toy for your kids.

SUPPLIES NEEDED

- **65lb. 8.5″** by 11″ cardstock. This should be shared according to the color you want. I made use of two sheets of black, one sheet of white as well as another sheet of orange.
- Rubberbands. A particular one should be in size 16 which is 2.5 inches long while the other should be in size 18- 3 inches long
- Your Tacky glue is also needed
- Hot glue
- Two dimes or tinny weights.
- 7" piece of wire, tweezers or even a hooked took like a crochet hook or something else.
- Your Cricut machine for cutting
- Patterns or cut SVG files from free resource library or your own designs.

STEP 1

First, you upload the SVG file on your design space. You click on the *Ungroup* button then change the two red layers having the score lines to *score*, next you would choose the red score layer plus its following black cut layer then click Attach. There is a need for you to join both sides of the red scored layers and the black cut layers also. This would allow the score lines to appear in the right places.

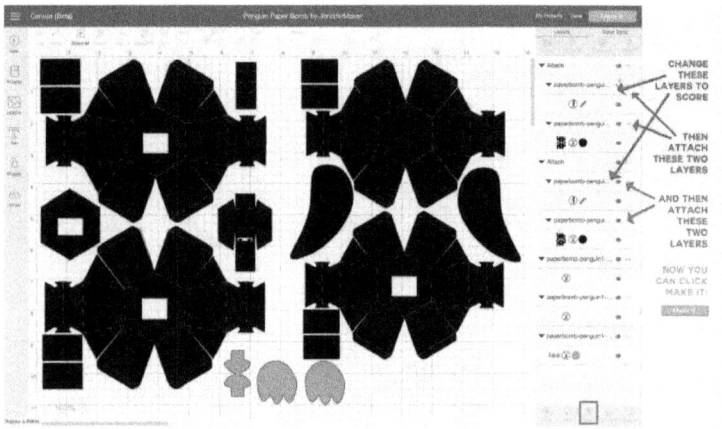

STEP 2

You start first by folding the top of the headpiece. This is the smaller round piece that doesn't have a hole in the middle. Then you would fold the other side from the tab inwards. You should not forget to crease each tab to get that good fold. There is also a need for you to fold in the triangle pieces also. Then you would fold the rubber band tabs in then up. Below is a picture of the folded piece.

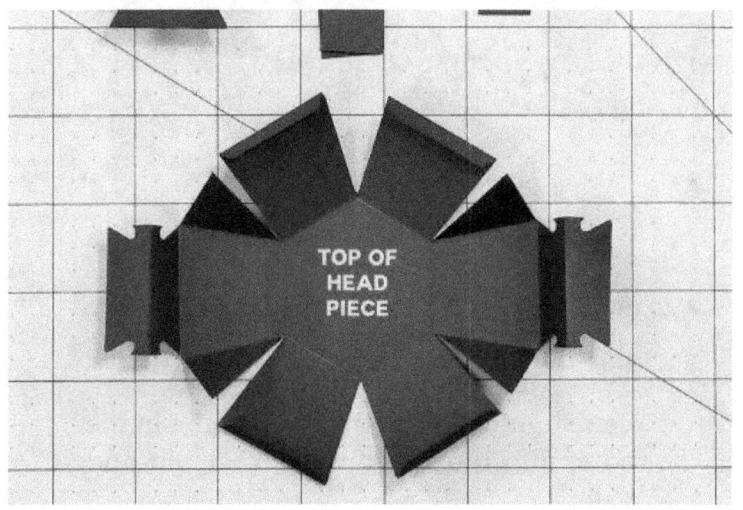

STEP 2

Next, you would glue down those triangles. Those rectangular side reinforcements should be on top each side having the triangles and the rubber band holders too. The photo below explains it all.

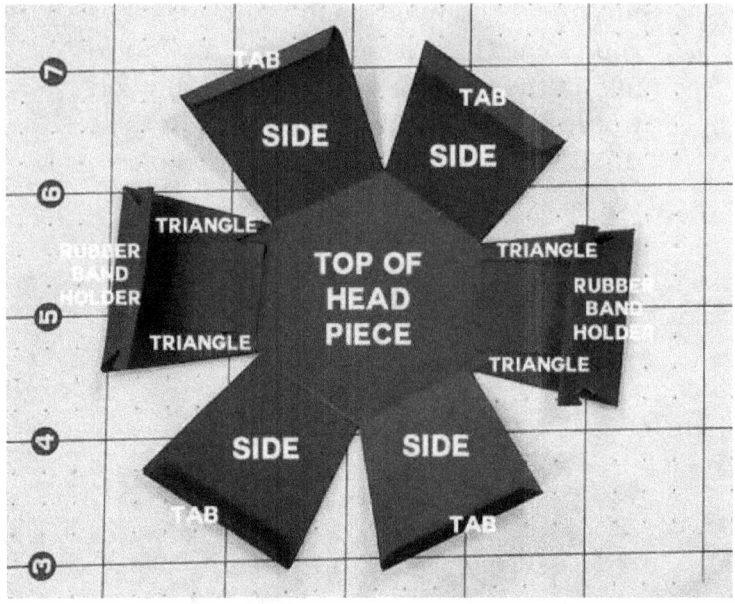

You should also do the same thing to the bottom of that headpiece. You fold and glue.

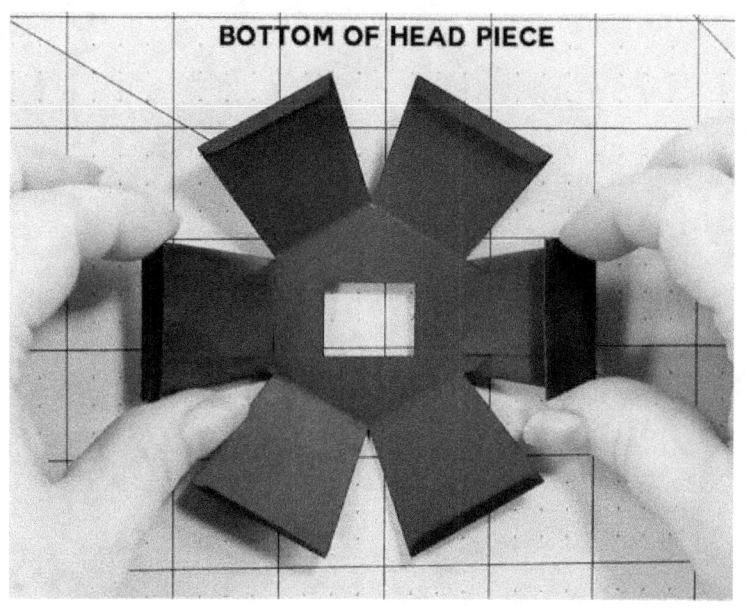

BOTTOM OF HEAD PIECE

STEP 3

Next, you would fold the paper spring mechanism, which is divided into two major parts. The first part looks so much like a rectangle having wing; this part would be folded and glued to the base. That part which is longer would go down again, just like it is in the picture.

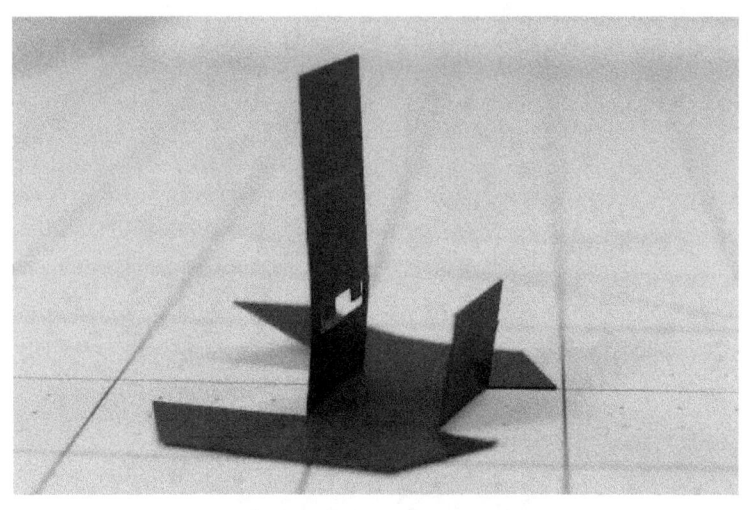

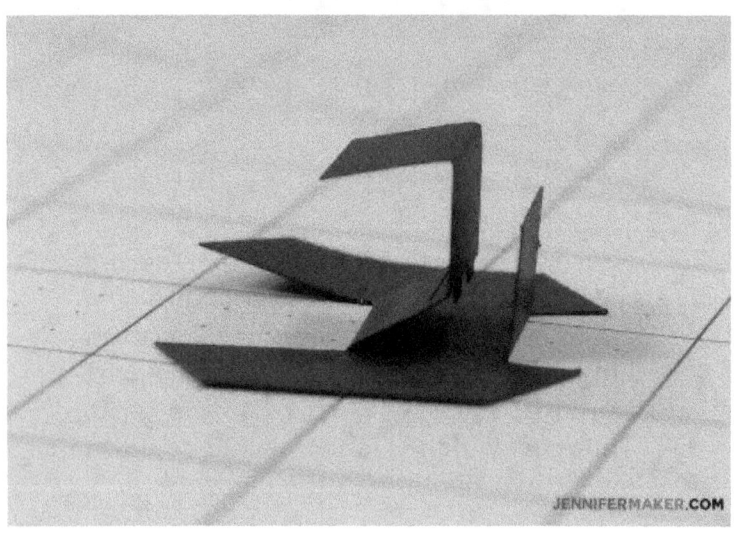

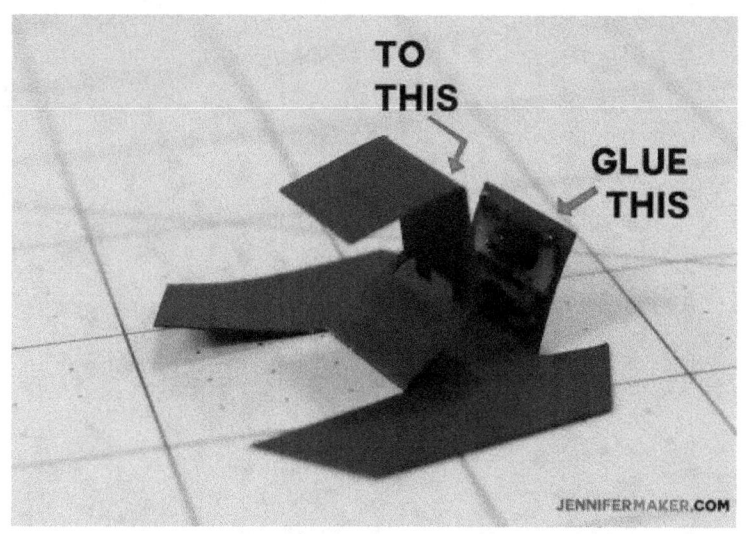

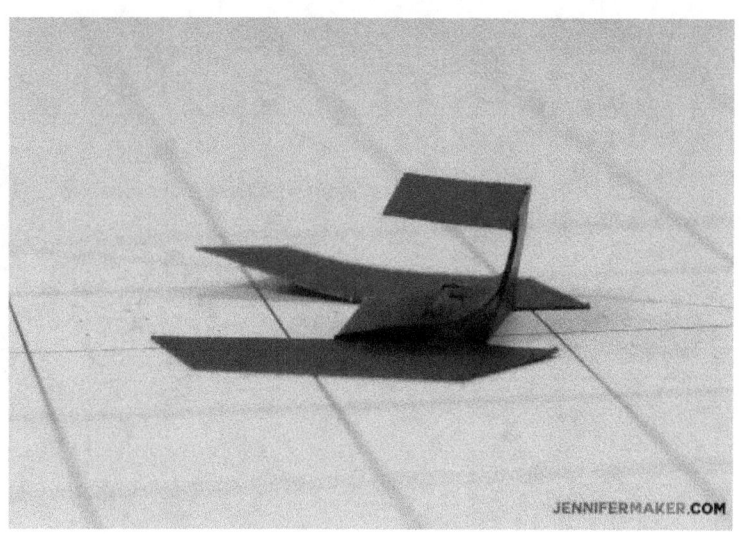

269

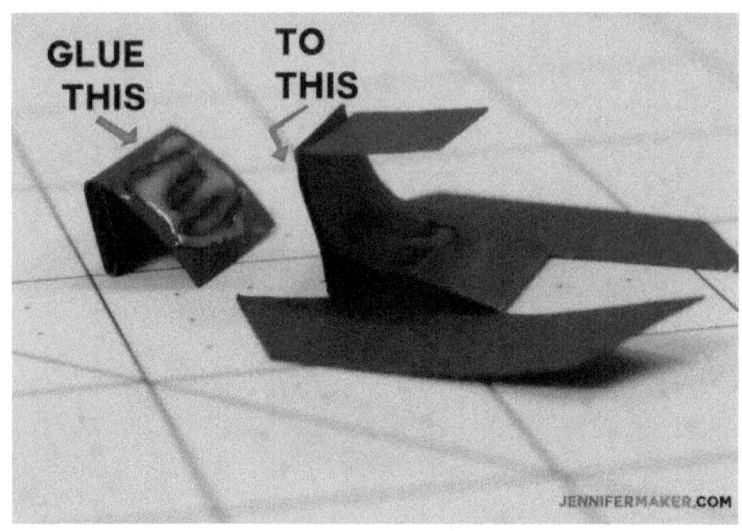

GLUE THIS   TO THIS

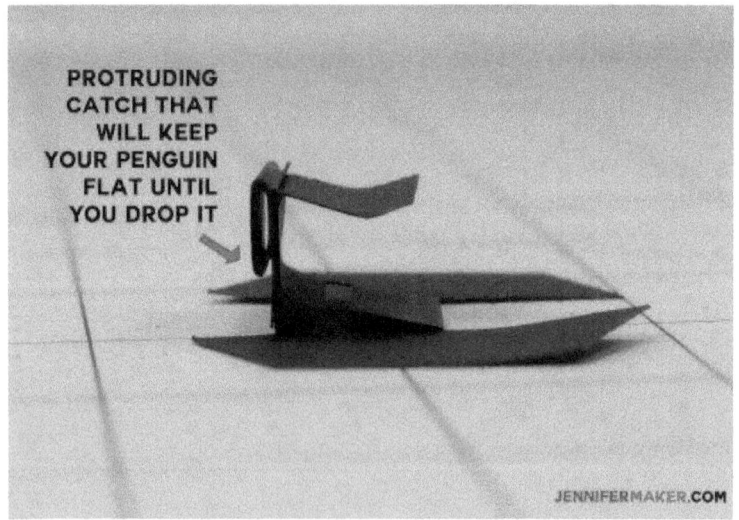

PROTRUDING CATCH THAT WILL KEEP YOUR PENGUIN FLAT UNTIL YOU DROP IT

STEP 4

Next, you would add your glue on the white-faced parts to the top and the bottom of the head piece like the picture below. You should pay so much attention to the orientation of those rubber band holders as you join the face parts to make sure they are in the right places altogether.

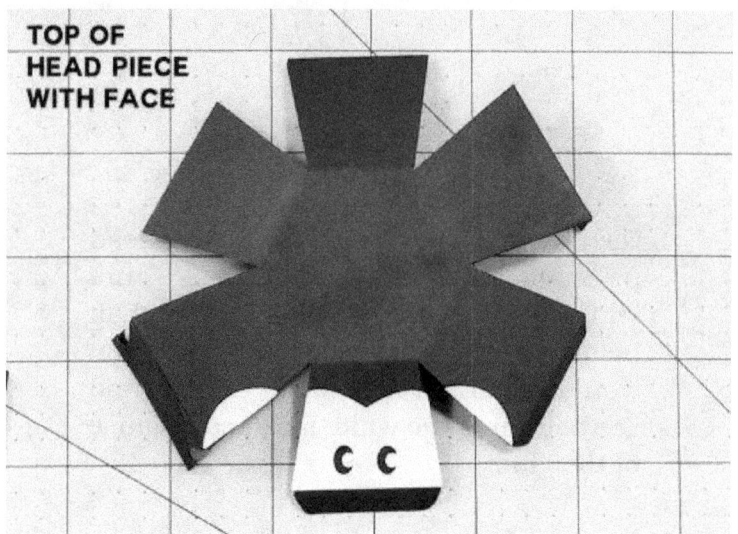

TOP OF
HEAD PIECE
WITH FACE

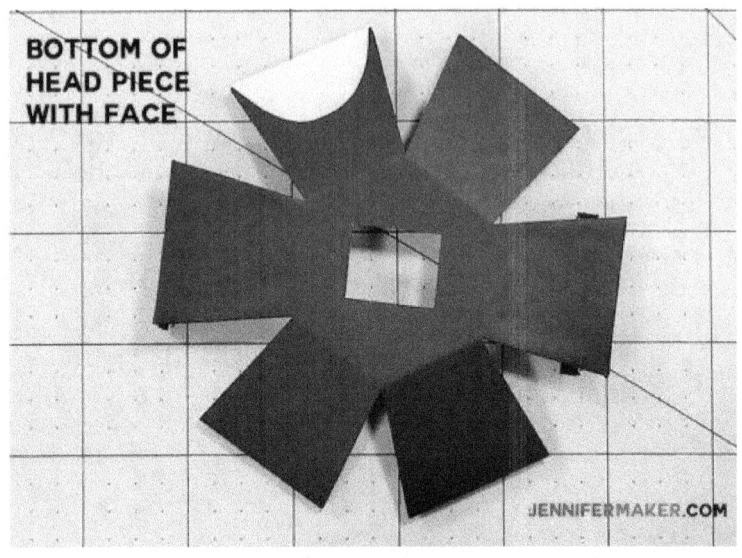

BOTTOM OF
HEAD PIECE
WITH FACE

JENNIFERMAKER.COM

STEP 5

Next, you would join these two head pieces together with glue but make sure you fold the orange bill piece in half before you glue it then close it. Next, you would sandwich it between the top and the bottom of the white face, making use of the glue.

After the two head pieces are connected at the face, you would fold it close then

272

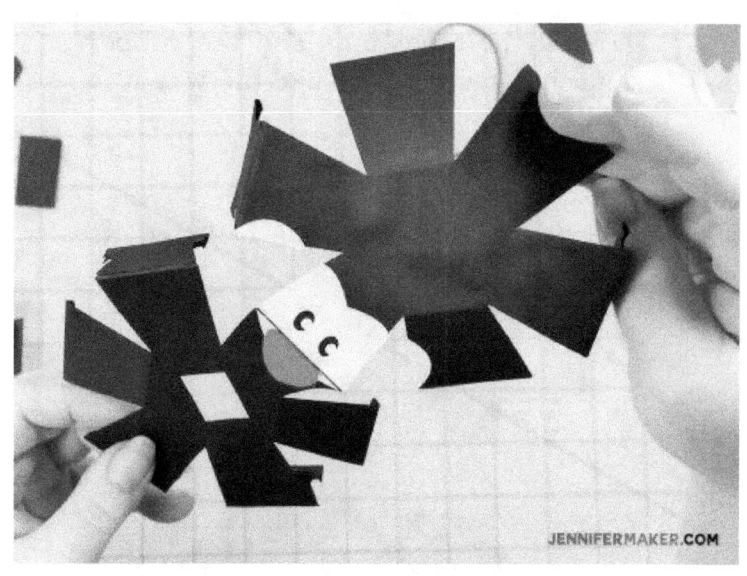

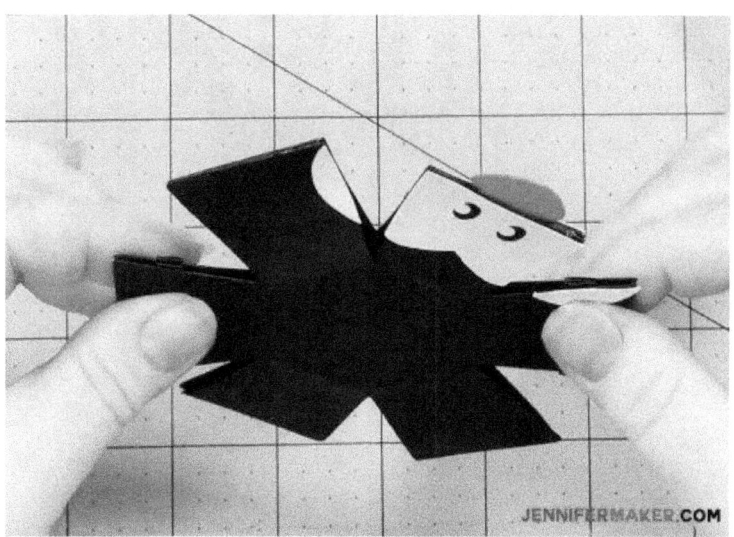

glue all the other tabs and the rubber band holders together like the way it is in the picture below:

The head piece would have gotten its shape by this time.

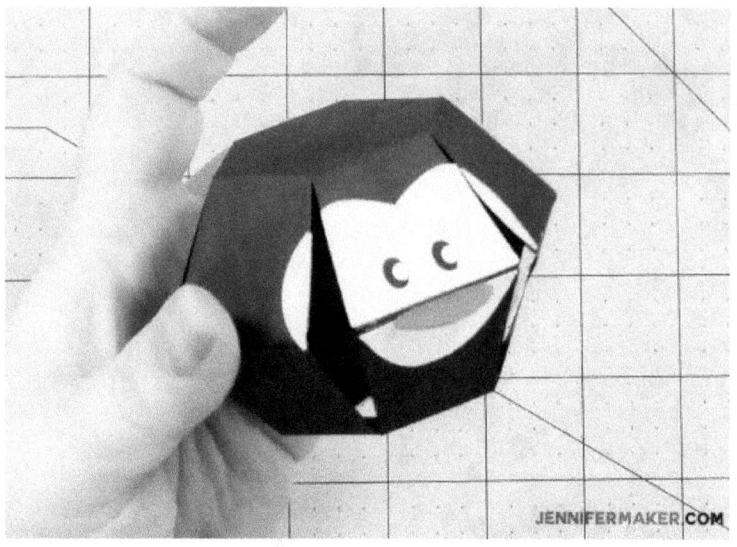

STEP 6

Let us make the *pop ability* now. Just add a smaller rubber band which should be around size 16 to about 2.5″ long then it would be folded and then drop it into the head so that one end of the rubber band would loop around on the end of the other rubber band loop.

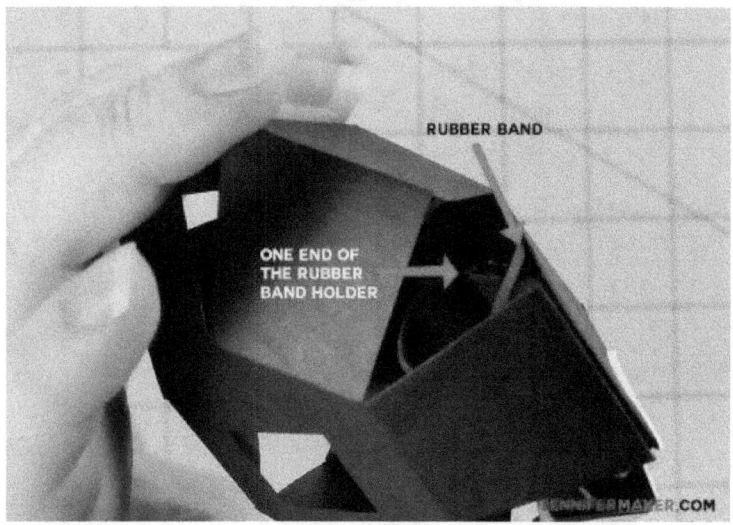

Next, you would reach into the head, gasp the rubber band then you would hook it around the other end of that rubber band holding.

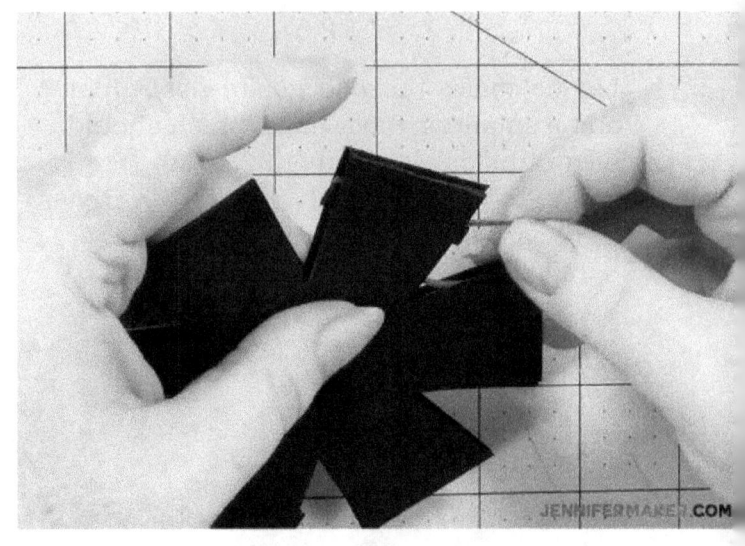

You may be having difficulties holding the rubber band. Just get a hook out of a small piece of wire like I did here.

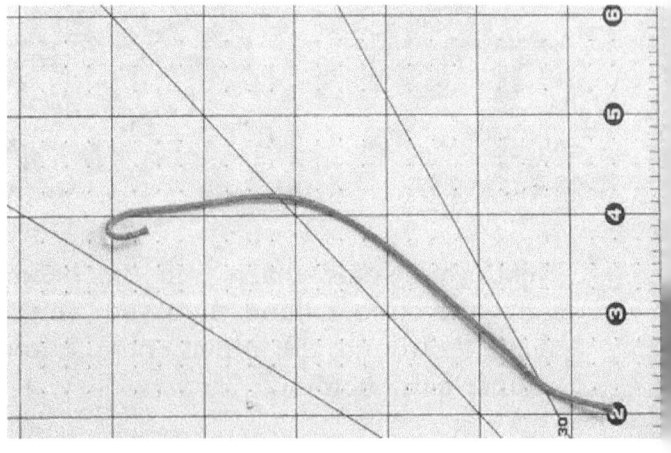

Make use of this hook to reach into the head, especially from the opposite side of where the rubber band is placed. Hold onto the end of the rubber band and carefully hook it around the rubber band holding from the first one. This can be tricky.

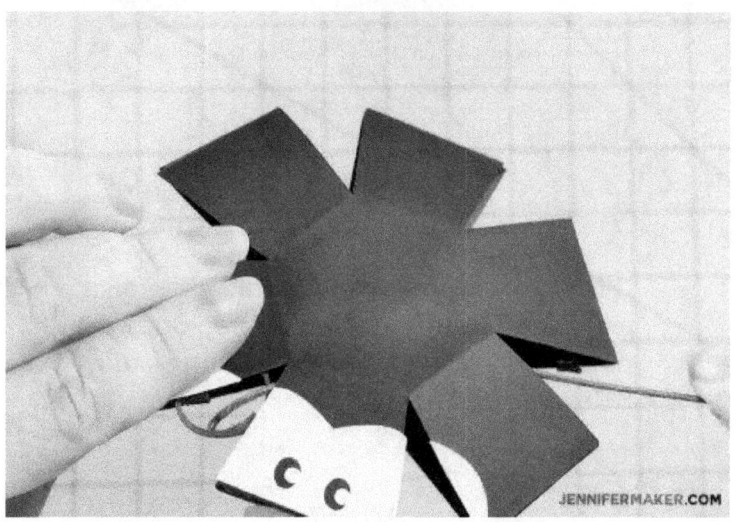

Next, you would reach for the inside with the hook you have been able to make from the other part. Then you'll get the rubber band and wrap it around the last end of the band holders.

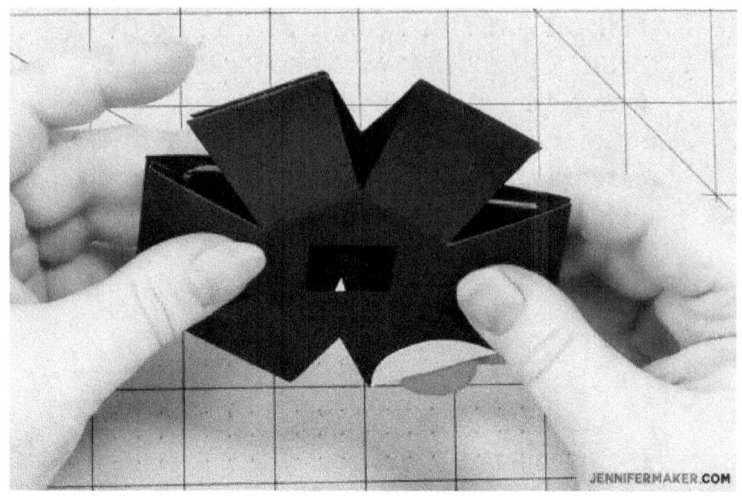

It is at this moment you would able to let go of the head, and it would pop out into place immediately. Something like below:

STEP 7

You flatten the head one more time and turn it over. You should be sure that the mechanism is sticking out. There might be a need for you to reach in and pull it out. Then you would allow the protruding side of the mechanism to capture that part of the bottom; this would always keep it flat.

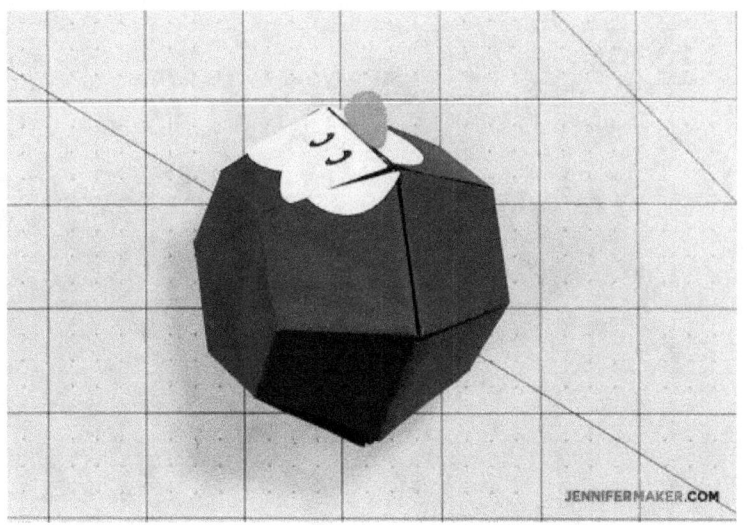

Now drop it, it is time to work on the surface mechanism on the other side down. Check to be sure that there is nothing impeding the mechanism from being pushed, especially when it lands on that work surface.

Next, you would fold the two halves on that penguin's body.

Glue down the triangles, as well as the side reinforcements pieces as well as rubber band holders. The same way you did for the head pieces.

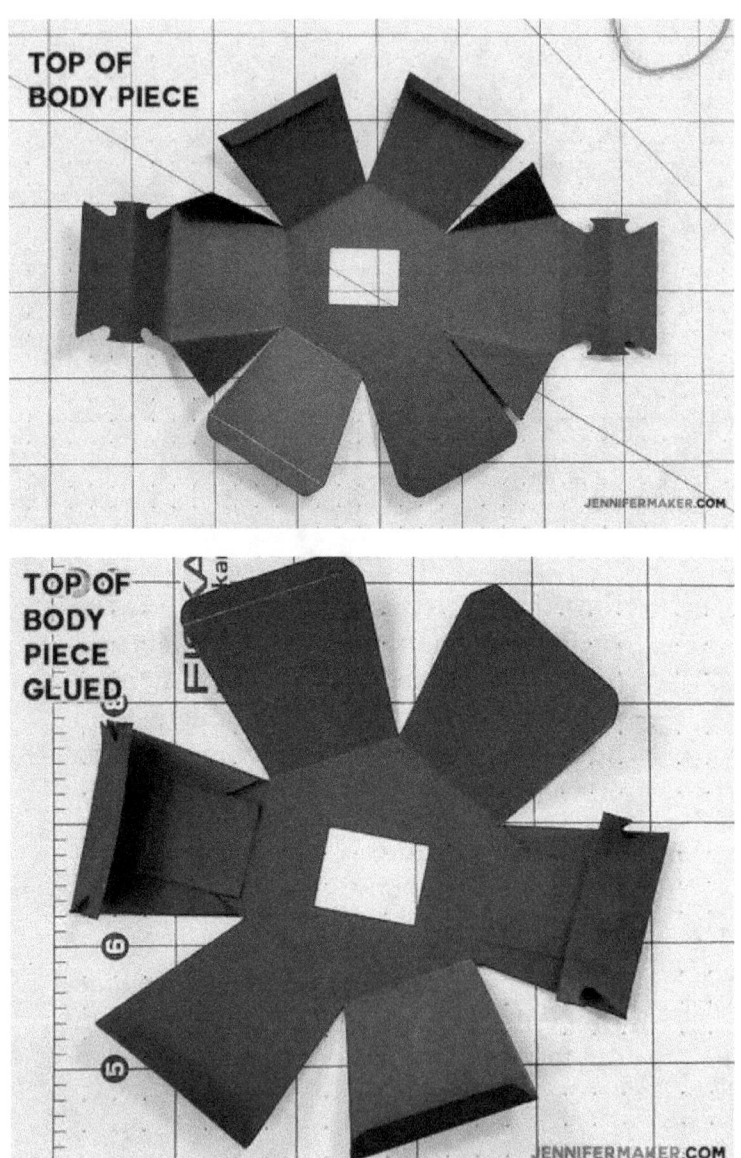

Attach the glue on the white body pieces. You should watch closely, the arrangement of the black body pieces. You can do the same orientation just like the photos

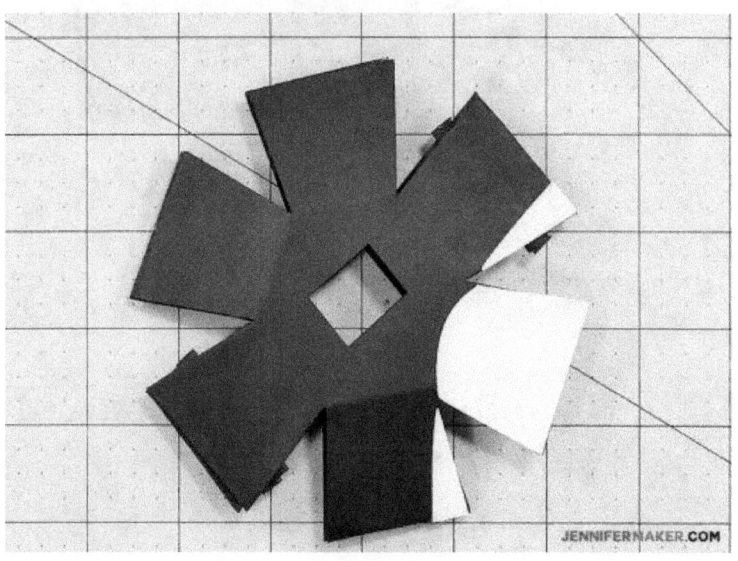

Now insert that hook and size 18 rubberband into the body in the same way you did for the head.

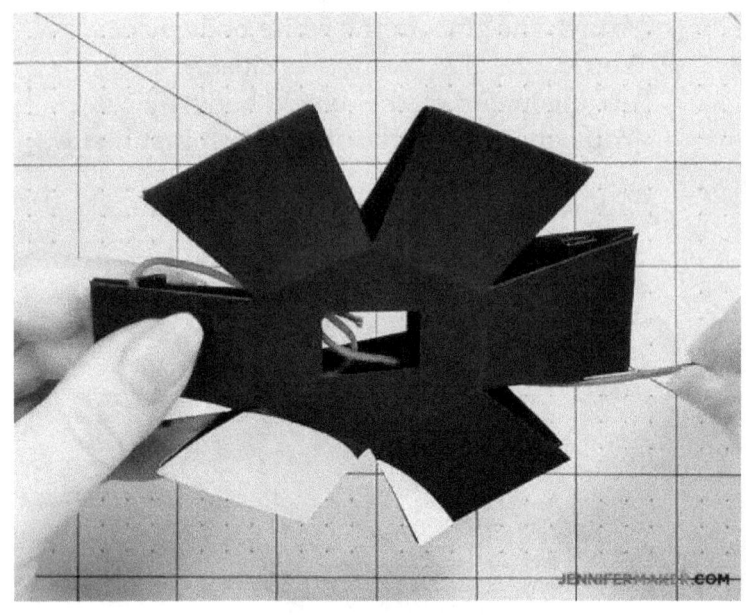

This is the body with the rubber band in one place

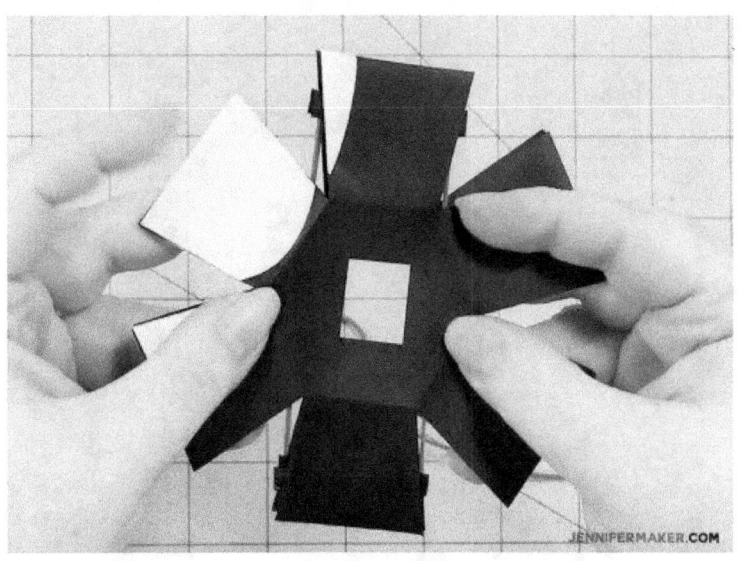

Next, you would use the glue to attach to the head of the body. Then line up the rectangles on each side so that they would match up. Then you would glue it. If the body isn't aligning to the right, you can turn it over and then try it once again. When you glue it, you should center that head on the body as straight as possible.

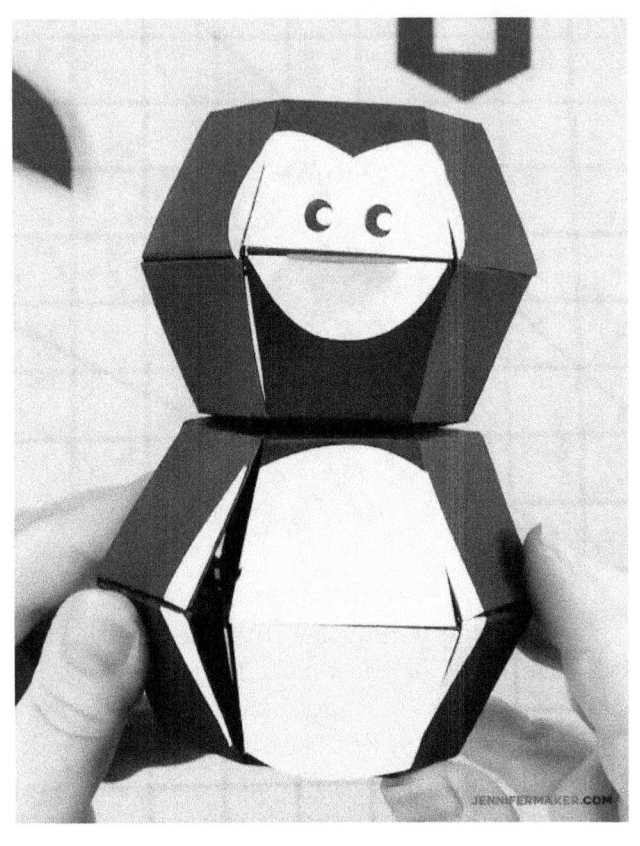

STEP 8

You would glue the reinforcement piece
onto the base of the penguin paper bomb
you should be careful not to impede the
mechanism present in the middle.
Check the picture below to see if it fits
properly.

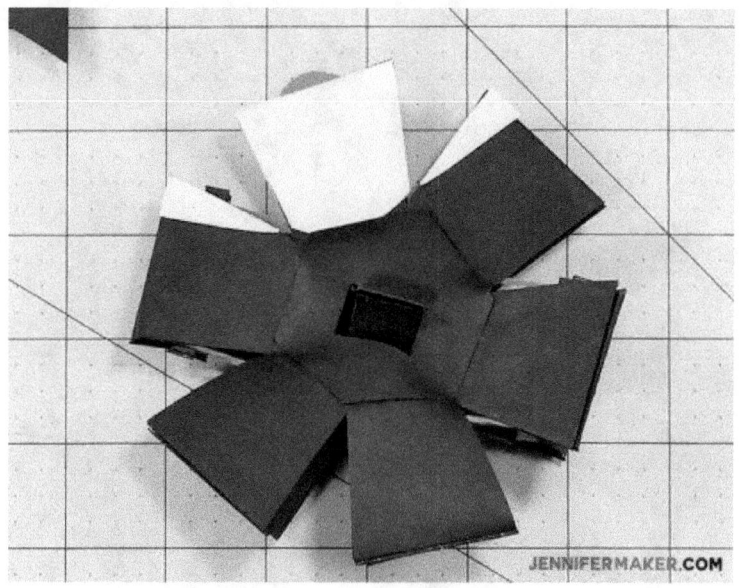

Then you would paste the orange feet so that they would stick out on both sides of the white part of the body.

Next, you would stand your penguin up, and you would paste the wings on both sides of its body. You should make use of strong glue so that the wings would not brush the ground. Furthermore, this would help the penguin when it jumps.

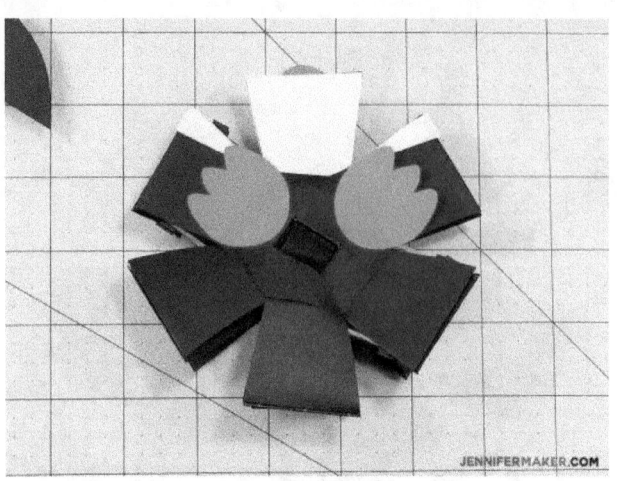

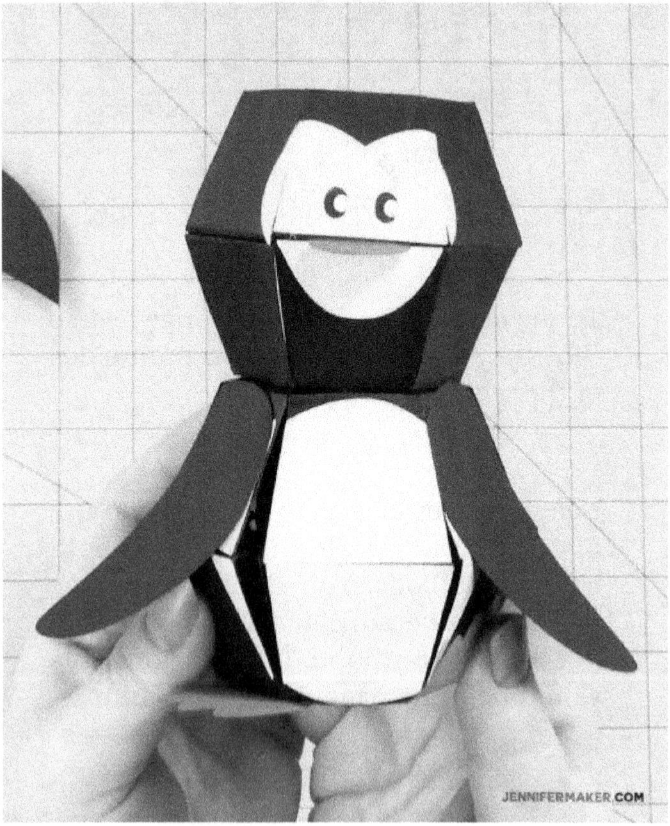

Another way you to increase stability is by placing two dimes glued onto the bottom. This would help it stabilize its weight when it pops up.

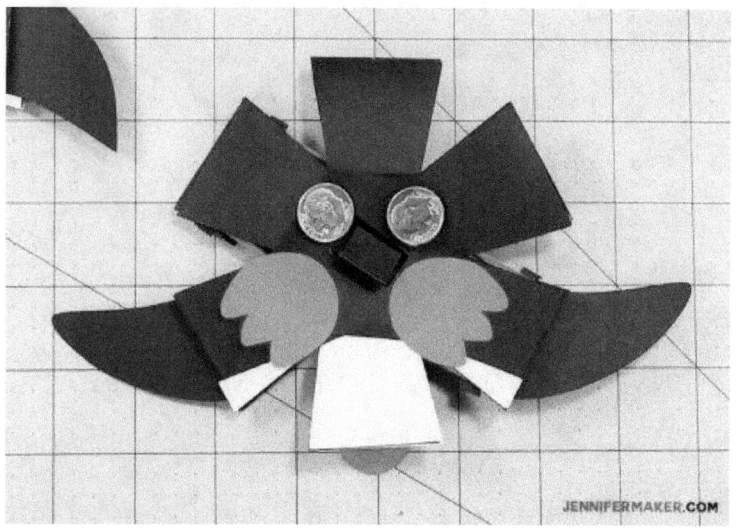

This time, you'll try it out if your penguin paper bomb is really a bomb. You flatten him then you would place that mechanism in place then drop it onto that surface. Did it pop u? be sure that there is nothing coming in the way of the tab. Free it, if you find something stopping it so that it doesn't impede the mechanism.

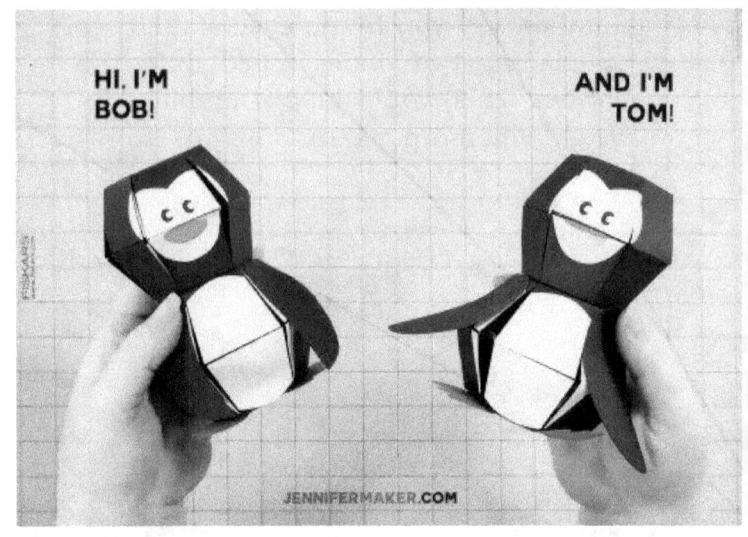

YOU CAN DO THIS NOW!

Notes

www.ingramcontent.com/pod-product-compliance
Lightning Source LLC
Chambersburg PA
CBHW072131170526
45158CB00004BA/1327